THE BEARS EARS

ALSO BY DAVID ROBERTS

Escalante's Dream: On the Trail of the Spanish Discovery of the Southwest

Limits of the Known

Alone on the Wall (with Alex Honnold)

*Alone on the Ice: The Greatest Survival Story
in the History of Exploration*

The Mountain: My Time on Everest (with Ed Viesturs)

*The Will to Climb: Obsession and Commitment
and the Quest to Climb Annapurna* (with Ed Viesturs)

*Finding Everett Ruess: The Life and Unsolved Disappearances
of a Legendary Wilderness Explorer*

K2: Life and Death on the World's Most Dangerous Mountain
(with Ed Viesturs)

*The Last of His Kind: The Life and Adventures of Bradford Washburn,
America's Boldest Mountaineer*

Devil's Gate: Brigham Young and the Great Mormon Handcart Tragedy

No Shortcuts to the Top: Climbing the World's 14 Highest Peaks
(with Ed Viesturs)

*Sandstone Spine: Seeking the Anasazi on the
First Traverse of the Comb Ridge*

On the Ridge Between Life and Death: A Climbing Life Reexamined

*The Pueblo Revolt: The Secret Rebellion That
Drove the Spaniards Out of the Southwest*

*Four Against the Arctic: Shipwrecked for Six Years
at the Top of the World*

Escape from Lucania: An Epic Story of Survival

*True Summit: What Really Happened on the
Legendary Ascent of Annapurna*

*A Newer World: Kit Carson, John C. Frémont, and the
Claiming of the American West*

The Lost Explorer: Finding Mallory on Mount Everest
(with Conrad Anker)

Escape Routes

*In Search of the Old Ones: Exploring the
Anasazi World of the Southwest*

*Once They Moved Like the Wind: Cochise, Geronimo,
and the Apache Wars*

Mount McKinley: The Conquest of Denali
(with Bradford Washburn)

Iceland: Land of the Sagas (with Jon Krakauer)

Jean Stafford: A Biography

Great Exploration Hoaxes

Moments of Doubt

Deborah: A Wilderness Narrative

The Mountain of My Fear

THE BEARS EARS

◄◄ ►►

A HUMAN HISTORY OF AMERICA'S MOST ENDANGERED WILDERNESS

David Roberts

W. W. NORTON & COMPANY

Independent Publishers Since 1923

For information about permission to reproduce selections from this book, write to
Permissions, W. W. Norton & Company, Inc., 500 Fifth Avenue, New York, NY 10110

For information about special discounts for bulk purchases, please contact
W. W. Norton Special Sales at specialsales@wwnorton.com or 800-233-4830

Manufacturing by Lake Book Manufacturing
Production manager: Anna Oler

Library of Congress Cataloging-in-Publication Data

Names: Roberts, David, 1943– author.
Title: The Bears Ears : a human history of America's most endangered wilderness / David Roberts.
Other titles: Human history of America's most endangered wilderness
Description: First edition. | New York, NY : W.W. Norton & Company, [2021]
| Includes bibliographical references and index.
Identifiers: LCCN 2020042614 | ISBN 9781324004813 (hardcover) | ISBN 9781324004820 (epub)
Subjects: LCSH: Bears Ears National Monument (Utah)—History. | Indians of North
America—Utah—San Juan County—Antiquities. | Sacred space—Utah—San Juan County. |
Cliff-dwellings—Utah—San Juan County. | Roberts, David, 1943– —Travel—Utah. |
San Juan County (Utah)—Description and travel.
Classification: LCC F832.S4 R625 2021 | DDC 979.2/59—dc23
LC record available at https://lccn.loc.gov/2020042614

W. W. Norton & Company, Inc., 500 Fifth Avenue, New York, N.Y. 10110
www.wwnorton.com

W. W. Norton & Company Ltd., 15 Carlisle Street, London W1D 3BS

1 2 3 4 5 6 7 8 9 0

For
Fred Blackburn
Vaughn Hadenfeldt
Greg Child
Of all my companions in my favorite place on earth,
You taught me the most

CONTENTS

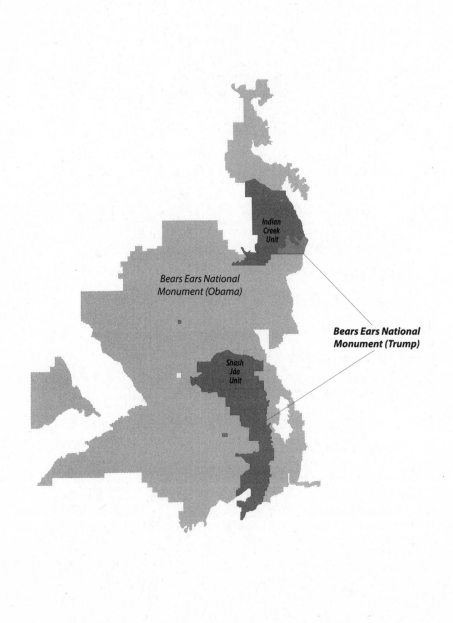

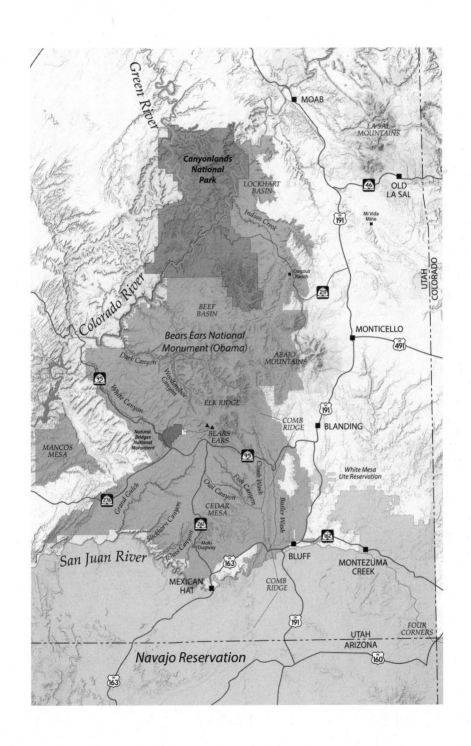

THE BEARS EARS

ONE

THE PLACE AND THE PROMISE

I n no particular hurry, we hiked along the rim of one of the canyons on Cedar Mesa in southeast Utah. Hundreds of feet below, the stream trickled across slickrock slabs and plunged into grassy hollows. I'd been friends with Vaughn Hadenfeldt for more than a decade. Along with his buddy Fred Blackburn, Vaughn had initiated me into the mysteries and glories of this 600-square-mile plateau, an upland quadrangle of piñon-juniper forest scored by a dozen sandstone gorges. The best place in the whole United States, they'd told me when we first met, to find prehistoric rock art panels and unrestored ruins.

I'd first arrived in 1992 to research a magazine article about a band of oddball wilderness devotees who were inventing a potent new discipline called "reverse archaeology" and lobbying hard for an ethic that Fred called the "Outdoor Museum." Instead of gathering up artifacts for curation in some research facility far from Cedar Mesa, Fred and Vaughn argued, you should leave everything in place, so that the next hiker who stumbled upon some dazzling relic from the past could share the magic of discovery.

I was instantly hooked. Long after my magazine piece was published, I kept returning to Cedar Mesa to prowl with Vaughn and Fred, and I brought my own friends out there to show them the things and places I had found.

On this breezy spring day in the late 2000s, as we sauntered along the canyon rim, Vaughn and I paused on promontories to raise our binoculars and train them on the far canyon walls—"glassing," as Vaughn called it. In 1995, Vaughn had founded Far Out Expeditions, pledging his life to guiding clients to ancient wonders on Cedar Mesa and beyond. And in 1996, I'd published *In Search of the Old Ones*, a memoir about my discovery of the prehistoric Southwest, with a chapter titled "In Praise of Cedar Mesa."

But on his off days, Vaughn loved nothing better than to go out looking for granaries and dwellings and friezes of petroglyphs he'd never seen before. I did the same on my semiannual pilgrimages to Cedar Mesa, and when we teamed up to search, the game took on a mildly competitive zest.

That day we'd already spotted a couple of minuscule granaries far off the ground on the nearly vertical opposite wall. We couldn't see any way to get to them except by rappelling, and the use of ropes to approach prehistoric sites on Cedar Mesa was interdicted by the Bureau of Land Management officials who regulated the place. More to the point was Vaughn's and my certainty that rappelling had not been the way the ancients had reached those two small ledges, on which they had mortared stones with mud to build bins to store the precious corn.

I was ready to hike on, but Vaughn had swiveled his binocs far to his right. "Check it out," he said quietly. "Somethin' right under the capstone layer. Way back, maybe half a mile." I raised my Leica Trinovids, found the spot, and focused. "Wow," I muttered. "Nice glassing."

It would take us another day to hike to the site, as we circled back almost to the head of the canyon before traversing the far rim. On the way, we discovered that the ruin could not be seen from directly opposite it. Nor was there any hint of it as we made our way along the capstone layer that guarded the elusive prize. We kept tiptoeing out to the edge of the cliff to peek sideways underneath its brim, never an easy task in the canyon country. As a landmark, we had memorized a pair of water streaks that gleamed silver in the sun on the side of the gorge we'd first walked.

They were easy to spot from across, but the locational anchor they offered gave us little help. We later realized that the ruin could be detected only from the vantage point where Vaughn had first seized it in his binocs. That invisibility had been a cardinal advantage for long-ago architects living in daily fear.

Just as we began to think we had overshot the site, we found a slope where dirt and stone rubble interrupted the capstone shelf. We scrambled down that chute, turned the corner—and there it was.

There are very few ruins anywhere in the Southwest that you can't really see until you're only thirty feet away from them. In that instant, Vaughn and I stared, wordless. What we beheld was a single unit of four large rooms sharing a clean façade, with a semidetached portal on the far end. But for a blown-out wall in the nearest room, the whole complex was remarkably well preserved, thanks to the huge natural ceiling that guarded it from rain and wind. The second room had a T-shaped doorway, and next to it a window that had been blocked up—some last-ditch remodel against a gnawing threat? We knew the refuge had been built in the thirteenth century, or at the very earliest the second half of the twelfth. For more than 700 years, after the small band who lived here had fled south in the great abandonment, the proud edifice had stood, intact and essentially changeless.

The most striking thing about the ruin, though, was that it was a solid two stories tall, stretching fifteen feet from the ruddy bedrock floor to the ocher caprock. Much of the wooden roof of the first story remained intact, and for a single second-story wall the builders had resorted to jacal— sticks and mud interwoven in a daub-and-wattle lacework. Black soot coated smooth the interior ceiling, the residue of generations of cooking and warming fires. As we poked our heads inside the several rooms, we saw rows of mortared sticks sprouting from the backside of the façade, like so many coat hooks in a closet.

Two-story ruins are rare on Cedar Mesa. This one looked like nothing else we had seen among all the dozen canyons. And here in the massive front wall, where the ancients might normally have stacked up whatever stones lay near at hand, the builders instead had conjured an abstract design by alternating clean white sandstone blocks with the usual brown chunks. We could only guess whether a sense of beauty had dictated the design, but to Vaughn and me, the dwelling was beautiful.

We were pretty sure that we weren't the first visitors since the thirteenth century to stumble upon this hidden ruin. For one thing, a paucity of potsherds strewed the runoff slope below the site. But by now, Vaughn had been guiding Cedar Mesa for almost two decades, and he'd never overheard the whisper of a rumor about this place. The Citadel and Moon House had long since become *vaut le voyage* stops on the imaginary Michelin tour of Cedar Mesa, even for the most casual dilettantes. Directions to those and a score of other ruins were starting to appear on the Internet, complete with GPS coordinates. It was about this time that Vaughn began to grouse about the burgeoning popularity of Cedar Mesa. "The whole place is goin' to hell!" I would hear him say every time we talked.

So finding this all-but-unknown ruin—and such a magnificent one to boot—seemed to prove that, after all, our cherished outback still had plenty of secrets up its sleeve, and that we might yet spend many a year searching for them. The immediate question, though—unspoken during the two hours we spent under the capstone, but hanging in our shared excitement—was, what should we do with our discovery?

I was pretty sure what Vaughn would do: take a select few clients to the site, surprising them with yet another prehistoric wonder no other guide could produce. But not just any clients—only those he knew would be struck by genuine awe as they turned the corner below the rubble chute and looked under the overhang. And only those who would never whip out GPSes to fixate the ruin, or publish their photos on the Internet. And he knew what I would do: write about the place, as I have here, in loving specificity, but without even naming the canyon in which we found it or giving the faintest hints how to get there.

And those choices—knee-jerk for both of us by now—raised again the troubling questions that had vexed me since my first excursions onto Cedar Mesa with Vaughn and Fred in 1992.

By the time of our late-2000s prowl along the canyon rim, both Vaughn and I would have said that Cedar Mesa was our favorite place on earth. It was impossible, though—at least for me—to separate the joy of finding the hidden ruin from a kind of covetous appropriation. When I had discovered the Citadel by accident in 1993, it was in the middle of a four-day solo backpack into Road Canyon during which I met not a single other hiker. At the bottom of the winding gulf whose intermittent stream flows eastward toward Comb Wash, I headed up a side branch, looked up the sheer wall on my right, and glimpsed, 500 feet above, the very top edge of a masoned suite of rooms. I actually said out loud, "Oh, my God!" It took me two hours and three false starts to work out a devious path up to that spectacular ruin on the crown of its own slender peninsular fin.

By the late 2000s, I expected to run into other hikers every time I went back to the Citadel, and one day several years after that, Vaughn took a couple of clients to the site, only to find (count 'em) sixty-five people in attendance, many jabbering away or spreading out their lunches on the ancients' bedrock porch. He fled.

In some way, Vaughn and I wanted to keep our new-found ruin a secret, to be shared only with the "right sort." In my case, at least, the elitism and ego-stroking of that impulse were hard to ignore. In *In Search of the Old Ones,* I had followed the journalistic ethic of the day (which still prevails), by not specifying where I'd found a certain wondrous artifact or ruin. But the popularity of my book inevitably increased Cedar Mesa visitation, especially as some readers treated *Old Ones* like a treasure map, showing up at the Kane Gulch headquarters and demanding that the rangers give them directions, for example, to "Roberts's pot."

One of my best friends, a writer as passionate about Cedar Mesa as I am, refuses to write anything about the place. It's his way, I suspect, of staying "pure," by doing nothing to encourage others to follow his lead into Grand Gulch or Slickhorn Canyon. But he's every bit as competitive as I am, and I've sensed in him the same gloating triumph that shivers my own shoulders when he plucks a perfect dart point out of the sand or glasses a masoned wall in an obscure cranny. We all want some part of our favorite place on earth to be *ours*, secreted from the rabble, tucked into the zippered pocket of our self-esteem.

Wilderness lovers have always decried the inroads made by latecomers on their landscapes of paradise. New roads are anathema: but Vaughn and I had taken for granted the road from which we started our rim-walk that day, as our friend Winston Hurst had not. Growing up in Blanding in the 1950s, Winston had been free to roam on foot all over the outback of Cedar Mesa, seldom encountering another pilgrim, and when civic boosters pushed through the new highway in 1976, blasting a hideous and unnecessary gouge through the Comb Ridge to accommodate even twelve-wheelers, he was outraged and depressed.

We all lapse easily into Vaughn's malediction that the place we loved is going to hell. Our favorite wilderness should always have stayed just as it was when we first encountered it. If we were born too late to discover the source of the Nile or the South Pole, we came along at just the right moment to explore Cedar Mesa. The illusion dies hard. . . .

◄◄ ►►

Like nearly all the prehistoric ruins and rock art panels on Cedar Mesa, the two-story dwelling that Vaughn and I found hidden beneath the top ledge of the long canyon was the work of the Anasazi, or Ancestral Puebloans.*

---

* In the late 1990s, certain Puebloan activists, mostly from Hopi, started objecting to the term "Anasazi," on the grounds that it was a Navajo word with pejorative connotations. In the Diné language, "Anasazi" means something like "ancestral enemies" or "enemies of our ancestors." Younger archaeologists proposed instead "Ancestral Puebloans," which quickly became de rigueur in academic discourse.

For many reasons, I've resisted this sanitizing of the taxonomy, and stubbornly gone ahead using the term "Anasazi." I won't repeat the arguments I appended to my previous books, except to make three new points. One: We are by no means sure that all the Anasazi became Puebloans. Two: "Navajo" is a Tewa word meaning something like "farm fields in the valley," which might

Those people, originally nomadic, later semisedentary, first arrived on the mesa around AD 200, although whether they were the direct descendants of Archaic or even Paleo-Indian predecessors whose artifacts have been found here and there scattered in the piñon-juniper forest remains an unsolved question. One measure of the Anasazi passion for this heartland is the fact that shortly before the abandonment—say, around AD 1250—more than a thousand men, women, and children flourished through all four seasons on Cedar Mesa. In 2020, the year-round population of the mesa is zero.

The greater Bears Ears region extends far beyond Cedar Mesa: on the east to the dramatic monocline called the Comb Ridge; north across lofty Elk Ridge and the Dark Canyon Plateau into Beef Basin and Lockhart Basin; along the corridor of Indian Creek, one of the country's premier rock climbing areas; even west to the detached segment comprising Moqui Canyon and the Red Rock Plateau. (See map, p. xi.) All these landscapes are virtually uninhabited today but incredibly rich in antiquities. Alas, the whole region is haunted by a 140-year-long tradition of illegal pothunting that has ravaged its prehistoric legacy.

Yet not long after the last Anasazi bands deserted this homeland, along with all of the Colorado Plateau, just before 1300, other Native American tribes—principally Utes, Paiutes, and Navajos—moved into the region and made it part of their own homeland. (Some would say those tribes overlapped with the Anasazi, but artifactual evidence is hard to find.) With the coming of the Spanish in the eighteenth century and Anglo-

---

sound pejorative to the far-ranging nomads the Navajo were at the time their sometime Puebloan enemies named them. But there's no movement afoot that I know of to purge "Navajo" in favor of "Diné." Three: Though I wholeheartedly endorse the replacement of "Eskimo" with "Inuit" or "Bushmen" with "San," that's because we value what the people call themselves. Nobody knows what the Anasazi called themselves.

Nonetheless, I'm regularly scolded by readers and reviewers for using "Anasazi," as if I were a rookie journalist who just didn't know any better. To these critics I say, Enough!

Americans in the nineteenth, the Bears Ears region became a vital place for non-natives. And in the last two decades of the nineteenth century, all of the twentieth, and the first two decades of the twenty-first, a protean medley of visitors and settlers with mutually incompatible goals swarmed across this outback. We're talking about gold, silver, and uranium miners; cattlemen and sheepherders; Mormon town-builders; oil and gas drillers; hunters; wood-gatherers; archaeologists; hikers and backpackers; and aficionados of the Anasazi such as Vaughn and me.

Starting in 2015, this stew of contradictory needs and desires reached a boiling point. With President Obama's declaration of the Bears Ears National Monument in December 2016, and President Trump's evisceration of the monument in December 2017, the conflict exploded into the most acrimonious wrangle over a national park or monument in American history. As of this writing, no matter how white-hot the bulletins streaming out of the controversy almost weekly, no final resolution is likely to arrive for years—and then, in all probability, in the verdicts of courts, only to be further appealed ad infinitum and ad nauseam. Yet all the while, the landscape that Vaughn and I and many others love best in the world, and for which others have quite opposite though equally heartfelt plans, lies fragile under the assault.

The controversy tends to align around predictable ideological fronts. Backpackers versus miners, drillers, and cattlemen. Environmentalists versus Mormons. Hikers versus ATVers and Jeepers. Democrats versus Republicans. Obama contra Trump.

Yet with the Bears Ears, a new phenomenon in America's history of preserving endangered lands emerged. For the first time ever, the initial thrust to declare a region off-limits to development came not from Anglo-dominated interest groups such as the Sierra Club or the Southern Utah Wilderness Alliance (SUWA), but from Native Americans themselves. In 2015, spearheaded by the work of an extraordinary Navajo activist named Mark Maryboy, a group called the Inter-Tribal Coalition proposed an area even larger than what Obama set aside to be protected, not as a national monument but as an official conservation area. (It was a proposal that many of us favored over monument status, since conservation areas never attract the mass tourism that in turn dictates stringent rules that forever change—and, we would say, inevitably trivialize—the quality of the visitor's experience.)

Roughly speaking, the Inter-Tribal Coalition aligned its priorities with environmentalists and low-impact recreationists, with the hikers and the Democrats. But this visionary Native American thrust put a new premium on oral history. If the landscape of the Bears Ears was sacred, it was so because of the unwritten but fervent record, passed down by word of mouth from one generation to the next, of what the place meant to native people before the first miner or Mormon or surveyor or archaeologist arrived on the scene.

By 2020, many articles and six books about the Bears Ears had been published. Nearly all of them leaned toward the environmentalist and Native American perspective. Several were anthologies of testimony from folks ranging from natives to archaeologists to artists and poets and guides, all pleading for the restoration of Obama's monument.

It's not my intention in this book to add to this chorus. Instead I hope to glide through the centuries as I evoke the complex human history of the magnificent Bears Ears landscape. Embedded in that history are all kinds of poignant ironies and surprising contradictions. Gold miners and cowboys, for instance, preceded the first true recreationists by half a century. Writers as diverse as Zane Grey, Edward Abbey, and Tony Hillerman embraced this wilderness, but saw quite different epiphanies written in cliff and canyon and butte. Outlaw cronies of Butch Cassidy fled posses across the plateaus or lay low in canyon nooks. Archaeologists worked in cahoots with pothunters. Other pothunters committed suicide. Navajos who escaped the genocidal Long Walk in 1863–64 hid out for five years in the Bears Ears. Cliven Bundy's son Ryan helped foment a Sagebrush Rebellion showdown in one of the canyons that ended up sending a county commissioner to jail. Mormons regularly push their Jeeps along the trail first blazed by the Hole-in-the-Rock expedition of 1879–80, the LDS founding myth of southeastern Utah. The tragicomic saga of the last

Indian war in the United States unfurled toward its denouement on the eastern edge of Cedar Mesa.

And Vaughn and I, no doubt, will head back to the Bears Ears year after year, searching for things we've never seen before, until we're so decrepit we have to crawl.

◄◄ ►►

So much partisan acrimony, so many broadsides and polemics, have already been generated by Obama's stunning creation of the national monument and by Trump's equally stunning destruction of it, that the weary reader might well complain, *Who needs another book about the Bears Ears?* Even though the controversy crystallizes a fundamental American schism in values that clusters around notions of land and property and wilderness and development—a schism that spans more than two centuries of our tenure on this continent "from sea to shining sea"—no manifesto is likely to clarify the mess. No Rachel Carson or John Muir is going to emerge to proclaim the just solution, and whatever becomes of the Bears Ears after the final verdicts dribble out of the courts years from now will leave the losers embittered for generations to come.

What I hope to do in this book is write a human history of this magnificent tract of canyons, plateaus, hoodoos, and basins. Lest this very idea conjure up some dreary textbook, with chapters marching chronologically from Paleo-Indian through Ute and Navajo, on to Mormon settlers and the "outdoor recreation industry," I promise to avoid that taxonomic straitjacket. I intend instead to jump around among the ages, muse on some of the heroes and villains of that history while ignoring others, and seize upon such tangled outbursts in the record as the pothunting career of Earl Shumway, or Posey's doomed war, or the mythic hegira of the Hole-in-the-Rock expedition. I'll try to bring the characters to life, not the lawsuits. A model for this book is Wallace Stegner's *Mormon Country* (1942), that deft and rambling grab bag of essays that somehow captures the essence of the culture of the Latter-day Saints in the landscape they chose for their New Zion.

Nor will I hesitate to interleave the passages about dramatic events and outlandish movers and shakers with accounts of my own adventures in the Bears Ears landscape, like the episode that opens this chapter. After all, this is the part of the world that I love most, the outback that if I were told I had only one more chance to see, I'd grab with both feet without a thought for any other choice. For me, the human history of the Bears Ears is inextricably tied up with the nearly three decades I've spent wandering, camping, and prowling across it. It's where I head instinctively when I sense the need to renew my sense of wonder. And wonder is the font of curiosity.

TWO

IN SEARCH OF A LOST RACE

As the Inter-Tribal Coalition and its allies began to put together their proposal to protect the vast backcountry domain they hoped to save from developers, they struggled to give it a name. The analogies of other Utah parks and monuments were at once helpful and frustrating. Canyonlands and Arches were apt names for national parks dominated, respectively, by narrow corridors and slots enclosed by towering cliffs and by natural bridges and windows worn by wind and erosion into the sandstone. Grand Staircase–Escalante, on the other hand, was an awkward mouthful, especially because even diehard visitors had a hard time identifying just what and where the Grand Staircase was. An amalgam of the place names of the component landscapes of the endangered region—Comb Ridge–Cedar Mesa–Elk Ridge–Dark Canyon–Beef Basin National Monument?—was obviously not going to work.

As early as 2012, the Navajo elders and other participants in the effort to preserve this wilderness, led by Mark Maryboy, had incorporated as Utah Diné Bikéyah (UDB), borrowing a phrase in their own language that translates as "the people's sacred lands." According to Gavin Noyes, an Anglo who is the executive director of Salt Lake City–based UDB, Diné Bikéyah reverberates with deeper, subtler meanings. "It signifies the relationship of all people to the earth, through the soles of our feet," says

Noyes. "That meaning is profoundly better than trying to pronounce it as an Anglo."

As a name for the proposed conservation area, though, Diné Bikéyah threatened to seem too arcane to non–Native Americans, and it was off-putting to members of other tribes such as the Utes and Hopi, because it seemed to give strong priority to the Navajo. "Actually," recalls Noyes, "everyone disliked the monument name from the beginning. Nobody could say it, and there is no way it was ever going to get the massive campaign behind it that we needed."

It was Noyes who came up with Bears Ears as a proper appellation. "What turned me onto the idea of the buttes was the effort to get all the tribes involved," he says. "Utes had never heard the name 'Cedar Mesa,' even though some of them had been born on it, and other tribes from farther away always zeroed in on the buttes. Eventually I studied the map, analyzed the topo lines, and realized you could see the land of the entire monument proposal from the top of the Ears. Then I asked all the tribes I knew for the name in their languages, and asked if it was suitable. Amazingly, they all said their names meant 'Bears Ears' in English, and the English version united everyone."

In the spring of 2017, after President Obama had announced the creation of Bears Ears National Monument, tourists began arriving from all over the country to see what all the fuss was about. Many of them alighted at Recapture Lodge in Bluff, where owner Jim Hook (my friend for the last twenty-five years) was happy to give directions. "How do I get to the Bears Ears?" they asked Jim, who pulled out a map and indicated state highways 261 and 95 and the dirt road that climbs north to the top of Elk Ridge. With a mixture of rue and mirth, Jim later told me, "You know how muddy that road gets in spring? Some of them got their cars stuck trying to get up to the plateau. And the ones who made it came back and complained, 'So what's the big deal about the monument? The Bears Ears are just a couple of bumps.'"

With Coronado's massive *entrada* from 1540 to 1542, for the first time Europeans made a major incursion into what would become the

American Southwest. (A few years earlier, the lost quartet of Spaniards led by Álvar Núñez Cabeza de Vaca, who during eight years of wandering and enslavement by Indians managed to cross the continent from Florida's Gulf shore to Mexico's Pacific coast, traversed southern New Mexico somewhere near the pueblo of Zuni. Their tales spurred the ambition of New Spain to explore and conquer the unknown lands to the north.) In 1598 Don Juan de Oñate defeated several tribes and set up a Spanish colony near the upper Rio Grande, moving its capital to Santa Fe in 1610.

Despite this stronghold in today's New Mexico, the governors and Franciscan priests in charge of the colony had such shaky control over the Puebloans whom they had suppressed and turned into servants and Catholics that for almost two centuries, no real effort to probe farther north and west was launched. It was only with the establishment of Spanish missions along the California coast in the 1760s and '70s that it became desirable to blaze a trading route from Santa Fe to Monterey. This grand campaign was entrusted to a pair of inexperienced explorers, the Franciscan padres Silvestre Vélez de Escalante and Francisco Atanasio Domínguez. Their epic seven-month, 1,700-mile journey in 1776 was a failure, in that the small team of twelve never came close to reaching California, but it remains one of the greatest voyages of European discovery in the New World. (My 2019 book, *Escalante's Dream*, recounts the forty-day retracing of the Domínguez-Escalante route that my wife, Sharon, and I undertook in 2017.)

As far as I can ascertain, the first mention in print of any part of the greater Bears Ears domain comes in a single line from Escalante's diary. On August 23, 1776, describing the course of what the team called the Río de San Pedro (today's San Miguel), the friar claimed that downstream the river joined the Dolores "near the small Sierra de la Sal—so called for their being salt beds next to it from which, as they informed us, the Yutas [Utes] hereabouts provide themselves." ("Sal" is Spanish for "salt.") Although the padres' party traveled as far north as current-day Provo and as far west as Cedar City, Utah, they never came closer than twenty-five

miles in a line to the vast tract that the Inter-Tribal Coalition would seek
to preserve in 2015.

Escalante never mentions seeing the La Sal Mountains, which rise
southeast of Moab, but the team could not have failed to do so from several vantage points, including the high Uncompahgre Plateau in western
Colorado. What's striking about the reference, however, is that apparently
the range was already known by a Spanish name before Domínguez and
Escalante came along. In the two decades just before the 1776 expedition,
New Mexican traders had made their own forays north and west into the
unknown. Because bartering with the Indians had been declared illegal
by the governor, those sly entrepreneurs were unlikely to commit their
voyages to paper.

In 1829–30, a team of sixty men under Antonio Armijo succeeded in
linking Santa Fe to California, thereby establishing what would become
the legendary Old Spanish Trail. But Armijo traveled well to the south of
the Bears Ears domain, as he threaded a path more or less along today's
border between Utah and Arizona. A year later, two other traders, Anglo-
Americans named William Wolfskill and George Yount, may have been
the first non-natives actually to cross the terrain of the future Bears Ears
monument, as they pioneered a northern variant of Armijo's trail.

The only surviving account of this journey emerges in a patchwork of
documents that were lost for almost seventy years. Late in life, in 1855,
Yount dictated a memoir of his adventures to a friend, Reverend Orange
Clark. Clark rewrote the story in the third person and tried unsuccessfully
to find a publisher. In 1922, the California scholar Francis Farquhar came
upon scraps of the Clark manuscript. A single page of this hodgepodge
covers the trek, which must have taken weeks, from Abiquiu to the team's
crossing of the Green River, probably near today's Utah town of the same
name. Yount (through Clark) offers no details of the passage that took the
party into Utah and along the eastern edge of the Bears Ears landscape,
except that his and Wolfskill's team of sixteen men with thirty-two horses
and mules was "quite large enough to thread the wilderness, much better than one more numerous." The men were on constant guard against

Indian attack, for "at the present time . . . the savages are provided with firearms which they use with great dexterity."

The Wolfskill/Yount variant on Armijo's Spanish Trail seems to have become a regular trading route between Santa Fe and California for about twenty years, though no subsequent travelers bothered to leave a written account of it. Yount's modern editor, Charles L. Camp, highlights the merits and drawbacks of the trek: "No wagon seems ever to have traversed the whole length of this difficult trail. It was preferred over more direct routes owing to Apache trouble in Arizona, the dangerous crossing of the Colorado [River] Desert, and the waterless stretches of northwestern Arizona." The great Western historian LeRoy Hafen salutes the Wolfskill/Yount itinerary as "the longest, crookedest, most arduous pack-mule route in the history of America."

It would take the US government almost three more decades to muster up any interest in the convoluted canyon country the traders on Wolfskill's trail traversed—and then the motive was not so much exploratory as military. Alarmed by Brigham Young's grand ambitions for a Kingdom of Zion in the mountain West—a Mormon empire autonomous from, and thumbing its nose at, the bureaucrats in Washington—President James Buchanan directed a poorly coordinated series of marches, threats, bluffs, and skirmishes that has come to be known as the Utah War of 1857–58. When all this bluster failed to bring Brigham to heel, Buchanan launched a trio of expeditions in search of better military approaches to far-off Zion.

In charge of a team, grandly titled the San Juan Exploring Expedition, that set out from Santa Fe in July 1859 was a captain in the Army Corps of Topographical Engineers named John N. Macomb. In addition to trying to find a practical new route into the land of the Saints, Macomb was charged with mapping the little-known territory and with discovering the well-hidden gorge where the two great rivers of the Green and Colorado joined. Macomb would prove to be an explorer of stunningly dim imagination. Fortunately for history, two of his assistants had souls in their breasts and wonder in their eyeballs.

Dr. John S. Newberry, trained as a physician and a geologist, had a keen interest in the traces of prehistoric peoples that his boss utterly lacked. In a characteristic passage from his journal, reprinted in Macomb's report, Newberry muses upon a basin "everywhere covered with fragments of broken pottery, showing its former occupation by a considerable number of inhabitants." He was even stirred to ponder "how they managed to exist" in such a barren locale, and why they had vanished "several hundred years ago." (Newberry's full journal has likewise vanished, perhaps thrown away by Macomb after he used it to beef up the report.)

Charles H. Dimmock was trained as a cartographer. It was he who sketched the splendid map that accompanied the report. In addition, Dimmock kept his own diary and made many excellent and precise drawings of the landscape. Lost for a century and a half, both the diary and the drawings were only recently rediscovered gathering dust in the archives of the Virginia Historical Society in Richmond by the Southwestern scholar Steven K. Madsen. Though constantly homesick for his wife and baby son left behind in Baltimore, Dimmock recorded the journey in prose that sometimes approaches the rhapsodic.

By mid-August the party was crossing the Great Sage Plain of eastern Utah, more or less on the Wolfskill/Yount trail. That epithet, still in regular use by the folks who live in Blanding and Monticello, was Newberry's coinage. On August 22, a scouting team of ten left the trail and struck out due west, some miles north of the Abajo Mountains, hoping to find the confluence of the Colorado (or Grand, as it was then called) and the Green. Macomb was in a foul mood, for once the men left the desert plateau and wound down into the canyons, it was obvious to him that this tortured labyrinth could never be smoothed into a military road bearing wagons.

The heat was intense. Stymied by a pouroff that halted all progress downstream, on August 23 six of the men climbed a 1,200-foot "pinnacle overhanging [the] river" in hopes of at least catching a glimpse of the fugitive confluence. The San Juan Explorers had followed Harts Draw down into Indian Creek. They were smack in the middle of the northern half of the tract of land that President Obama would declare the Bears

Ears National Monument in 2016. For modern visitors, this is one of the most sublime corners of the Southwest. The road along the creek delivers tourists to Canyonlands National Park, established in 1964. Clean vertical fissures in the sandstone cliffs along the right side of Indian Creek test the best rock climbers in the world with splitters, off-widths, and layback cracks. And nooks and crannies on all sides served more than 700 years ago as canvases for visionary petroglyphs and pictographs.

Barring the unrecorded wanderings of a few trappers and traders before 1859, Macomb's scouts were perhaps the first Anglo-Americans ever to behold this wilderness. The soaring towers of Canyonlands blocked all but the most partial view of a mighty river far below in the west. Wrote Macomb in disgust, "I cannot conceive of a more worthless and impracticable region than the one we now found ourselves in."

Newberry and Dimmock, on the other hand, were transported. The former claimed he was witness to "the wildest and most fantastic scenery on the globe. . . . Scattered over the plain were thousands of . . . fantastically formed buttes . . . pyramids, domes, towers, columns, spires, of every conceivable form and size." Wrote Dimmock, "[L]ooking around there met our eyes such a view as is not to be seen elsewhere on earth."

The summit on which the men stood, 4,899 feet above sea level, later identified as a promontory to which has been given the name Newberry Butte, stands near the border of Canyonlands National Park and the proposed Bears Ears monument. The view from on high wrote a finis to the expedition's search. The next day the party would start its long journey back to Santa Fe. In Macomb's jaundiced view, the whole enterprise had been a failure, for no military road could have been engineered along this approach any closer than 200 miles as the crow flies to Brigham Young's temple in Zion.

◄◄ ►►

On a cool, cloudy day with intermittent spits of rain, Sharon and I drove south from Moab in our rental SUV. A few miles beyond La Sal Junction, we were more or less following the old Wolfskill/Yount trail, though in reverse. Opposite the bulbous tower of tawny sandstone called Church Rock, we left US Highway 191 and turned west onto State Highway 211, also known as the Indian Creek Corridor Scenic Byway. That road meanders northwest for thirty-three miles before dead-ending in Canyonlands National Park.

It was May 2016. We were following the Toyota Tacoma operated by our friends Greg Child, Shannon O'Donoghue, and Greg's daughter, Ariann Child. For the last fifteen years Greg had been my companion on many a jaunt in southeast Utah (and northeast Arizona) in search of prehistoric ruins and rock art. In 2004, Greg and I had joined with Vaughn Hadenfeldt to make the first end-to-end traverse of Comb Ridge, 125 miles of slickrock backpacking through eighteen days in September, most of them in ninety-degree heat.

Now, as we drove along Indian Creek, we paralleled the journey Captain Macomb's party had prosecuted 157 years earlier, in their futile search for the great confluence and for a military road to Salt Lake City. As they pushed down Harts Draw, Macomb's scouts traveled about six miles north of the future Route 211.

Fifteen miles in along the scenic byway, as the road joins Indian Creek and turns abruptly north, a pullout on the righthand side beckons travelers to inspect Newspaper Rock, one of the most famous petroglyph panels in the Southwest. A metal fence, hung with an injunction ("Do Not Climb on Fence"), tries to keep visitors at a healthy distance from the panel, where as early as 1892 Anglo passersby etched their calling cards alongside the ancient runes. The wayside cliff is both a Utah State Historical Monument and a National Historic Site. Across the road, picnic tables invite stays more leisurely than the five minutes most visitors devote to the rock art. "Feel free to bring your dog" urges one online site celebrating the place.

That gray morning, however, neither the Childs nor Sharon and I stopped at Newspaper Rock. We'd all seen the panel before (Greg and I many times), and the touristic packaging of what must once have been a numinous shrine felt off-putting. Which is not to say that the gallery isn't an amazing complex of disparate visions. Archaeologists have counted some 640 distinct images on the relatively small surface of the panel. Nearly every square inch of available stone has been appropriated. Anasazi evocations of shamans with horned headdresses, bear-paw prints, and bighorn sheep pierced with atlatl darts mingle side-by-side with bison and with Ute or Navajo hunters on horseback wielding bows and arrows. Woven through it all are wavy lines and constellations of dots whose meanings are forever lost. The experts guess that, barring the modern graffiti, the designs on Newspaper Rock range in age from 2,000 years to a mere century.

The Navajo name for the panel is Tse' Hane', which translates as "The Rock That Tells a Story." *Okay, fellas,* I imagine addressing some absent Diné sage, *so what story exactly does it tell? I'm all ears. Bears Ears, in fact.*

Rich though it is, Newspaper Rock has never captivated me. With all its vignettes crowded into a single slab of Wingate sandstone, the panel is just too *busy* for my liking. It is of course the height of dilettantism, or of cultural myopia, to apply a photo editor's sneer to a panoply of signs and symbols graven by many different artists across a span of twenty centuries. But that May morning, Sharon and I, as well as the family in the car ahead of us, were in search of more esoteric links to the Old Ones.

Exactly a year before, Greg, Sharon, and I had joined with four friends for a five-day llama trek into lower Fish Creek, on the eastern edge of Cedar Mesa. We'd poked among half a dozen ruins and found as many walls covered with pictographs and petroglyphs (brilliant negative hand-prints in white kaolin powder apotheosizing one major ruin), though untimely heat rendered us all more lethargic than we liked to be. As we hiked out, I was already planning a return to Cedar Mesa in the fall.

The twelve months after our Fish Creek outing, however, turned my life upside down. In June 2015, just a couple of weeks after the llama trip, I noticed a lump in what I thought was a lymph node in my neck. It turned out to be stage 4 throat cancer. At the Dana-Farber Cancer Institute in Boston, I was plunged into radiation treatments and chemotherapy. That autumn, rather than hiking in Utah, I spent weeks in the hospital, suffering from everything from aspiration pneumonia to mucositis to colitis. Unable to swallow normally, I had a feeding tube inserted in my chest, and for the next seven months took nearly all my food in the form of bottles of Ensure Plus and Osmolite poured down the tube. I had half-hour coughing fits, vomited regularly, and fainted several times, striking various parts of my body on hard surfaces. There was a lot of pain, and a lot of morphine, and at one point in the hospital I reached a dim threshold where I thought it might not be so bad to let go of it all and succumb to the cancer.

For half a year, Sharon and I ventured no farther than fifteen miles from our home in Watertown, Massachusetts. We attempted only a single meal in a restaurant. In November, after the last radiation zapping and chemo infusion, I tried to exercise, but a stumbling walk most of the way down the block, with frequent rests on neighbors' walls, was the best effort I could muster.

In March 2016, however, a techie at Brigham and Women's Hospital pulled the feeding tube loose with an audible *pop* and a spurt of blood. By May we'd decided to try to hike once more in Utah, with only the shortest and easiest forays as a goal. And so it was that that damp, overcast day we found ourselves driving along the Indian Creek byway behind the car that Greg was piloting.

We parked beside a mileage marker that Greg and I had remembered as the clue to a hidden panel. The hike up to the cliff required an ascent of no more than a hundred feet, but I had to stop several times, plant my hands on my knees, and reduce my gasping to mere deep breathing. The Childs and I had visited this site before, but it was new to Sharon. And now it felt new to me: for cancer gave me the gift of gratitude that I could still stumble to a *locus mirabilis* whose access I had always taken for granted.

Unlike Newspaper Rock, this vertical slab of dark sandstone bore an aggregation of designs that hinted at a coherent whole: a mere thirty or forty images, not 640. Archaeologists like to use the sterile term "anthropomorph" to avoid anthropomorphizing human-looking creatures that, in the mind of the artist, could have conjured up anything from the scary dart-slinger next valley over to an ancestor discovered in a dream to a god who appeared in datura visions in some grotesque parody of human form. The three big dudes that centered this panel ran the gamut of anthropo-ness. The one on the right had the massive quadrilateral chest, the square head with hair bobs dangling off either ear, the broad sash across the waist, the vestigial dangling arms and missing legs of a classic Basketmaker II honcho-morph. He (it?) could have been carved any time between 1500 BC and AD 50. But the hulking guy in the center and his smaller compa-dre on the left looked more like robots than men: yes, pendants dangled from their pencil necks onto their blank chests, but their heads were fea-tureless squares. Center guy had a plume sprouting from the top of his forehead—an antenna to catch the music of the spheres?

In the upper left-hand corner, three tiny bighorn sheep romped toward the show. No mistaking them for mythic beasts; no ovimorphs, they. But in the lower left-hand corner, a clown seemed to mock the whole stately composition. He danced on splayed, froglike feet that were as big as his torso. His left arm twirled toward the sky, while in his right he held a curved stick. A fending stick, to ward off unwelcome missiles? Call him a scurramorph.

But just as I was tempted to squeeze the whole panel into a story, I had to reckon with the snake wriggling all the way across the composition from right to left. Its sinuous body writhed through a remarkable twenty-one bends, and its head seemed poised to strike deep into the left cheek of the junior robot-morph. What I could not ignore was that the snake had been etched on top of all the images it crossed. It had been added to the panel sometime after the three big dudes—months after, or maybe centu-ries. No one can be sure what superimposition signifies in Southwestern rock art. It could be, as with Aboriginal art in Australia, that being seen is not the point, so much as being performed. Carving new images atop old ones is simply conserving canvas. Or it could, in some cases, signify an act of negation, of revisionism—the new design canceling the power and the meaning of the old one under it.

The more I studied the panel, the less confident I was that I could stuff it into a story. I was reminded of the pithy words of the great archaeologist Earl Morris almost a century before, as he stared at a panel of spiral pictographs in Navajo Canyon, south and west of the Bears Ears domain. "There is no key to the meaning of these ancient rock markings," Morris wrote. "Conjecture is interesting but fruitless."

The only thing I could be sure of was that the panel was pure Anasazi, no matter when and by whom it was etched. Just left of the slab, a clean-cut chimney a little wider than my body formed a corridor deep into the bedrock ridge from which the cliff hung. Even inside that slot, on the left-hand wall, the Old Ones had limned a couple more anthropomorphs, these with pinheads, legs and feet, and arms spread akimbo like those of defensive linemen closing in to sack the quarterback. Just above those fellows Ralph Hurst had patiently scratched his name in capitals, with a date of 1911. The "P" in "RALPH" threatened to decapitate one of the pinheads.

I guessed that Ralph (at the time of our visit to Indian Creek, 105 years had passed since he had left his Kilroy on the stone) was a good old boy from Blanding. Three years later in the Blanding cemetery I would come across his grave, indicating that the man, born in 1892, had celebrated his ninetieth birthday before expiring in 1982. Ralph was one of seventy-one Hursts interred in the graveyard. I wondered if he was some kin—a great-uncle, perhaps?—to my friend the brilliant and iconoclastic Blanding archaeologist Winston Hurst. A few weeks later, Winston filled in the lacuna by e-mail: "Ralph was my Dad's first cousin. Worked on a gov't survey crew as a chain man, I believe, at the time he left that inscription." Far from a good old Blanding boy, then, Ralph was only nineteen when he'd carved his graffito. It was what you did back then after a hard day surveying the road.

A rain squall swept in from the south. We found an unmarked stretch of cliff where the wall overhung, crouched there, and ate a meager lunch. I was happy to have revisited a panel I'd first discovered about a decade before, but Greg had another plan for the afternoon.

We drove a few miles farther along the Indian Creek Byway, then parked opposite a tributary canyon. The creek was running high with spring rains, and the only way to cross it was on a fallen log that stretched barkless and level from the near bank to the far. Following her dad's lead, eleven-year-old Ariann pranced across the log, but I felt so unsteady on my feet that I resorted instead to an ungainly shuffle astride the dead tree, riding it like a dude-ranch tourist.

An old trail led up the side canyon, but almost at once Greg veered off to the right through a field of bunch grass scattered with small piñon pines. After a quarter mile, he stopped beside a single boulder about ten feet tall. One clean face of orange-brown sandstone bore a pair of superbly rendered humanoids, their features reduced to stylized slashes and curves. The heads were bucket-like trapezoids each sprouting a pair of spikes or horns; eyes were mere horizontal slits, mouths and noses smudged together in rude vertical gashes. A single outline rendered the armless trapezoidal bodies, which ended in feet splayed outward. Yet across the chest of each figure dangled five or six drooping rings (necklaces or breastplates?), with spherical pendants hanging from each. It was as if the person carved into stone were transmogrified into a pectoral display that defined his or her status in the world.

What dazzled me at once was the recognition that these anthropomorphs were not Anasazi at all. They sprang from another culture, the Fremont, almost all of the other manifestations of which are found well to the north and west of Indian Creek. I had seen kindred priests or shamans or ancestral spirits etched on panels as far from here as Vernal, Utah, and Dinosaur National Monument on the border of Utah and Colorado. But among the thousands of humanoids carved and painted that I had beheld in the canyons of Cedar Mesa, not one had the Fremont stamp.

In other words, here in the center of the soon-to-become Bears Ears monument, we were face-to-face with an ancient frontier between two cultures that had overlapped in time but lived in fundamentally different ways.

It was a lawyer turned Harvard archaeologist named Noel Morss who identified the distinct culture in the late 1920s, naming it after the Fremont River in central Utah where the sites he was digging puzzled him with their diagnostic differences from the well-codified patterns of the Anasazi. There are still a few experts who reject Morss's distinction—one of them (whom I highly respect) likes to call the northern phenomenon "hillbilly Anasazi," though only off the record. But textbooks and conferences nowadays devote pages and hours to the Fremont. On the many days in the early 2000s that I had spent hiking in Range Creek and rafting Desolation Canyon on the Green River, I had compiled my own checklist of Fremont differences from the Anasazi.

The pottery bears little or nothing in common. Such stunning late Anasazi styles as Tusayan Polychrome and Mesa Verde Black-on-White look nothing like Uinta Gray or Ivie Creek Black-on-White. Fremont dwellings are hard to find, and generally unimpressive—nothing compares to such multistory Anasazi wonders as Pueblo Bonito or Square Tower House. The granaries of each culture have distinct styles: Anasazi with doors in the front façade, Fremont top-loading. And in general, the Anasazi made their granaries hard to raid by building them on scary, high, hard-to-get-to ledges, while the Fremont were at pains to hide them in esoteric nooks, tucked among jumbles of boulders, even camouflaged to look like mere rocks.

With a shorter growing season farther north, the Fremont never fully gave up a nomadic way of life, as the late-stage Anasazi did. Growing corn and beans and squash was too uncertain a gamble on which to stake a whole band or village's survival. And so, hunting and gathering must have remained essential for the Fremont. And warfare?

It is in the realm of rock art that Fremont culture shows its glory. The humanoids carved on the walls near McKonkie Ranch and McKee Springs Wash in northeastern Utah seem designed to intimidate: warriors carrying shields, adorned with headdresses and breast-plate jewelry, dangle "trophy heads" from their hands—possibly the decapitated heads of enemies killed in battle. There are certain unique Fremont artifacts, among them an array of extremely fragile figurines made of unfired clay (drop one in a pot of water and it would dissolve within an hour). None are more splendid than the set of twelve figurines discovered by a rancher named Clarence Pilling in 1950 inside a small alcove in Range Creek. (In my 2015 book *The Lost World of the Old Ones*, I lavished half a chapter on the Pilling figurines, their miraculous survival through decades of being carted from motel to bank to courthouse as part of a curio road show, and the enigma of their meaning and purpose.)

Up the side canyon off Indian Creek that overcast day in 2016, the five of us spent several hours admiring the Fremont anthropomorphs. With the depredations cancer had inflicted on me, I had started to despair of ever again hiking far enough into the back country to find new prehistoric wonders—new to me, at least. But on this day, within a mile of a paved road, I'd been blessed to witness two masterpieces of ancient art.

And to ponder their juxtaposition. It is next to impossible to date rock art, but I couldn't help wondering: had the Fremont and Anasazi coexisted here, in this narrow but well-watered corridor under the cliffs and buttes of Indian Creek? Had they traded, or even intermarried? Or had they waged war upon each other? The archaeologists have no definitive answers.

Most beguiling is the ultimate fate of the neighboring cultures. We know for a certainty that after the abandonment of the Colorado Plateau just before AD 1300, sizable cohorts of Anasazi men, women, and children migrated south and east and ultimately assimilated with the Pueblos along the Rio Grande and west to Hopi. The Fremont lasted only as long as the Anasazi, or a little longer, in their vast northern domain. But what happened to them, none of the experts can definitively say. They may have merged with Numic tribes—Utes, Shoshone, Paiutes—moving in around AD 1300 from the Great Basin to the west. Or they may have migrated elsewhere (one respected archaeologist sees the Fremont "becoming" the Kiowa on the western Great Plains). Or they may have died out completely, whether by massacre at the hands of Numic interlopers, or through starvation. What they left behind, like the shaman/seers staring at eternity from the boulder up our nondescript side canyon, haunts us with lost significance.

◄◄ ►►

Sixteen years after Captain Macomb's frustrated stab across the canyon-lands in quest of a secret wagon route to attack—or at least keep tabs on—the runaway kingdom of the Latter-day Saints, a far more ambitious government expedition set out with an altogether different mission: to survey and map the Great West, in anticipation of its settlement by Americans. This grand enterprise was entrusted to Ferdinand V. Hayden, who divided his teams into four divisions, each with its territorial mandate. An ardent geologist and explorer, Hayden had already won his spurs on an 1867 survey of Nebraska. By 1875 he was director of the US Geological and Geographical Survey of the Territories, which soon became known simply as the Hayden Survey.

Hayden put William Henry Holmes in charge of his Southwestern or San Juan River Division. Trained as an artist and geologist, Holmes would go on to a stellar career as the first director of the Bureau of American Ethnology after John Wesley Powell and later as the director of the National Gallery of Art. Along the way he taught himself archaeology and anthropology, and his publications are still taken seriously by experts in those fields today. Rounding out Holmes's small party were two junior topographers, two mule packers, and a camp cook.

In charge of his own division was the pioneering photographer William Henry Jackson, whose hard-won glass plate images of wonders such as the Mount of the Holy Cross and ruins on Mesa Verde built a public enthusiasm for the West that has never waned. Jackson's magpie intelligence seized upon everything to do with the wilderness, and he wrote well both about science and his own adventures.

With far more optimism and a far broader mandate than Macomb's secret probe against the Mormons, Holmes's Southwestern Division set out from Denver in early June 1875. By the first week of August the men were working their way down the San Juan River toward the future corner of the Bears Ears domain. But any appreciation of the landscape was subjugated to the party's worries about the Indians they kept running into.

Holmes's comments on the natives who pestered his survey win him no points for cultural sensitivity today.

Not only did they stay all night boldly in the camp to which we had tracked them, but at noon rode coolly down to our camp, dismounted, and seated themselves in a half circle in the middle of the camp and proceeded to scrutinize every object in the outfit, to beg for this and pretend to wish to "swap" for that. . . . One old scamp had the audacity to nudge me with his elbow and order me to bring a pail of "agua" (water). . . . These fellows came more nearly up to my notion of what fiends of hell ought to be than any mortals I have seen.

A month later, the Gardner Division of the survey, exploring farther north, also ventured to the edge of the Bears Ears domain as they climbed some peaks in the La Sal Mountains. Along for the ride was a *New York Times* reporter named Cuthbert Mills. In a fashion that mirrors the attitudes of most of Hayden's explorers (though not William Henry Jackson), Mills links the hostility of the landscape to the depravity of the "savages." In a dispatch to the paper on September 9, he wrote,

Nearly the whole of this canyon region is a burning, death-like desert in which nothing thrives but sagebrush and piñon pine. No man can live there, not even the Indian, but many fly to it as a safe sanctuary. They live on the edge of the mountain slopes and only descend to the lower portions when pursued or pursuing. . . .

It will be easily seen that such a region presents nothing which is ever likely to attract other inhabitants to it than it has now. . . . Being on the boundary lines of the ranges of three tribes, the Utes, the Paiutes, and the Navajos, the most desperate rascals from each congregate there for mutual protection and plunder when they dare not openly appear anywhere else.

Travelers such as Mills were so preoccupied with the "thieving" Indians that attached themselves to the survey that they remained oblivious to all the signs of much earlier Native Americans strewn across the landscape. Those relics alone should have given the lie to Mills's notion (shared by other Hayden explorers) that the "burning, death-like desert" was uninhabitable. The exception was Jackson, who during the same weeks was making his own happy jaunt southward along the eastern edge of the Bears Ears region, exposing his photos as he went. Recalling those days in a memoir many years later, Jackson wrote,

> The ruins were so numerous now that frequently one or more were in view as we rode along. Arrow points were so plentiful that there was an active rivalry as to which one of us found the greatest number. Broken pottery of all kinds and beads and other trinkets also were collected.

In 1875, scooping up not only arrowheads but "beads and other trinkets" right and left was not merely the sport of itchy-fingered collectors—it passed for science in the nascent discipline of archaeology.

Some days later, farther south, Jackson's team discovered one of the greatest Anasazi ruins in Utah. As the photographer reminisced from the gilded perspective of seven decades,

> In a long shallow cave . . . we discovered a whole little town of sandstone dwellings. Although it had been abandoned centuries before, the accumulated debris was rich in relics. Glazed pottery (mostly fragments), hollowed stone grinding basins, ax heads, arrow tips, and spear points abounded. Only our need to travel light kept us from departing with an immense haul.

Even by 1940, when Jackson wrote these words, he saw no need to be embarrassed about making "an immense haul." If the Hayden surveyors

justified their collecting as adding data to the great storehouse of the prehistoric past, already by the 1870s pothunters with no pretensions to scientific motives were scarfing up Indian curios for their private collections.
Hayden's team not only gathered what lay on the surface of the Anasazi
ruin: they dug in the midden, the rich trash heap on the slope below
the dwellings. There they uncovered "seven large earthen pots of rough
indented ware." These goodies were too big and fragile to load into the
mules' saddlebags, "so we put them by for future investigators."

Forty-eight years would pass before the first true archaeologist worked
in the remarkable ruin Jackson's team had plundered. In 1923, Samuel
Guernsey, a Harvard professor serving under the aegis of the university's
Peabody Museum, discovered hundreds of important artifacts Jackson's
men had failed to unearth. All of those relics are stored in climate-
controlled drawers in the Peabody today. But Guernsey was dismayed to
see that vandals had broken down walls in the dwellings to get at the treasure. As for the seven earthenware jugs Jackson had laid aside, they "had,
of course, disappeared."

By the late 1880s, several men were turning the avocation of digging in
the ruins into something like a part-time job. The more ambitious of them
had discovered that Grand Gulch on Cedar Mesa, far from the nearest
settlement, was a canyon astoundingly rich in antiquities. Richard Wetherill, eldest of five Quaker ranching brothers from Mancos, Colorado, led
two extensive expeditions to Grand Gulch in the 1890s. Competing side-
by-side with the Wetherills were their friends, Durango miners Charles
McLoyd and Charles Cary Graham.

Those men, inured to hard work, were no mere pothunters. Their practice in the field lay somewhere on the spectrum between curio-mongering
and self-taught archaeology. All of them believed that the artifacts they
dug up, including well-preserved Anasazi mummies, should end up not
in private homes but in museums. (Of these oft-vilified but misunderstood
pioneers, more below.)

By 1890, plans were under way for a gala 400th-anniversary celebration
of Columbus's "discovery" of America, to take place in Chicago in 1892.

(As it turned out, snags of all kinds delayed the opening until May 1893.) The organizers of the World's Columbian Exposition reflected a startling attitudinal shift: with the final defeat of Geronimo's Apaches in 1886, the American Indian could be transformed from savage enemy into object of anthropological delight. Thus the Exposition planned to include many dioramas and exhibits to show off the splendid varieties of the country's indigenous cultures.

Seizing this opportunity was a coterie of entrepreneurs from Ohio, led by one Warren K. Moorehead, an archaeologist attached to the Smithsonian Institution, who had previously excavated a mound in the Ohio Valley and traveled to South Dakota to study the Ghost Dance of Sioux shamans who conjured up a messianic future free from the White Man. Moorehead and his cronies quickly signed a contract with the *Illustrated American*, an ambitious, text- and photo-heavy monthly published in New York City— a kind of proto-*Life* or *Look* magazine. The team promised to send dispatches from the field every week or two.

Moorehead and his cronies also won the support of the Smithsonian, the Peabody Museum at Harvard, and the American Museum of Natural History in New York. The goal of the expedition, besides entertaining readers of the *Illustrated American* with breathtaking accounts of triumphs and adventures in the Southwest, was to secure a cache of relics to display at the Columbian extravaganza.

All this credential-polishing went to the heads of Moorehead's stalwarts. In the very first magazine dispatch, while offering token nods to the previous fieldwork of government employees such as Holmes and Jackson, the unsigned author sneered at the team's predecessors as "travelers," insisting that "no articles of scientific value have been contributed to the intellectual wealth of the world."

The same dispatch defined the Ohioans' field of inquiry: "The ... Expedition will begin its labors in the San Juan country and work its way to the southwest, following the line whereon the cliff dwellings are located." Readers were assured of the quality of Moorehead's team: "The members of the expedition have been selected with great care. They are young men, enthusiastic and skilled in their several professions; of excellent repute, sound in mind and body; and accustomed to 'field-work.'" Each dispatch was headed with a title H. G. Wells or H. Rider Haggard might have savored: "In Search of a Lost Race."

By mid-April 1892 the team had rendezvoused in Durango: eleven men, two wagons, and a pack string of burros loaded with supplies for more than a month's toil. The first destination was Noland's, a trading post on the San Juan River near the Four Corners. Even at the time, a straightforward road—pretty much following the line of today's US Highway 160—could have conveyed the team across those eighty-two miles. But Moorehead decided to take two of his companions and raft the Animas River from Aztec, New Mexico, down to the San Juan—in a boat constructed on the spot for that enterprise.

It's at this point that the Illustrated American Exploring Expedition (IAEE) starts to shade from bold discovery into comic farce. Five miles into their float trip, the crew hit rapids that tossed the "clumsy scow" from bow to stern. Suddenly Charles Smith, a local whom Moorehead had hired as a guide just days before, shouted a warning: "Great heavens, boys, look ahead!" A fallen cottonwood lay across the churning Animas. Powerless to pull to shore, the terrified trio "dropped to the bottom of the boat." Clinging to the steering oar, Clinton Cowen, the team's surveyor, had his hands raked and bloodied, but the boat survived its passage under the strainer.

So the river journey proceeded. At one point, a rancher, hearing the men shouting to each other over the roar of the rapids, came down to the bank and "strongly urged us to abandon our project." Still the men careened on toward Farmington and the San Juan. "On the way," Moorehead admitted, "we totally lost control of the boat, and bumped into headlands, rocks, and trees." Half a mile north of Farmington, as they hit a patch of slow water, the rafters called it quits. "Here we made a landing and set up camp, tired, bruised, and bleeding, and with aching arms." The next day an unspecified party drove the survivors of the river in a wagon alongside the San Juan down to Noland's to join the rest of the team. "We were received with great demonstrations of joy," Moorehead claimed, "by those who had given us up as lost."

Nowhere in the dispatch does Moorehead explain the thinking behind the disastrous raft trip. If he hoped to discover more "cliff dwellings" along the way, he was disappointed. But rather than own up to the folly of the side trip, the *Illustrated American* saluted the intrepid trio for having pulled off "[t]he most dangerous feat of river navigation attempted since Major Powell and his party floated down the Colorado River."

From their camp at Noland's, the team poked northward, investigating such ruins as the massive valley-floor pueblo of Yellow Jacket and the striking towers curated in today's Hovenweep National Monument, as well as other ruins "known only to wandering cowboys and Indians." At Hovenweep, the team attempted something like a serious survey, and the magazine's sixth dispatch is filled with enough architectural minutiae ("Hollow Boulder C stands opposite the junction of the upper two cañons, and is 39 feet long and 20 feet high") to make the reader long for more river misadventures. (That reader would not have long to wait.)

On May 5 the team packed up their camp near Noland's, intending to head out in the morning for Bluff City (as the town, founded by Mormons in 1880, was then called), forty-two miles northwest along the San Juan. It had been raining heavily, but the men, in a festive mood, built the campfire high and regaled each other long into the night with grizzly stories. The merriment ended abruptly as "we were suddenly confronted by the camp-boy, scantily attired; he was greatly excited, and as he ran toward us he cried: 'The bank is caving in just back of the tent!'"

There followed an all-night battle with the overflowing river, which the river won. The men hauled tents and gear inland, built levees to forestall the flood, but ended in panicked retreat: "We carried our clothes, valises, and blankets to the cook's wagon, and, returning, pulled down the tent and stored it on top of a deserted Indian clay lodge near at hand. . . . There was no more sleep for us that night, and we passed a very cheerless time of it waiting for the daylight."

The journey to Bluff City demoralized the men even further. From Camp F. W. Putnam (named after the director of the Peabody Museum), a mile downriver from Bluff, Moorehead wrote a dispirited report that for the first time conveys just how out of sorts these explorers from Ohio were with the desert landscape of southern Utah.

> There is no interest whatsoever in camp life here, excepting archaeo-logical matters. The country is wild, the scenery full of grand, strange beauty, which interests the traveler for a few days, but he soon tires of the same cañons, with their sandstone cliffs and the sandy plains, which stretch day after day along his route. When he has tramped or ridden from sun-up to sunset, with nothing to quench his burn-ing throat but a canteen of water which, when divided among eleven persons, scarce leaves him half a pint, he will conclude, no matter how desirable the country may have been for the cliff-dwellers, it is no place for him.

The Exploring Expedition was having a lot of trouble finding potable water. Moorehead's complaint goes on: "Even when one does find a camp-ing place, the water is sure to be muddy or to contain alkali. Then wood is very scarce, and on the mesa there is nothing to burn but sage brush. Without wood and water, there is about as much fun in camping as in going duck hunting when there are no ducks."

The fact is that the explorers, the men "selected with great care," all young, enthusiastic, skilled, and "accustomed to 'field-work,'" were home-sick for Ohio!

> At night the members of the party retire early. There is not as much story telling as there was during the first month. Everyone comes in tired and hungry. The main desire on the part of every one is to get through as rapidly as possible and return to the delights of the East.

Out of the semipermanent Camp Putnam, in early May the men made short forays north and west. Nearest at hand was the great monocline of the Comb Ridge, bordered on the east by the shallow valley of Butler Wash. The east face of the angled Comb was a prime habitation region for the Anasazi, and it was here, if anywhere, that the IAEE made real discoveries. As far as we know, they were the first scientists (no matter how thin their credentials) to investigate such important sites as Monarch Cave, Cold Spring Cave, Eagles Nest, and Giant Cave. They named the first three, while Giant Cave (called Fishmouth today) had been dubbed by local Mormon ranchers. And as the team dug in these ruins, they were determined to record their deed for posterity. On the back wall of each alcove, in immodestly large letters, they chiseled such boasts as "I. A. E. Exped., MONARCH'S CAVE, 1892." Those inscriptions catch the eye of the visitor 128 years later.

By mid-May, the explorers had had enough. They were back in Bluff City on the twenty-first, and their eagerness to get to Durango and board the train to the East knew few bounds. Yet a dawning awareness of how much more the team might have accomplished emerges in the last lines of the tenth dispatch, written by Lewis W. Gunckel, the team's geologist.

> As a conclusion, we would say that there is no richer locality in this country for the ruins of cliff-dwellings than Butler's Wash, Comb Wash, and the unexplored regions to the south and west. A rich reward awaits the archaeologist who thoroughly explores the more remote cañons and gorges in this desolate and unknown region.

Out of all their hard work, the IAEE managed to ship back east to Putnam only forty-six "items" from their digs in Anasazi ruins. Those artifacts were duly put on display at the Columbian Exposition in 1893. After that they reverted to the Field Museum in Chicago. Whether any scholars track them down in their storage drawers today, or learn from them anything they don't already know, is a question few can answer.

THREE

MANUELITO'S DIRGE

Manuelito, one of the greatest Navajo leaders of the nineteenth century, was born near the Bears Ears around 1818. According to tribal oral history, it took him four days to be born, and his kin at once prophesied that he would grow up to become a Naat'aani—a headman, but also an orator, a singer, and perhaps a shaman. Among the epithets his people bestowed on him during his long life were "Holy Boy," "Bullet Hole" (supposedly for a gunshot wound in his chest inflicted in a skirmish with Comanches), and, after he led his comrades in battle against Mexicans, Puebloans, and Americans, "Warrior Grabbed Enemy."

While still a youth, Manuelito married a daughter of the chieftain Narbona, and according to Navajo custom, moved to her family's homestead near today's town of Tohatchi (Navajo: "scratch for water"), in the Chuska Valley north of Gallup, New Mexico. That early relocation has led some historians to dispute whether Manuelito was actually born near the Bears Ears. As the controversy over the new monument waxed hot after 2015, the warrior's birthplace became a political playing card in the larger question of Navajo historical presence in southeast Utah.

For the Navajo Nation, the 1830s were a decade of glory, played out in dazzling triumphs in battle against their foes. Ever since the Spanish colonization of New Mexico in 1598, troops had waged unrelenting warfare against the nomadic tribes—the *indios bárbaros*—whom the Spaniards regarded as unredeemable: not only Navajos, but Apaches, Comanches, and Utes. (Theologians argued the question of whether these "savages" even possessed souls.) At the same time, the colonizers tried to convert and assimilate the *indios de pueblos*, on the grounds that, as sedentary natives who constructed real towns out of stone and adobe, they might be brought into the Catholic fold. By the nineteenth century, however, Navajos had endured almost two centuries during which women and children captured in battle were sold into slavery as far south as Mexico City, 1,500 miles from their homeland.

In 1821, Spain relinquished its crumbling hold on the colony Cortés had won for the Crown with his conquest of the Aztecs three centuries earlier. Mexican independence signaled a triumph of Enlightenment-driven escape from Old World oppression, but it left the northernmost outpost of the former Spanish empire intensely vulnerable to attack by the "barbaric" nomads. Still a youth, no older than seventeen, Manuelito rose to fame among his people in the pitched battle at Washington Pass in northwestern New Mexico.

In February 1835, an overconfident Mexican captain set out from Santa Fe with a force of 1,000 soldiers and Puebloan allies, on a slaving expedition into Navajo territory, with the added goal of wiping out the Diné altogether. Instead, the Navajos utterly routed the Mexican army, killing its captain and his two lieutenants and forcing a Jemez chieftain to jump off a cliff to his death. The defenders were led by Narbona, Manuelito's father-in-law.

(In 1992 Washington Pass was officially renamed Narbona Pass. State Highway 134 winds its way today between the New Mexico hamlets of Crystal and Sheep Springs, up through piñon and juniper groves into ponderosa forest, topping out at 8,730 feet on the divide. No road sign announces the crest as Narbona Pass, but someone has painted a mural of Narbona, staring wistfully west across the virgin forest, on the triple doors of an abandoned storage shed.)

Two years later, Manuelito played a pivotal role in the Navajo attack on

Oraibi, which "almost depopulated" the ancient Hopi village, in the words of historian J. Lee Correll, whose researches into the life of Manuelito give us the best understanding of the Naat'aani (the powerful leader/shaman his people deemed him) outside of Diné oral tradition.

Another historian, Frank McNitt, deftly analyzes the supreme confidence that Navajo warriors enjoyed in the 1830s, and that carried over into their first encounters with American troops in the next decade.

If the muskets and cannons of the Americans were superior to Navajo muskets and bows and arrows, the American horses were not. Most Navajos now and for some time to come regarded themselves superior to the Bilagáana [white man] in both numbers and fighting ability. They had no understanding whatever of the overwhelming resources the United States could bring against them.

The outcome of the Mexican-American War in 1846 brought into being a confusing new state of affairs for the Navajo Nation. Seeking to seal a treaty with the tribe, Colonel Alexander Doniphan explained to the Diné, as if lecturing children, that once Americans had defeated an enemy, they treated the losers as friends. In McNitt's paraphrase, "[I]n the future if the Navajos stole property from the New Mexicans they were stealing from Americans; if they killed New Mexicans they were killing Americans." Among the provisions of the treaty was the declaration that henceforth New Mexicans and Puebloans were to be regarded as "American people," though the Navajos were excluded from that honor.

Dubious and bewildered, fourteen Navajo headmen, including Manuelito and Narbona, signed the treaty with their Xs marked on paper, though one of them, Zarcillos Largos, eloquently pointed out the absurdity of the terms.

We have waged war against the New Mexicans for several years. We have plundered their villages and killed many of their people, and made many prisoners. We had just cause for all this.... We cannot see why you have cause of quarrel with us for fighting the New Mexicans on the west, while you do the same thing on the east.

With Doniphan's treaty—ignored by white authorities almost as soon as it was signed—Manuelito began a lifelong course of veering between implacable opposition to American rule and sincere efforts to comply with it, always guided by the ultimate goal of saving his followers from harm and death. But only three years after he had marked his X on the paper, he tasted the bitterest of treacheries at the hands of the Bilagáana.

In July 1849, several Navajos murdered a Jemez sheepherder and drove off a large part of the flock. In Santa Fe, the military governor, Colonel John Washington, decided that this crime warranted a wholesale expedition of reprisal against the Navajos who roamed the Chuska Valley, far to the west of Jemez pueblo. Washington thus subscribed to the fallacy that would bedevil American relations with Native Americans throughout the nineteenth century: the conviction that a tribe was a unified people, guided by a "big chief," rather than (in Diné reality) scattered bands each loyal only to a local headman.

In late August, Washington's troops confronted several hundred Navajos just east of the pass that would later bear the colonel's name. When the officer berated the natives for "the murders and robberies they had committed," one of the Diné headman responded that "these were the actions of lawless men whom they were powerless to control." Nonetheless, they offered to give up however many cattle and sheep the Americans claimed they had stolen, and promised to try to find out who had killed the Jemez sheepherder. The Navajos, led by Narbona and three other headmen, insisted that they wanted peace.

The confrontation might well have ended in a bloodless impasse, but for a disgruntled lieutenant who upped the ante by claiming that one of the horses being ridden by a Navajo man had been stolen from the American militia. In the confusion that followed (who knows what linguistic gulfs muddied the exchange?), Washington demanded the immediate return of the horse. Narbona and his fellow leaders turned and fled on horseback.

The Americans opened fire with muskets and a howitzer that had been wheeled into place. When the smoke cleared, Narbona and seven other Navajos lay dead in the ravine where they had sought escape.

Later, filing his official report of the skirmish, Washington expressed not an iota of regret. "Among the dead of the enemy left on the field," he wrote, "was Narbona the head chief of the nation who had been a scourge to the inhabitants of New Mexico for the last thirty years."

Manuelito's reaction to the death of his father-in-law has escaped the Anglo record, but it is not hard to divine. In Diné lore, he had always been wary of Narbona's predilection for peace and for bargaining with the Bilagáana. Now the great headman's conciliatory instincts had led only to his death, without even a fair fight against the presumptuous enemy. Whatever grief Manuelito, still barely thirty years old, might have felt, it would transmute into a passion to keep his people free.

◄◄ ►►

Mark Maryboy, the Navajo man who would ignite the movement that led to the Inter-Tribal Coalition, Diné-Bikéyah, and Obama's declaration of the national monument in 2016, was born on the reservation near Bluff, just south of the San Juan River, in 1955. His father and two older brothers worked in the uranium mines that proliferated across San Juan County in the 1950s and early '60s, and Maryboy's mother often moved her six other children to temporary camps in nearby canyons, well north of the reservation, to support the miners. Maryboy's father would die of lung cancer, almost certainly a victim of exposure to the radioactive ore.

Mark Maryboy traces his awakening to an event in 1967, when he was eleven. That year Robert F. Kennedy, already pondering a presidential run, visited the Navajo Reservation. For years Kennedy had championed the cause of Native Americans, and had made it a point to visit reservation schools and councils. As early as 1963, as attorney general, he had addressed the National Council of American Indians in North Dakota, where he proclaimed, "It is a tragic irony that the American Indian has for so long been denied a full share of freedom—full citizenship in the greatest free country in the world." In Window Rock in 1967, speaking to the Navajo Nation, he drove home another injustice: "Is it not barbaric to take children as young as five and send them a thousand miles from their families to a boarding school?"—prompting an elder to shake the then senator's hand and swear, "I've waited my whole life for a White man to say that."

In 2018 Maryboy recalled Kennedy's visit to the Rez, claiming the senator had stopped to address a group of elders on the south bank of the San Juan, right where the Maryboy clan tended their sheep. "I was just a kid running around all over the place, climbing around on those trees," Maryboy told journalist Rebecca M. Robinson. "Then all of a sudden, my dad [said] . . . 'Son, all of those old people, they're going to be gone pretty soon. Listen to them. Listen to what they have to say.'

"So I sat down for a moment, and watched those old people talk, and I noticed that they were talking about the land": places such as the Abajo Mountains, Monticello, the Great Salt Lake, and the Bears Ears.

"They told Bobby Kennedy, 'Those are very important . . . and the land is who we are. It's something that's sustained us for millions of years. . . . Never, ever forget us."

In 1984, Maryboy won election as one of the three commissioners for San Juan County, making him the first Native American ever to serve on that board. He lasted as commissioner for twenty-six years, retiring only in 2010. At the age of fifty-five, he thought he was done with politics, planning instead to "lead a quiet life, free of controversy, and focused on family." But the splinter that Bobby Kennedy's visit had lodged under his skin at age eleven still festered. In his retirement from public office, Maryboy began seeking out Navajo elders and asking them about their connections to lands beyond the borders of the reservation. Soon he paired up with a Utah-based nonprofit organization called Round River Conservation Studies, which already had fifteen years of comparable advocacy for Canada's First Nations under its belt.

Gavin Noyes, second-in-command at Round River, recalls the collaboration with Maryboy. "The ethnographic mapping interviews at Bears Ears began in 2010, after several months of designing these elder interviews to meet the needs of the local communities," Noyes told me in 2019. "Mark got permission in the form of Chapter House resolutions from all seven Utah Chapters, and he administered each of the interviews. . . .

"Many [of the interviews] happened in the Diné language. Some questions were map-based and Mark drew their responses onto maps that my team digitized and organized. Interviews ranged from two hours to six hours in length. About seventy-five elders were interviewed. . . . There were not many surprises due to the research and years of investment into relationships that led up to these interviews. However, one mistake is I limited elder responses to San Juan County (that was our map extent) and it turns out that elders had ties well beyond SJC. Also, the ceremonial use of the Diné was far more extensive than I ever would have guessed. I expected that with hunting, herb collection, and stories, but the ceremonies blew me away!"

A comparable effort to document Navajo connections to the landscape had been carried out in the 1960s, thanks to a remarkable scholarly enterprise called the Doris Duke American Indian Oral History Program. Using interpreters whose first languages were the same as the subjects', scores of interviewers recorded short biographies of some four thousand Native Americans. All the speakers began by identifying the places where they were born and where they subsequently lived.

Thus in January 1961 a Navajo woman testified: "My name is Desbaa', 'Warrior Woman'. . . . I am 71 years old [born ca. 1889]. I am of the Bit'anni clan"—the Folded Arms People, the same clan as Manuelito. "I was born on Bear's Ears Mountain, and lived in this country until about 25 years ago, when we were forced to move by the Mormon settlers in that area. From Bear's Ears we moved to the vicinity of John Ismay Trading Post, where we have lived ever since." The Ismay trading post, derelict today, sits on the Colorado-Utah border at the junction of Hovenweep and McElmo Creeks, fifty miles as the raven flies from the Bears Ears.

Desbaa' recounted vivid associations with the landscape where she had spent her first forty-five-odd years. A place called "Rock Springs," east of the Bears Ears, was a shearing ground for Navajo sheep. A place farther west called "Lonely Tree" was also known as "Navajo woman gave birth to a child." There Desbaa''s mother kept her sheep, "and when I was old enough, I herded those sheep."

Throughout the 1850s, conflict between Navajos and Anglo settlers supported by the American army radically intensified. In 1862, Brigadier General James H. Carleton organized a roundup aimed at capturing every single Navajo in the West, with the intention of sending them on a forced march to a newly built concentration camp 300 miles to the east. (Of this genocidal campaign—the greatest tragedy in Diné history—more below.)

Many Navajos escaped the roundup and spent the next five years in hiding. As Desbaa' recalled in 1961, "My father's mother was named Nakai Asdzaan, 'Mexican Woman'. . . . She died over in the Bear's Ears country, and is buried there. She did not go to Fort Sumner [Bosque Redondo], because she was with the group that hung out with Kaayelii in the Haahootso." K'aayelii was Manuelito's brother. Kigalia Point and Kigalia Canyon, high on Elk Ridge north of Cedar Mesa, are named after him.

At the end of her testimony, Desbaa' made a passionate plea for the Bears Ears as a Navajo homeland. "I would like to add that the old people used to tell us that they lived freely in the Bear's Ears and the Blanding Mountain country," she told her interviewer, "and that this was our country; that we should try to hold it; make whatever we could out of it; don't let anyone beat us out of the country that our ancestors lived on for years before the white people took control of the Navajos, and rightfully belongs to the Navajos."

Also in January 1961, the Doris Duke program interviewed Kit'siili, or "Old Ruins," an eighty-nine-year-old Navajo who had been born on the south side of the Bears Ears. While he was still a child, his family had moved to a new range north of the San Juan River, but still regularly returned to the Bears Ears for summer camp. During the Long Walk and the ordeal at Bosque Redondo, both Kit'siili's mother and father, as well as his maternal grandmother and great-grandmother, hid out near the Bears Ears, in the place called Haahootso, or "Canyon to Escape from Enemy"—the same sanctuary in which Desbaa''s grandmother eluded the Navajo roundup.

About those long-ago days, Kit'siili added, "The headmen, and other Navajos of that time, made their living by raising sheep, cattle, and planting wherever they could find a place suitable for a farm. They also hunted antelope, deer, and mountain sheep. There was a lot of wild game in this country at that time. They usually hunted around Bear's Ears."

And so on. Taken together, the work of Mark Maryboy and the Round River Conservation Studies team with Navajo elders after 2010, and of the Doris Duke researchers more than forty years before, establishes beyond the scintilla of a doubt that the Diné had a rich ancestral connection to the greater Bears Ears domain long before any Spaniards or Americans arrived in the region. But with the controversy spawned by the Obama-Trump flip-flop over the national monument, all kinds of voices began to clamor against that legacy, fueled by arguments more emotional than rational.

◄◄ ►►

Mark Maryboy insists that he is Manuelito's grandson. When I first read that assertion, I was skeptical. Born around 1818, Manuelito died in 1893. One of his sons, Bob Manuelito, was interviewed in 1960 at the age of ninety-nine, by scholars working for another American Indian oral history project out of the University of New Mexico. The son was thus born around 1860, shortly before the Long Walk. But Mark Maryboy was born in 1955. Even if Manuelito fathered other children in his extreme old age, the gap between the 1890s and John Bell Maryboy, Mark's father, seemed too great to bridge.

Perhaps Maryboy's claim should be taken less literally. In another interview, veteran Southwest journalist Rob Schultheis reports only that "Maryboy's people have always been leaders. His family are related to the legendary Navajo hero Manuelito."

Oral history is only one source for documenting ancestral Navajo occupation of the Bears Ears region. All across that landscape, very old forked-stick hogans and small sweat lodges testify to the Diné presence. In 2008, Fred Blackburn and I spent several days looking for old hogans and Navajo rock art on Cedar Mesa. In one part of the plateau, near the small sandstone tower called Hat Rock, we found five or six unmistakable Navajo structures. Whether they date from the 1860s, the decade when refugees hid out from the army roundup, only tree-ring dating would verify, but there's no disputing the conclusion that when those hogans were built and occupied, no Anglos were living anywhere near Hat Rock. And we know from both anecdotal and historic record that scores of hogans over the years were burned as firewood by cattlemen and even by recreational campers.

Despite the recorded testimonies of so many elders about their ties to the Bears Ears, it is the linkage with Manuelito, as one of the greatest of all Navajo leaders, that came to take on a huge symbolic weight after 2010. And thus a certain faction of locals who opposed the monument, mostly Mormons from Monticello and Blanding, began to question Manuelito's linkage to the twin buttes on Elk Ridge.

Robert S. McPherson is to my mind the most curious case. A professor of history at Utah State University–Blanding, he is also a prolific author. No historian has done more to bring the Navajo legacy and culture to a larger audience, in excellent books mixing oral history and fieldwork on the ground such as *Sacred Land, Sacred View*; *The Journey of Navajo Oshley*; and *A Navajo Legacy: The Life and Teachings of John Holiday*. Yet McPherson is also a bishop in the LDS church and a Boy Scout leader in his hometown, and a subtle but persistent Mormon bias threads through his works.

In early 2019, I started an e-mail conversation with McPherson about Manuelito. In a 2011 book, he had stated without qualification, "Manuelito, born five miles south of the Bears Ears around 1820, grew to be one of the most prominent Navajo war leaders. . . ." By 2019, he was of a different mind. As he e-mailed me:

There are always surprises, but I can just about guarantee—based on Van Valkenburgh's work with old timers born around the Fort Sumner period and others' interviews, that Manuelito had little if anything to do with the Bears Ears. No doubt he might have visited his brother living there, but I think he was much more invested in the Chuska-Tunicha area—the Manuelito Springs region. Van had the responsibility to unearth who was living where—to include north of the San Juan—and there just is no evidence for Manuelito.

The work McPherson cites is Richard Van Valkenburgh's *Diné Bikéyah*, a pioneering 1941 investigation of Navajo ethnohistory. But what Van Valkenburgh actually wrote is ambiguous—or so I argued with McPherson. The crucial sentence—under the topic heading "Manuelito's Spring," a tiny settlement in Coyote Canyon, between Gallup and Crownpoint, New Mexico—reads, "Manuelito was born near 1818 and died at Manuelito's Spring, in 1893." I thought that line, with its apparently missing words, could mean either "Manuelito was born near [here in] 1818," or, alternatively, "Manuelito was born [around] 1818"—probably somewhere else.

An early book by McPherson, *A History of San Juan County*, is shot through with comments that subtly undercut the Diné insistence on centuries of presence in the Bears Ears region. Thus the opening sentence of a chapter called "Navajo Conflict and Boundary Expansion, 1880–1933" states, "Following their release from Fort Sumner in 1868, Navajos returned home and then pushed beyond their reservation borders in search of water for agriculture and grass for their livestock." The implication is that the Navajo "home" or homeland was coterminous with the somewhat arbitrary reservation boundaries the US government set up in 1868 for the Diné returning from Bosque Redondo. Thus Navajos who "pushed beyond their reservation borders" were illegal aliens trying to squat on land that belonged to someone else—in this case, the Americans living in southeast Utah, and maybe the small band of Utes who would later settle on the White Mesa reservation south of Blanding.

McPherson goes on to say that "only the Utes could justify a strong aboriginal claim to the area [southeastern Utah]." This is simply not true, as the Doris Duke transcripts and the Mark Maryboy and Round River interviews with Navajo elders so abundantly demonstrate. In 1884, President Chester A. Arthur enlarged the Navajo reservation to include all the land in Utah south of the San Juan River. According to McPherson, Arthur simply legalized a fait accompli—"that the Navajos had expanded far beyond the 1868 reservation boundaries." And yet, in McPherson's view, even this addition to the Rez failed to satisfy the land-hungry Indians, for soon "the expanding Navajo population, growing herds of livestock, and the discovery of precious metals eight years later would drastically change the situation."

And: "By 1892 Navajo agent D. L. Shipley noted a tendency for Navajos throughout the reservation to leave their confines and move onto the public domain." The very vocabulary of *A History of San Juan County* betrays McPherson's bias: "expanded beyond," "reservation boundaries," "pushed beyond," "drastically change," "leave their confines," and so on. No such innuendo attends the Mormons who started homesteading in San Juan County in the 1880s. Indeed, when Brigham Young first led his caravan of Saints into the valley of the Great Salt Lake in 1847 to build his New Zion in the wilderness, he was invading a foreign country, for that land still belonged to Mexico.

McPherson repeats and endorses the oft-cited Navajo belief that the quadrangle defined by the four sacred mountains defines the true Diné spiritual heartland. Those mountains are the San Francisco Peaks in Arizona, Mount Taylor in New Mexico, Blanca Peak in Colorado, and Hesperus Peak, also in Colorado. Yet that trapezoid very poorly matches the boundaries of the Navajo reservation established in 1868 and modified several times between 1878 and 1913 and again in 1933. Blanca Peak, in fact, stands a full 155 miles northeast of the nearest corner of today's reservation. The Dinétah, a region in northwestern New Mexico where most anthropologists and archaeologists think the Navajo first made a lasting appearance in the Southwest, lies wholly outside the reservation.

Since November 2018, Phil Lyman has served San Juan County as a representative in the Utah legislature. Before that, he was a longtime San Juan County commissioner. In 2014 Lyman became famous—or infamous, depending upon one's take on such things—for defying a BLM mandate against riding ATVs through an archaeologically sensitive stretch of Recapture Creek, just outside Blanding. The protest ride was reinforced by Ryan Bundy, of the notorious Sagebrush Rebellion Bundys. (Of this, more below.) Although Lyman insists he was a somewhat reluctant participant in the ride, he was convicted of a federal misdemeanor and served a ten-day jail sentence. His martyrdom earned him new acclaim as a populist hero in and around Blanding.

Within days of being installed in the legislature, Lyman enacted a sly revenge on his persecutors by introducing a bill that would impose a jail sentence "on anyone who 'knowingly places or authorizes the placement of a temporary or permanent barricade' on any public road, including disputed routes claimed by Utah counties across public lands." Lyman had strenuously argued that the road through Recapture Canyon was a public thoroughfare of long standing. (As of this writing, the fate of the bill was undecided.)

In January 2019 I started an e-mail dialogue with Lyman. The question of Manuelito's birthplace came up early on. In one of his first messages, he passed on the new doubts about the Bears Ears dug up by fellow Blandingite Robert McPherson, "a great friend and a truly great historian." We kicked the controversy back and forth. At last, in characteristic exasperation, Lyman wrote,

> Here's the problem, as I see it; We have a long and proud story of Manualitto's [sic] birthplace. All my kids have been taught and have embraced the story. But when politically motivated outsiders strut in and start using that info as leverage for an arbitrary federal declaration, it becomes proper to vet that info. I would love to know the truth.

The dig at Mark Maryboy, Lyman's fellow county commissioner for many years, was impossible to miss.

The nadir of the Mormon perspective on Native American presence in the Bears Ears region came in a meeting in Bluff in July 2016. Secretary of the Interior Sally Jewell hosted the public forum, which was meant to gauge the local temperament vis-à-vis the possible national monument that President Obama would decree five months later. After several speakers vigorously supported the idea of a monument, longtime San Juan County commissioner Bruce Adams approached the lectern. Without preamble, he claimed that when his (Mormon) ancestors first homesteaded in southeast Utah in the 1880s, "Nobody had really settled there before them." Adams's remark was greeted with raucous laughter from the crowd.

Vaughn Hadenfeldt later told me, "I was outside under the tents along with many Navajos when the sound system broadcast Adams's statement. The group was taken aback. Several Navajos looked around and asked, 'What did he just say?'"

◄◄ ►►

During the 1850s, embittered by the treachery that had cost the Diné the life of their great leader Narbona, Manuelito led many a raid and attack on Americans and on other tribes. Sometime during that decade, he received the wound to the chest that, according to Anglo historian J. Lee Correll, earned him the sobriquet "Bullet Hole." Correll reported that Comanches had stolen Manuelito's favorite horse, so he enlisted a small squad of allies to hunt down the miscreants. The battle took place somewhere north of Tuba City, Arizona. After Manuelito was shot in the breast, in Correll's account, "His brother, Cayetanito, rescued him. The bullet was removed by a captive Mexican blacksmith who had long been a member of Manuelito's band."

But in 1969, Manuelito's aged son told a quite different story. According to Bob Manuelito, his father was alone, near his adopted homeland around Tohatchi, New Mexico, when the Comanches attacked. He was, the son insisted, outnumbered twenty to one.

> He sure fought like a cat. When he downed about 16 men that he killed alone; there was a few left about 5 or 6 left, he started to chase away but he made a mistake that he went right in the midst of it, there was another wounded man that shot him with an arrow in the chest right below his breast. This is where he got hurt and went back, he was hurt very bad, the arrow was in his chest, he was bleeding to death by the time when he got back. He just broke the arrow off but the point was still in his chest.

The warrior staggered home, but he lingered near death for a month and a half. Manuelito's wife fed him corn meal in tiny portions, but a stronger cure was called for.

> Everybody was sent out for medicine throughout the country, they brought medicine from each ... different direction. ... [T]here were about 5 or 6 medicine men working on Manuelito. Finally about something around two weeks time or more, Manuelito start to come back a little. People never did sleep for quite a few days, they been watching him day and night, feeding him every way that they can know how, trying to save him. And in two weeks time or a little over, Manuelito all of a sudden woke up and he started to gain back. The sore was lots better with the medicine that he's been treated with. His sore was washed off every once in a while and was covered back with clean buck skin.

In maturity Manuelito was very tall for a Navajo (some say six feet six inches). A studio photograph, shot in 1874, when the man was in his sixth decade, still conveys the will and strength of the man in his prime. He sits bare-chested, clad in buckskin leggings, a Navajo blanket across his lap, as he cradles in his right arm a rifle cased in buckskin, its butt planted on the ground. Several necklaces dangle on his upper chest. His arms are spread rigid, shoulders cocked. He squints into the distance, with the hint of a mustache on his upper lip, a few tendrils of hair floating loose near his ears. The portrait embodies defiance tempered by a stoic awareness of his people's fate.

By the early 1860s, as American miners and settlers began to covet the lands that would become western New Mexico, northern Arizona, and southern Utah, the "Navajo problem" increasingly vexed military leaders and territorial officers. But it would take a fanatic to devise a final solution. Brigadier General James H. Carleton, appointed as military commander of the New Mexico Territory in 1862, was described by one historian as "tyrannical," "unscrupulous," and "abrasive," a demagogue who "believed it his duty and destiny as a good Christian gentleman to tame the 'savages' and to make civilized beings of these 'barbarians.'" A photo of the man at the time, seated in full uniform, vividly projects his monomania. His head is cocked unnaturally to his left, as if he had just been startled by some ominous intrusion. But it is Carleton's eyes, afire with missionary zeal under bushy black eyebrows, that capture the trance of unwavering conviction. They are the eyes of Big Jim, the crazed prospector in the classic silent film *The Gold Rush*, without the slightest trace of Chaplinesque humor.

Carleton's plan had two crucial phases. The first was to gather and incarcerate all the Navajos across their sprawling homeland inside the walls of Fort Defiance, the outpost established in 1851 by Carleton's predecessor on today's border between Arizona and New Mexico, to serve as the pivot point in the campaign against the Diné. The second was to escort all the captives on a 300-mile-long forced march east to the "round grove," or Bosque Redondo, on the Pecos River far out on the New Mexico plains, where the general planned to build Fort Sumner, the concentration camp in which he hoped to turn the "savages" into law-abiding citizens.

The epic tragedy that unfurled as the Roundup and the Long Walk— the most searing episode in Navajo history since the advent of the white man—has served as the doleful subject of more than a few books. Most of these treatises are grievously one-sided, since they are based almost entirely on the army records of the campaign and the reservation "experiment." A crucial corrective emerges in the oral history passed down to their descendants by the Diné who suffered under Carleton's regime. Besides the transcripts of interviews curated in sites such as the Doris Duke American Indian Oral History Program (some of them quoted above), two valuable books compile the accounts of grandchildren of men and women who survived the Long Walk and Bosque Redondo. They are *Navajo Stories of the Long Walk Period* and *Oral History Stories of the Long Walk*.

Carleton's campaign might never have gotten off the ground had he not appointed the canniest soldier in the West to carry it out. At age fifty-two, Kit Carson had wearied from his successive careers as trapper, scout, guide, and Indian agent. But as a colonel in the Union army who only months before had fought in a decisive battle against Confederate troops at Valverde, near today's town of Socorro, New Mexico, he felt duty-bound to accept Carleton's commission. The severity of the commander's policy, as formally expressed in orders initially aimed at Mescalero Apaches, but soon to be applied to the far more numerous Navajos, shocked Carson deeply: "All Indian men of that tribe are to be killed whenever and wherever you can find them: the women and children will not be harmed, but you will take them prisoners. . . ."

In the field, Carson ruthlessly burned Navajo hogans and crops and hunted down refugees; persistent but unverified Diné lore adds that he cut down all the precious peach trees in the Diné stronghold of Canyon de Chelly. But he refrained from killing the men, so rigorously that most of the Ute scouts he had enlisted in the hunt quit in disgust when they learned that the colonel would not allow them to slay their traditional enemies. One of the plangent ironies that lingers more than a century and a half after the campaign is that most Navajos today revile the memory of Kit Carson, while very few of them have ever heard of James Carleton.

This chapter is not the place to revisit in any depth the five-year agony of the Long Walk and Bosque Redondo. A handful of vignettes will serve to underline the gulf between the Army and the Diné comprehensions of what was going on. Thus one officer arriving at the Bosque admitted that 110 men, women, and children had died along the trail from Fort Defiance, but insisted that on arrival the "Navajos were greatly delighted and expressed great satisfaction with what they saw." But Curly Tso recalled his grandfather's account of the grim march across New Mexico: "People were shot down on the spot if they complained about being tired or sick, or if they stopped to help someone. If a woman became in labor with a baby, she was killed. There was absolutely no mercy." For three years, Carleton continued to issue rose-tinted assessments of Bosque Redondo, even while its prisoners were starving because their corn crops failed two years running, the women exhausted themselves hiking as far as twenty miles to gather firewood, the alkaline water of the Pecos gave everyone severe intestinal problems, and a measles epidemic swept the camp. In addition, many Navajo women were raped by the soldiers guarding them. In the 1970s Mose Denejolie remembered a detail his grandparents had told him about life inside the Bosque: "The U.S. Army fed corn to its horses. Then, when the horses discharged undigested corn in their manure, the Diné would dig and poke in the manure to pick out the corn that had come back out."

From the start, Carleton focused on Manuelito as one of the two or three key Navajo leaders it was critical to lure to Fort Defiance. For almost four years from the inception of the campaign, Carson and other officers periodically thought they had the warrior in their grasp, only to see him slip through their fingers. Manuelito feigned willingness to surrender, but he wanted to hear from other Diné who were at the Bosque who could give a truthful reckoning of the conditions there. At the slightest hint of treachery on the part of the soldiers, he led his band of forty or fifty men far to the west, beyond Zuni, to the canyon of the Little Colorado River, where he felt safe and free.

Yet even as he remained at large, Manuelito and his men were debilitated by the scarcity of food and the anxiety of constant vigilance against the arrival of the bluecoats. In November 1865, while Manuelito was away on a solo hunting trip, Utes led a surprise attack on his camp. According

to Lee Correll, the Utes stole twenty-seven horses and mules and a sub-
stantial herd of sheep. Even worse, "Most of the men in Manuelito's band
were killed but no Utes lost their lives. . . . [M]ost of the survivors including a large number of women and children were taken as captives back to
the Ute country."

Manuelito rallied the remnants of his band and retreated to another
sanctuary, only to have an attack by Hopi warriors follow close on the
heels of the Ute onslaught. More Navajos were killed, and Manuelito was
badly wounded. (Rumors that he was dead reached Fort Defiance.) At
last, on September 1, 1866, the great leader surrendered, his left arm dangling useless at his side, bringing with him only twenty-seven allies who
had survived the Ute and Hopi attacks. That surrender signaled the end
of the four-year-long Roundup.

Carleton was pleased to believe that he had corralled the entire Navajo
Nation, but Carson knew better. His superior, Carson maintained, had
always underestimated the numbers of Diné spread across their homeland,
and as he resigned from the campaign he had always found distasteful,
Carson averred that many—even thousands—of refugees remained on
the loose. At today's remove from the frantic events of the 1860s, accurate
statistics are hard to come by. A best estimate gives the following numbers.
More than 8,000 Navajos were forced to make the Long Walk. Both en
route and at Bosque Redondo, between 2,000 and 3,000 of them died. But
as many as 4,000 escaped the dragnet, hiding out in remote canyons for
five years undetected by Carleton's soldiers.

Among the Navajos who escaped the Roundup and hid out until 1868
was K'aayelli (as a group of his descendants based in Aneth, Utah, spell
the name). Manuelito's brother and a headman in his own right, K'aayelli
camped near the Bears Ears, at the spring that bears his name today,
under the Anglicized spelling Kigalia. As the oral histories in the Doris
Duke collection tell us, many other Diné hid out in the same region, given
heart by the power and resilience of K'aayelli.

The most legendary of the Navajos who escaped the Roundup was
Hoskinini, or Hashkéneinii, to spell his name closer to its Diné pronun-

ciation. In 1863, at about age thirty-five, Hashkéneinii fled from Carson's troops with sixteen companions—men, women, and children—armed with a single rusty rifle, having only a single horse to ride, and driving a mere twenty sheep. The pursuit of this ragged band does not appear among the official dispatches Carson wrote (or rather dictated, since he was functionally illiterate) to Carleton. But Navajo lore has it that the soldiers chased Hashkéneinii's refugees north to the banks of the San Juan River, which in all likelihood the Navajos crossed by a secret ford. The soldiers waited three days for the swollen river to subside, then gave up. Some Diné swore that Hashkéneinii escaped via a tunnel *under* the river.

Robert McPherson claims that during the next few years, Hashkéneinii often visited K'aayelli near the Bears Ears. But more contemporary sources—in particular an interview with Hashkéneinii's son, Hoskininibegay, conducted by historian Charles Kelly in 1925—indicate that shortly after evading the army, Hashkéneinii doubled back, recrossed the San Juan, and went into hiding along the skirts of 10,320-foot Navajo Mountain. The best guess as to the location of that refuge is a few miles to the southwest of the peak, in an area of convoluted slot canyons and domes called the Kettle Country.

In 2013 Greg Child and I spent five halcyon days exploring that little-known region. The country into which we plunged seemed at once bucolic and fierce: open glades lush with ungrazed grasses alternated with soaring sandstone walls and towers, and the main stream dead-ended in a pouroff where the waters surged into a deathtrap chute. Though the area is uninhabited today, we found abundant signs of Navajo presence, ranging from dates and initials scratched on the walls to one-stone cairns placed atop boulders to mark vestigial trails. To our surprise, only a scattering here and there of faint petroglyphs testifies to an Anasazi habitation earlier than the Navajo.

Our great discovery was three very old but superbly built hogans—not the "male" forked-stick hogans, but "female" hogans, octagonal or hexagonal cribbings of juniper logs mortared with mud and stones, a narrow door facing east, a smoke hole in the roof. The logs had clearly been hewn with metal axes, but not a single nail had been pounded into any of the three structures. Could these well-hidden dwellings be ones that Hashké-neinii's band had built and lived in during their almost five years of exile? Greg and I wanted to think so, even as we chided ourselves about wishful thinking or confirmation bias. Only tree-ring dating from cores bored out of the juniper logs could give the true answer, and that is not a project likely to happen soon.

In 1868, as they learned of the closing of Fort Sumner and the return of the captives to their homeland, Hashkéneinii's troupe emerged from hiding. Thanks to the headman's inspired leadership, their numbers had swelled to scores; they tended a herd of a thousand sheep, from whose wool they had made robes and blankets; and they had harvested more corn than they could eat in months. As Hoskinini-begay later told Charles Kelly, they had become "the richest Navajos in the country," and the impoverished return-ees straggling home from Bosque Redondo were stunned to meet them.

Two years earlier, as he had surrendered at Fort Defiance, Manuelito was in the grips of a dark, fatalistic mood. According to his son, interviewed ninety-four years after that surrender, Manuelito lashed out at his fellow captives, many of whom he recognized as having attended a Squaw Dance years before when he had admonished them about how to live.

> [H]e told them that he was right, he was very right, that they should never have done a thing like that because he said that this never been happen. If you had listened to my order, listen to me this time, [that] never should have been happen, we should live different way. But today, we are going far away, he told his people. We don't know if we will ever return, back to our land or not. . . .

Just what "order" Manuelito had given his followers at the Squaw Dance remains unclear, but the thread of gloom and collective self-blame running through the headman's scolding opens a window to an aspect of Diné culture I had first discovered decades earlier. In 1996 Alan Downer, then the Anglo Historic Preservation Officer for the Navajo Nation, told me,

"The Navajo Way hangs on a belief that the Navajos are given a way of living by the Holy Beings, and that there are real and nasty consequences for not living in that way. . . . I wouldn't be surprised to find Navajos who blame themselves for the Long Walk."

Sure enough, in the oral histories collected from descendants of the Diné who were imprisoned at Bosque Redondo, there are examples of that self-castigation. Seventy-two years old when he was interviewed, Charley Sandoval insisted, "It was the Diné's own fault to be rounded up. The Diné, using bows and arrows, had been having war with other tribes. That was the reason why they were rounded up by the military army. . . ."

At Fort Sumner, in recognition of his sway over so many followers, Manuelito was placed second among the twenty-two "chiefs" delegated to speak for all the incarcerated Navajos. Few details of his two years at the Bosque survive in either army or Diné accounts. By 1866, even New Mexicans who approved of the Roundup and the Long Walk had begun to recognize that the concentration camp on the Pecos was a dismal failure. Carleton's own officers had started deriding the general's utopian dreams, nicknaming the camp Fair Carletonia. Carleton himself had requested reassignment from New Mexico to Texas months before Manuelito arrived at Fort Sumner. Carson had resigned his post in the campaign even earlier, complaining that army bureaucracy left him "no power or control over the Indians or their affairs, except a moral one."

By 1867, the Navajo leaders in the camp had started pleading vigorously for their people's return to their homeland. In May 1868 they won a significant concession, as several of them, including Manuelito and Barboncito, who was famed for his eloquence, were carried by train to Washington, DC, to argue their case before President Andrew Johnson, who ended up making no promises. Matters came to a head only after General William Tecumseh Sherman, at the head of a peace commission charged with assessing Fort Sumner, was appalled at the conditions he encountered there. "I found the Bosque a mere spot of green grass in the midst of a wild desert," he wrote. The Navajos "had sunk into a condition of absolute poverty and despair."

Finally, in May 1868, Sherman met with seven Navajo leaders, including Barboncito and Manuelito, to decide the question of the tribe's relocation. The conference stretched over three days, made cumbersome by the need for one interpreter to translate Diné to Spanish, another Spanish to English, and vice versa. By prearrangement, Barboncito did almost all the talking for the Navajos.

It was by no means a foregone conclusion that the captives would be resettled in their homeland. Sherman dangled the alternative of the Indian Territory in what would become Oklahoma, soon to serve as America's dumping ground for "troublesome" indigenes ranging from Cherokees to Chiricahua Apaches. With honeyed words, he tried to tempt the headmen with promises of cattle and cheap corn and schools to teach the children to speak English.

Barboncito responded with two sentences that have come down through the ages as a quintessential cry of sovereignty: "I hope to God you will not ask me to go to any other country except my own. It might turn out another Bosque Redondo." On June 1 the headmen inked their Xs on the treaty, against the signatures of Sherman and the Indian Peace Commissioner. The Long Walk home began in mid-June.

Bob Manuelito left a vivid account of the beginning of the journey back to the homeland, as remembered by his father:

> The day came of their return. [E]verything was ready for them to start. The little ones were to be hauled back and some of them had to carry each other, carry their own babies. And they were started back from Fort [Sumner] all the way on back and the Navajo people were singing and dancing. The first night of their camp, they had a big pow-wow that night, that they were so happy that they didn't know what to do. Finally for two nights they have been dancing and singing. The third night, they had done the same, dancing and singing. The fourth night, they had dancing and singing. There are some songs that they still remembers during the time of their returning back from Fort Sumner. Some good songs that is known, that I don't

think that you would care about the songs so I will just tell you the story of what they have done, moving back. The fourth night was supposed to be the end of the Squaw Dance celebration in their ceremony celebration. On the end of four days, they said that, it shall be kept secret. . . .

Manuelito's feelings when the procession first came in sight of Mount Taylor, one of the four sacred mountains defining the corners of the heartland, were recorded by an Anglo observer: "When we saw the top of the mountain from Albuquerque we wondered if it was our mountain, and we felt like talking to the ground, we loved it so, and some of the old men and women cried with joy when they reached their homes."

Manuelito would live for another twenty-five years, vacillating between his passion to preserve the cultural integrity of his people and the effort to adjust to the demands of an America run by white men. It was a balancing act that would not end well.

◄◄ ►►

Since the early 1990s, I've hiked extensively on the Navajo Reservation— on some forty one-day outings, as well as on more than fifteen backpacking trips ranging in length from two to eighteen days. Quite a few of those excursions I undertook alone, wringing a deeper rapport with the landscape from solitude and silence. To hike anywhere on the Rez, you need a permit from the Navajo Nation, which used to require a postal back-and-forth with the Parks and Recreation offices in Window Rock or Cameron, Arizona, but which can now be managed online. That low bureaucratic hurdle seems to weed out casual recreationists, including folks who need a guidebook to tell them where to hike. But as I've observed over the years, a stronger disincentive lies in the gut-level suspicion that for Anglos the Rez is an alien place, too much like what we used to call the Third World (now euphemized as the "developing nations"). On only one of my backpacking trips, and on none of my day hikes, did I run into any other Anglos.

The Navajo homeland is every bit as densely imprinted with the ruins and rock art of the ancients as is the Bears Ears domain—chiefly those of the Anasazi, but also, on its southern and western edges, of their contemporaries the Mogollon, Hohokam, and Sinagua. But throughout the Rez, one finds a state of preservation of antiquities that can be matched nowhere else in the Southwest. That preservation stems from a belief that runs deep in Navajo culture: that places of the dead are dangerous, and that the relics of Those Who Came Before are to be left alone. Even the potsherds and projectile points that generations of Anglo visitors have picked clean from places like Cedar Mesa remain by and large in situ on the Rez.

In their 1946 treatise *The Navaho*, Clyde Kluckhohn, the leading Diné ethnographer of his day, and Dorothea Leighton write,

> Death and everything connected with it are horrible to The People. Even to look upon the bodies of dead animals, except those killed for food, is a peril. Dead humans are buried as soon as possible. . . .
>
> This intense and morbid avoidance of the dead and of everything connected with them rests upon the fear of ghosts. The other Earth Surface People who have fearful powers—witches—are also very terrible, but they are, after all, living beings who can be controlled in some measure and, if necessary, killed. Ghosts are, as it were, the witches of the world of the dead, a shadowy impalpable world altogether beyond the control of the living.

In general, after a Navajo has died, none of his relatives or friends will ever again speak his or her name, resorting instead to circumlocutions to refer to the one who is gone.

Kluckhohn and Leighton's analysis betrays a bit of the academic pontification of the day, with its whiff of condescension ("intense and morbid"). But they were among the first outsiders to focus on the Navajo fear of the dead, and to analyze it within the logic of Navajo religion and cosmology. There is no question that that fear, and the linked avoidance of places of death, are central to Diné belief.

On several of my reservation trips, I traveled with a Navajo as guide or companion. From those outings, I learned firsthand how carefully today's Diné deal with the ruins and rock art and artifacts of the ancients who preceded them. But first, a quick reminder of that chronology.

For at least two millennia, and in all likelihood for much longer, the Anasazi and their ancestors (stretching back to the periods archaeologists label Archaic and Paleo-Indian) flourished across a vast region stretching from what is now central Utah to central Arizona, as well as most of north-central and northwest New Mexico and the southwest corner of Colorado. But thanks to a multiplicity of factors that made life perilous or unsustainable—a complex of environmental maladies and cultural mandates that is still poorly understood—the entirety of the Colorado Plateau (which includes all of the Bears Ears region and most of the Navajo Reservation) was abandoned within the last two decades of the thirteenth century AD. Abandoned for good, except for the occasional pilgrimage of a descendant to a never-forgotten shrine in the lost homeland. That when they left, the Anasazi migrated south and east, and that many of the refugees assimilated with the Pueblos along the Rio Grande and westward to Zuni and Hopi, is unarguable. But it is not the whole story, and the missing chapters have yet to be written.

No one doubts that the Navajo are an Athapaskan-speaking people. In today's Southwest, only the Apaches share that language group. But both Navajos and Apaches are close linguistic kin to a host of Native Americans (or First Peoples) who live today in subarctic Canada and Alaska: Chipewyan, Tłı̨chǫ Yatıì (formerly Dogrib), Gwich'in, Koyukon, and Tanaina, among others. Indeed, many of these tribes call themselves the Déné ("The People"). Tanaina, in fact, is an Anglo rendering of Dena'ina. In the Southwest, the Navajo and Apache languages are completely unrelated to Ute, Paiute, Comanche, or Shoshone tongues, or to any of the several different languages spoken by today's Puebloans.

Nearly all anthropologists who have studied the question conclude that both Navajos and Apaches migrated from some subarctic homeland, though by precisely what routes in exactly which time period are issues fiercely debated. The temporary dwellings and fire pits and tent rings of nomads are notoriously hard to date, but no conclusive proof of a Navajo presence in the Southwest before AD 1500 has been established. Partisans of an earlier arrival would push that date back by one or more centuries.

The inevitable conclusion, then, is that when the Navajo arrived in the parts of the Southwest they would make their new homeland, the Anasazi had already departed. Much Diné lore reinforces that idea, as the newcomers muse on abandoned homes and a vanished people. Yet at headlong odds with this version of history is the bedrock Navajo belief that they have *always* ("since time immemorial") lived within the quadrangle defined by the four sacred mountains. Other legends dramatize Navajos witnessing the Anasazi abandonment of the Colorado Plateau.

On a couple of occasions, I challenged my Navajo guides with this paradox. In Canyon de Chelly in 2008, on a blissful hike down the White Sands trail with Kalvin Watchman in charge—a hike I could not have undertaken without a Navajo guide—I queried him out of the blue: "How long have the Diné lived in Canyon de Chelly?" Without missing a beat, Kalvin answered, "Since the 1300s."

I probed on: "Were the Anasazi still here when the Navajo arrived?"

"No," said Kalvin.

"What happened to the Anasazi?"

"They angered the Holy Ones."

In my smug reportorial brain, I was putting Kalvin down. The earliest tree-ring dates retrieved from hogans in Canyon de Chelly hover in a cluster no earlier than AD 1750, and few anthropologists would place the Diné in the Southwest as early as the 1300s. But I kept my silence.

It was a good thing I did so. At the end of two happy days hiking into little-known corners of the twin-pronged canyon, as Kalvin and I edged toward a friendship, I asked him, "Do you ever get clients you just can't stand?"

"Yes," he said.

I imagined spoiled kids with no attention spans, or obese adults who couldn't handle the steep trails. "What are they like?" I asked.

"Folks who say, 'That's not what I've read in books.' They think they know more about the place than I do."

On some of my outings with Navajo guides or companions, I've seen their aversion to prehistoric ruins vividly played out. In 1994, Jon Krakauer and I hired Eric Atene to horsepack our supplies into a remote basin north of Navajo Mountain, so we could set up a base camp for what we hoped might be the first descent of a tortuous slot canyon that snakes down to Lake Powell. Eric proved to be a jokester with a bite. As we hiked along beside his pack animals, he commanded us like dudes at a guest ranch. When I swatted the rear end of a recalcitrant horse too gently, he got down and thwacked the animal himself. "Indian pony," he editorialized. "He knows his master."

Along the trail, Eric kept bragging, "I know this country like the back of my hand." But I'd hiked the same route the week before, on a recon for our assault on the slot. As I pointed out the chute that led to the remote basin, Eric seemed to see us in a new light. "How do you guys know about this place?" he wondered.

We dumped our gear in a clearing just outside a massive alcove facing north. On my recon, I'd explored the recesses of the arching shelter, finding all the diagnostic signs of a major Anasazi site from the Basketmaker II period—sometime between 1200 BC and AD 50. Now Eric dismounted and stared at the alcove. His mood had darkened; the jokester was absent. "Those Anasazi people, we don't know how they lived," he said, as much to himself as to us. "We can't go up there. If I go over there"—he touched the fingertips of one hand to the other, aimed at the alcove—"I break the bond."

"They had their power," he went on; "we have our power. There's unseen spirits over there. Only a medicine man can go into those places, and he has to prepare himself."

Two years later, Fred Blackburn and I organized a week-long probe into the Lukachukai Mountains, a little-traveled range in northeastern Arizona, close to the New Mexico border. Among the friends we invited was Wilson King, a young Navajo man Fred had befriended during previ-

ous trips out of Cove, Wilson's hometown on the other side of the Lukachukai divide. He would not serve as our guide, for he knew the canyon
we hiked up (with Fred's two horses packing our gear) no better than we
did. We hoped instead to benefit from Wilson's Diné take on the wilderness, so different from our Anglo apprehension of the world.

The object of our quest was a legend passed on in the pages of Ann
Axtell Morris's charming 1933 memoir, *Digging in the Southwest*. The
wife of Earl Morris, one of the greatest hands-on archaeologists who ever
toiled in the Southwest, Ann recounted the fable of "The Lost City of the
Lukachukais," a massive, lordly Anasazi ruin discovered by accident by a
pair of Franciscan missionaries in 1909 but never conclusively identified
thereafter.

On the third day of our trip, at the corkscrew dead-end of the canyon,
I spotted what might be the source of the legend—a sizable Anasazi ruin
in apparently pristine condition tucked inside a high alcove that could be
seen from very few vantage points. But getting up to the ruin was a challenge. The crux came in the last fifty feet below the lip of the alcove, where
a blank sixty-degree slab had been gouged by the ancients to craft a hand-
and-toe trail, some of whose steps had flaked or eroded off during the
centuries. The only climber in the group, I managed to solo the sketchy
route, then belayed the others up one by one with a rope.

Wilson had been visibly anxious about making the climb up to the
ruin, but the enthusiasm of the gang won him over. Like many young
Navajos, he was torn between the lore and culture passed down to him by
his parents and grandparents and the rational scientism he had picked up
in Anglo-run schools. But while we explored the forty-room ruin, raving
about its felicities, Wilson was subdued. I heard him softly mutter, "I hope
these guys forgive me."

Then, as we were about to leave, in a drift of loose dirt below the ruin,
I stumbled upon a human leg bone. Though I didn't touch the bone, I
recognized that here a human burial had eroded to the surface. Back in
camp, Wilson told me how that incident had unnerved him, and went on
to recount a strange and doleful story.

The year before, he had been hired by a salvage archaeology team excavating the path of a soon-to-be-built highway. On his very first day of work, he had dug up the skeleton of a fifteen-year-old Anasazi girl. Two months later, he woke up feeling paralyzed from the waist down. "I had to crawl across the floor," he told me. "It hurt so bad."

Wilson went to a medicine man, who performed a complex curing ritual. But when his wife subsequently lost her child after a five-month pregnancy, he blamed it on his misdeed with the salvage team.

Now, because of the leg bone, Wilson felt that he had to perform certain propitiatory deeds. "When I go home," he said, "I'll change clothes, and I'll wash everything I have before I handle my kids. And I won't tell a lot of people about the place. I'll keep it to myself."

On the last night of our trip, I developed an intense stabbing pain in my right knee. In the morning, I could barely walk. I made it out the fifteen miles to our cars only after popping a heavy dose of painkilling drugs. In the emergency room in Cortez, Colorado, a doctor diagnosed my malady as a deep anaerobic infection caused by a tiny splinter entering my knee as I had bushwhacked through a tangle of scrub oak. Left untreated, it could lead to the amputation of my leg, but with antibiotics, I would be cured, though it eventually took three weeks for the pain to go away.

Though he never said a word to me, Wilson knew better. It was all about the leg bone in the ruin.

Anglos so seldom hike on the reservation that for locals to bump into them in the backcountry can be a great surprise—or worse, a disturbing event. At the end of a two-day backpack down a sandstone corridor west of Canyon de Chelly, a passage lined with enigmatic rock art, as my two friends and I emerged from the narrow chasm onto gentler slabs and ledges, we turned a corner and met a Navajo family out for a Sunday picnic: Mom and Dad and two grade-school-age kids. Their startlement and unease were unmistakable. I felt vaguely guilty that we hadn't somehow warned them of our advent, so I tried to make small talk. They kept staring east, up the chute out of which we had materialized. At last Mom asked, "But where did you come from?" My answer, all geography, was meaningless to her.

In the middle of our eighteen-day traverse of the Comb Ridge in 2004, Vaughn Hadenfeldt, Greg Child, and I stopped to rest at one of the infrequent springs along the way. We were eating lunch when we heard the barking of dogs; then sheep started scurrying over a nearby hill. They were followed by their shepherd, a lean, weather-beaten, very old man. He was beyond startlement: genuine fear claimed his features. We managed to learn his Anglo name, but he spoke almost no English.

Mortified by the sense that we had somehow taken possession of *his* spring, we tried to make up for the intrusion by offering him some of our food. He turned the items over in his fingers, as though he had never seen a banana or a peach before. His hands shook, and his whole body trembled. One of us said, "We'll get out of here so you can take your sheep down to the spring," but it was obvious that he understood nothing of what we spoke.

Later we heard from an Anglo woman who had worked with folks on the Rez and knew the old man we had interrupted in his daily round. We had gotten his name wrong: it was Maxie Black, not Maxie Platt (as I had written in my published account of the traverse). Sadly, the sheepherder died less than a year after our encounter.

It's tempting to play the amateur anthropologist and come up with a pat explanation for the kind of fear we provoked in the Sunday picnickers and the old man herding his sheep. Navajos believe in skinwalkers, one of the species of Kluckhohn and Leighton's "witches." Skinwalkers are usually medicine men who have performed unspeakable acts and then dedicated themselves to evil. They appear as normal human beings, but can suddenly transform themselves into wolves or coyotes or ravens, or into other human beings. (Tony Hillerman gets great mileage out of skinwalkers in his deft mystery novels set on the Navajo Reservation.)

But did the Diné whom we so upset as they carried out their normal activities see us as skinwalkers? Did they go home and tell others about the strangers with white skin who appeared out of nowhere, or did they keep their silence? It's not for me to know.

The official headquarters of the Navajo Nation are in Window Rock, a small town near the southeast corner of the reservation. But it's common knowledge among those of us who hike on the Rez that a paper permit from Parks and Recreation may not cut the mustard with a Navajo grazing his cattle near Kaibito or Oljato. Some friends of mine had told me gloomy stories of being ordered off the premises by irate locals, permit be damned. But in decades, I'd never had such an encounter myself. Several times a Navajo man had accosted me as I locked my vehicle and started on a hike, but when I showed him the piece of paper signed by some clerk out of Window Rock, he let me go my way. Once an old-timer detained me briefly as I headed in to an obscure branch of Navajo Canyon for a five-day solo backpack, but after scrutinizing the permit and asking what I hoped to find, to my great surprise he took my map and pointed me toward two or three alcoves in which the Anasazi had worked their architectural wonders.

I had begun to dismiss the warnings of other reservation-hiking veterans as over-cautious, or even paranoid. Until 2018.

On a blue-sky gem of a day in September, Sharon and I and two friends who were new to the Anasazi world left our rental car at the end of a dirt road vectoring west off Route 191, some ten miles south of Bluff. Our goal was a side-canyon shortcut into lower Chinle Wash, where an enigmatic pictograph panel nicknamed Baseball Man and several handsome ruins lurked. I'd been to that same stretch of the culturally rich Chinle three times before. Vaughn and Greg and I had camped there on the eleventh night of our Comb Ridge traverse. A week before the traverse, in fact, I'd made a quick trip in from the same dirt road off Highway 191 just to check that a vital spring was running free.

On this September day in 2018, I asked a Navajo woman who lived at the end of the road if I could park nearby. I offered to show her my permit, but she waved the paper away, then suggested I station the car in her driveway. I thanked her and gave her a twenty-dollar bill. It was a gesture I'd made countless times before on the Rez, and it seemed to jibe with a Diné sense of decorum. Yet there was a nervous edge in the woman's conversation that perhaps I should have heeded.

The four of us spent a rapturous seven hours on our looping trek into the Chinle. The ruins and rock art were new to Sharon, and John and Alissa were dazzled by the Anasazi achievement. In late afternoon, we trudged, weary and content, across the bare plateau toward the car. But something was wrong. In the distance, I saw a man riding a canary green ATV toward us, slaloming recklessly through sand drifts as he came. When he got closer, I realized that he was screaming at us. He dismounted and confronted me. The man was about forty, stocky, muscular, and his face was dark with rage.

"You got no business out here!" he shouted into my face from two feet away. "You trespassin'! This is Indian land!"

"I've got a permit," I said, reaching for the paper tucked into an outer pocket of my pack.

"Don't matter! That's no good here! You got no right. You trespassin'! You 'sposed to come up from the river." I knew he meant the San Juan, which defines the border of the reservation. It was thus that I had first approached the lower Chinle in 1995, in the middle of a seven-day raft trip.

My normal manner would have been to plunge into the argument, but something told me to back off. "I'm sorry if we were trespassing," I said softly. "We meant no harm."

No apology would mollify my antagonist. Sharon, John, and Alissa stood mute nearby, stunned at the man's invective. "You just lucky you didn't mess with those guys over there," he went on, pointing at a house a few hundred yards away. "They got the guns!"

"I'm sorry," I meekly protested. Out of the corner of my eye, I saw the woman who had given us permission to park in her driveway peering out of her half-closed front door.

"Get out of here!" the man flung after us as we climbed into our car. "You lucky this time."

As we trundled slowly back to Bluff, John said, "Whew. What was that all about?"

Three months later, I read in the newspaper that a Navajo man had been arrested for murder. In April 2018, five months before our Chinle hike, another Navajo, driving in his van with his wife and seven-year-old son on their property as they searched for a lost pet, got into a dispute over trash dumped on their land with a man parked nearby in a white truck. As the dispute escalated, the second Navajo got out his gun, fired it in the air, then, as the landowner started to get back in his van, shot him in the back of the head, killing him. According to the paper, the murder occurred "about 2 1/2 miles from state Route 191 south of Bluff."

Only in December did a lucky sighting of the white truck and notation of the license plate number lead authorities to the suspect. His name was Perry Maryboy. John, Alissa, Sharon, and I studied the mug shot of the suspect, but couldn't decide if he was the same guy who had screamed at us out on the dirt road west of Route 191.

Beyond the unfathomable tragedy of killing a fellow Navajo over a trivial dispute about trash lies another perplexing conundrum. Perry Maryboy, who as of this writing still awaits a trial, is the brother of Mark Maryboy, the activist who started the inter-tribal movement that generated the Bears Ears National Monument, and of Kenneth Maryboy, the San Juan County commissioner who, with his fellow Diné commissioner Willie Grayeyes, has been the leading voice in Utah in the campaign to overturn Trump's gutting of the monument.

From the same family, such different paths of destiny? Aeschylus would understand.

◄◄ ►►

The deepest insight I ever got into the Diné feeling about land and landscape came on a single day's outing in 1999. Fred Blackburn, who in his years as BLM ranger, backcountry guide, and self-taught archaeologist had befriended many a Navajo, arranged the rendezvous with Jimmy Austin. The complex canyon system called the Tsegi, in northeastern Arizona, enfolds some of the most impressive Anasazi ruins in the whole Southwest. Two of them, Keet Seel and Betatakin, were incorporated in 1909 as the raison d'être of Navajo National Monument. Today, small squares of federal land fence off those matchless ancient villages, but all the rest of the Tsegi lies within the Navajo Reservation.

The several branches of the Tsegi converge in a single ravine that issues south, escaping the gateway pillars of Skeleton Mesa, then bends eastward to form Laguna Creek. That gateway, just below Marsh Pass on US Highway 160 between Kayenta and Tuba City, is the obvious portal to the whole of the Tsegi. But Jimmy Austin had lived for four decades at Marsh Pass, and he'd made it his business to turn back Anglo interlopers who longed to explore the Tsegi, accosting them before they even got started. So Fred's invitation to join Jimmy for a day poking around his outback was a rare privilege.

I was only slightly disappointed that we would head up the Tsegi in Fred's battered old Ford pickup. The choice was Jimmy's. As I was beginning to learn, even a traditional Navajo will push his truck into every bend of the backcountry he can drive. Where a pickup can't go, he'll ride his horse. Only as a last resort will he hike.

Sixty-eight years old that bright May morning, Jimmy was tall, barrel-chested, with a strong, weathered face and short, spiky gray hair mixed with black. He wore a straw ten-gallon hat, a checked flannel shirt, blue jeans, and hiking boots. When he got out of the truck to examine the vestigial track ahead of us, he walked with an old cowboy's careful bow-legged gait.

Fred was driving, but Jimmy, riding shotgun, called the shots. Each time the truck crossed the shallow stream of the Tsegi, he made signals with his hands where to strike the ford. On a hairpin in soft sand, he bellowed abruptly, "Move on that side! Gotta know how to drive!"

A few miles in, on a lower stretch of streambed, Jimmy grew reminiscent. Waving his hand out the window, he said, "When I was six or seven, we'd run out of sugar or coffee or salt. My ma sent me to run down the canyon here to get sugar from our relatives. I used to be scared to death of this herd of longhorns—they were real mean." Our journey, I realized, was like watching a flashback reel of Jimmy Austin's life.

A little farther on, we paused beside an old gate in the fence. "Nearly got killed here when I was a kid," said Jimmy. "Dad opened the gate here, and my horse spooked and started jumping. I got the rope tangled around my chest, couldn't get loose. Dislocated my hip, and my chest hurt for three years."

We ran into fifteen or twenty of Jimmy's cows—Angus bulls mixed with Hereford and Beefmaster crosses. The cattle looked up expectantly. "They still want me to feed 'em hay," Jimmy mused. "In the winter, I carry hay into Wildcat Canyon. But if you feed 'em in a corral, they just get skinny. If you take the hay back in the canyons, they get fat fast.

"These guys are on their way back from up just below Keet Seel. They always go up there—some of 'em were born right there. That's why they come back."

To me, a cow was a cow—a far less interesting creature than, say, the elusive coyote that occasionally crossed my path. But to Jimmy Austin, the animals lay at the heart of a way of life. "When I was a little kid, my grandpa told me to take care of cows, because they'll take care of you. If you don't, you'll starve. He used to say, 'When I die, those cattle gonna be your grandpa.'"

Our guide pointed out the distant mouth of Wildcat Canyon, a far eastern tributary of the Tsegi. "I was born up there in 1931," he said. "A while back, I went up there to look at the hogan where I was born. Just the two front poles left. I guess somebody hauled it off for firewood."

We passed under a high cleft in the eastern wall that hid, I knew, a remarkable ruin called Scaffold House. On a previous hike, starting at the monument headquarters rather than Marsh Pass, a friend and I had spent rapt hours exploring the site, with its dazzling pictograph panels and the enigmatic wooden structure, wedged fifty feet up a flaring chimney, that gave the place its name. As a boy, Jimmy had lived beneath the ruin for several seasons, but he had never climbed up to it. Nor would we today. Glancing at the high cleft, he said, "My grandma told me, 'Stay away from there. There's dead people there. When you're young, your mind isn't fully grown. You go up to those places, they might catch your mind.'"

Though all its canyons still served as grazing land for Jimmy and his relatives, by 1999 no one lived year-round in the Tsegi. Over the decades, the pull of Highway 160—of the "civilization" that came to northern Arizona, in the form of jobs and schools and grocery stores and movie theaters—proved irresistible. The cultural watershed was when the pickup truck began to replace the horse.

For Jimmy himself, the pivotal turn came at fourteen. Friends his age had returned from school in Tuba City, bedecked with a worldliness it was hard not to envy. "My ma told me not to go to school—it was a bad place," Jimmy recalled. "But I had to see for myself. I walked out to the highway and hitched a ride to Tuba City. At fourteen, I didn't speak a word of English. In the school, nobody was allowed to talk Navajo, so I just kept my mouth shut. If you spoke Navajo, they put this yellow Napa soap in your mouth and made you chew it."

From Tuba City, Jimmy went on to a Bureau of Indian Affairs school in Riverside, California. His adult career betokened, in one sense, a full engagement with the Anglo world. He fought in the Korean War, surviving a battle in which many of his fellow soldiers were killed. For twenty-two years, he worked as foreman and crane and dozer operator for Peabody Coal, the gigantic mining operation atop Black Mesa, just south of Jimmy's home in Marsh Pass.

In addition, Jimmy performed for many years as an extra in western movies such as *She Wore a Yellow Ribbon*. Remembering those gigs, he deadpanned: "You see, the white man and the Indian, they like to kill each other. I killed a lot of white men in the movies, but they came back alive."

Yet Jimmy Austin, I saw, was no Navajo assimilated into white American life. The old beliefs and ways he grew up with retained a paramount importance for him. For decades he had been a medicine man, curing others with traditional healing ceremonies, many of them using peyote that he journeyed to Texas to collect.

By early afternoon, six miles up the tributary Jimmy called A Tah'a Biko (Keet Seel Canyon on the maps), we reached the end of drivable streambed. "We got an old hogan near here," Jimmy said. "Nobody uses it any more."

We left the pickup and climbed the steep arroyo bank, Jimmy moving fast with his bowlegged limp. On the grassy shelf above stood a rickety brush corral, one wall formed by a sandstone cliff, and a skeletal hogan, the turf that had chinked the cribbed logs of the ceiling washed away by the rains of the decades. We sat on the ground beside the structure.

"This was my grandma's hogan when I was a boy," said Jimmy. "We used to come up here every spring. We'd bring up the sheep. The corral was for the sheep babies. But nobody's lived here since about 1944. After that, we used to come up here, use it as a camp for hunting deer."

With his toe, Austin nudged an old stove lying in the grass, cunningly modified from a section of road culvert. The object stirred the man to a meditation: "They say if you live in a hogan with an open fire, you live a long time. That fire, it keeps you alive. If you eat your own peaches and melons and potatoes, it will take you a long way. If you buy food from the store, buy those medicines, you won't last long. You'll go up to eighty or so, and age will take you. My grandpa lived to a hundred and seven."

Five horses abruptly appeared on the bench above us. Jimmy glanced at them. "Used to belong to my brother. They gone wild."

The sun warmed our backs as we sat on the shelf. White-throated swifts and violet-green swallows darted on the breeze. For the third time that day, I said, "God, this is a beautiful place."

And for the third time, Jimmy ignored my effusion. Instead he nodded at a nearby shrub and soliloquized, "Greasewood'll make the cattle real fat. Sagebrush won't—they just eat a little bit of it."

I realized that none of my preconceptions about this landscape matched Jimmy's. His indifference to the canyon's beauty might have disappointed me, but I sensed how much I had to learn from it. Jimmy saw the Tsegi not so much aesthetically as in moral and pragmatic terms. It was the quality of life that could be lived here that mattered, not the momentary wonder or inspiration of a brief journey through it.

Faced with Jimmy's hard-earned view of the Tsegi—a good place for cattle and sheep, with plenty of grass and water, and secret patches of the medicinal herbs he used to cure the sick—I felt my own notions about landscape and adventure undercut. In that unsettling moment, I wondered for the first time: was backpacking a mere upper-class Anglo luxury? Was the very passion for wilderness, as opposed to land to be lived with, a Romantic fixation?

Yet there was no mistaking a certain wistfulness that our trip had provoked in Jimmy Austin. "The water never dries up here," he said now. "Other people wish they had places like this. When we lived here, we never used to get sick. When people moved out, they started to get sick.

"There were special places way back in, where the people would pray in spring, before any Anglos came here. They used to talk to the land. And the old people, they said it was the land that made us human."

◄◄ ►►

If, as the more skeptical anthropologists believe, the Navajo have occupied the Southwest for less than 500 years, what explains the prevailing belief among the Diné that they have lived there "forever," within the trapezoid of the four sacred mountains?

One answer might spring from a tendency of peoples all over the world who, in the absence of a written language, document their pasts through oral tradition: namely, to project the present backward into an origin story that validates the deep intertwining of a culture and a terrain by positing that it was "always" so, in this place, from eternity until now. Thus the Lakota Sioux, having seen the 1851 treaty with the US government that guaranteed them the Black Hills violated by gold-rush prospectors backed by the soldiers under General Custer, fiercely resisted the theft of a landscape that had become central to their existence. In a sense, both Sitting Bull and Crazy Horse were martyrs to that conviction. The Sioux today still clamor for the return of the Black Hills.

Yet all the anthropological evidence argues that the Lakota arrived in what is now western South Dakota only after 1765, having been pushed out of Minnesota by the Ojibwa, whom Europeans had armed with guns. As they migrated west, the Lakota in turn pushed the Cheyenne and Kiowa out of the Black Hills, which soon acquired the numen of a sacred homeland for the newcomers.

Eurocentric notions of "truth" do not fit well with certain kinds of Native American tolerance of ambiguity. I had seen this duality play out often on my visits to the Pueblo villages in New Mexico and Arizona. Many Puebloans believe that all of humankind emerged from a hole in the ground, which the Hopi call the *sipapu*, as the subterranean Third World gave way to the Fourth World of the present. In 2003, as I joined a group of visitors on the standard tour of Sky City, the butte-top ancestral village at Acoma pueblo in western New Mexico (my fifth such tour, all of them yielding fascinating insights into oral lore), I was baffled by the comments of our guide, a stocky, middle-aged fellow named Leo. Near the end of the walk-through, Leo explained the *shibop*, the Acoma version of the *sipapu*. "The original *shibop* is just over there," he said, waving his hand toward the west. I knew that Acomans traditionally located the orifice of creation in a specific spot in the canyon of the Little Colorado River, as it joins the Colorado River in the Grand Canyon. But in the next moment, Leo added, "It's also believed that the *shibop* is across the Bering Strait in Siberia. That's where we migrated from."

A Western rationalist, I could never get my head around such syncretism, as the welding of apparently contradictory beliefs (like Catholicism and the kachina religion) is often called. But Leo, who had apparently absorbed the archaeological account of the peopling of the New World by migration across the Bering land bridge, seemed untroubled by his dual *shibops*.

Likewise with the Navajo. Once I felt I had gotten to know a guide or a companion well enough to ask such an impudent question, I would throw out my query point-blank: "Do you believe the Diné migrated from subarctic Canada?" Some responded with a firm "no"; others with a hesitant "perhaps" or "probably." But some, like Kalvin Watchman in Canyon de Chelly, seemed to have it both ways, and showed no confusion about mingling what their grandparents had taught them with what they had picked up from books and in schools. (I later regretted that I had failed to nudge Jimmy Austin with my question as we rode Fred's pickup through the Tsegi.)

Although I restrained the impulse to challenge the "subarctic deniers" among the Navajos I queried with citations from scientific journals, I clung to my firm belief that the Diné had made their way thousands of miles from the homeland of such Athapaskan kin as the Chipewyan or the Gwich'in to the Southwest within the time span that in Europe stretched no farther back than Tudor England, or at most the House of Valois in France. A corroborating source fell into my hands by accident when I read Helge Ingstad's *The Apache Indians*, a book that South-western anthropologists have mostly ignored—most likely because although it was published in Norway in 1945, an English translation did not appear until 2004. A maverick explorer and ethnographer, and the man who discovered the only fully verified Viking settlement in North America, at L'anse aux Meadows on the northern tip of Newfound-land, Ingstad spent four years in the early 1930s as a trapper among the Chipewyan people in Canada. Near the end of his sojourn, on a cari-bou hunt that was part of the yearly round of the tribe, Ingstad listened to an old chief named Tijon soliloquize about the former greatness of his people, when they "ruled all the northern country" and defeated all their enemies in battle.

"How did the tribe lose its power?" Ingstad asked.

"Long ago," said Tijon, "many Indians traveled away. This was before the white people came to the country."

"Where did they go?"

"South," answered the chief, pointing with a wave of his hand.

"How do you know this?"

"The old ones say so."

This revelation seemed to dovetail with the standard theories of Navajo and Apache migration from the subarctic. It reinforced the linguistic arguments with the oral memory of the Athapaskans left behind, as their brethren in large numbers abandoned the northern homeland, never to return, reducing a once-dominant tribe to a more marginal existence.

Then in 2012, seemingly out of the blue, a radical new explanation of Navajo origins threatened to rewrite anthropological orthodoxy. In a scholarly volume devoted to Athapaskan migration, a chapter titled "Emergence of the Navajo People" appeared. Readers might have dismissed the paper as a wild-eyed riff on the edges of the hypothetical, but it was the work of David M. Brugge, who during his long career had become the Anglo ethnographer most universally acclaimed for his understanding of Navajo culture. (Brugge died in 2013 at the age of eighty-six, only a year after his radical theory appeared in print.) As my mentor and friend Steve Lekson told me in an e-mail,

> Brugge was the preeminent non-Navajo expert on Navajo history. He had a long association with the Navajo Nation, working on their behalf for the Federal Land Claims. In his later years Dave tied his hair in the traditional Navajo tsiiyéé or bun (NOT the hipster's man-bun!). He credits their belief that the Navajo emerged, as a social entity, in the Dinetah homelands south of the San Juan River. But Brugge sees a far more complicated ancestry than most anthropologists, who derive the proto-Navajo as a late in-migration from the far north.

Brugge's paper thoroughly analyzes all the evidence for that migration from the subarctic. There is no disputing the fact that the Navajo and Apache languages are Athapaskan tongues, in some cases still close enough to their northern counterparts that many terms and phrases are mutually intelligible. Brugge concludes that the northern tribe that bears the closest affinity to the Diné is the Chipewyan—a finding that nicely corroborates Ingstad's account of the old chief's story.

But from this common theoretical ground, Brugge departs, as he analyzes a trio of facts that other ethnographers have long puzzled over. Among the Athapaskans in the Southwest (Navajo, Jicarilla Apache,

Lipan Apache, Western Apache, Mescalero Apache, and Chiricahua Apache), the Diné have a far stronger genetic overlap with Puebloan peoples than any other group—though only in the mitochondrial DNA of their maternal line.

The second observation has to do with clans. Among Southwestern Athapaskans, only the Navajo and the Western Apache have clans at all, while that form of social organization is central to Puebloan culture. Moreover, none of the northern Athapaskan peoples have clan systems of any kind. Even more strikingly, writes Brugge, "the Navajo clan system seems to *derive* from the Western Pueblo [i.e., Hopi, Zuni, and Acoma] of the Southwest" [emphasis added].

The third anomaly that Brugge highlights has to do with Navajo creation stories, of which there are two distinctly different versions. The first has the people emerging from a hole in the surface of the earth, though in the Diné version, that place lies not in the gorge of the Little Colorado River, but at a location called Hajíínáí in the San Juan Mountains of Colorado. But in the second origin story, the world is created by Changing Woman, the most important Navajo deity. The first humans given life by Changing Woman are the ancestors of the four to six original Navajo clans.

It is out of these baffling elements that Brugge builds his theory. As he writes, "The two creations suggest two creation stories from two different peoples that merged to found the Navajo Nation." And here's the startling hypothesis: "that the early Navajo were not initially Athapaskan speakers but instead originated with the hunting-and-gathering cultures already in the Southwest."

I've greatly oversimplified Brugge's argument, which is complex, nuanced, and technical. But there's no mistaking the core of the theory. When I first read "Emergence of the Navajo People," I had to revise the picture of the ancient Southwest that I'd sworn by for decades, that clicked into my brain each time I stared at certain rock art panels in Utah or Arizona, or found a chert projectile point half-buried in dirt. Yes, those early ancestors of the Anasazi, sliding from the Archaic (before 1200 BC) into

Basketmaker II (1200 BC to AD 50), were gatherers of wild seeds and nuts and hunters of deer and bighorn sheep. But if Brugge was onto the truth, I could no longer visualize those Old Ones as seamlessly evolving into the Puebloans who grew corn and beans and squash and built villages of shaped stone and mud.

I had instead to imagine a certain population of early Southwesterners being, as it were, "left behind." They would have clung to the hunter-gatherer life even as their neighbors created a sedentary civilization. In Brugge's view,

[T]hey may well have been peoples who were in many ways still Archaic in culture who lived in the hinterland around and about the developing pueblos, probably trading the products of hunting and gathering to those engaged in farming as their major economic activity. . . . They did not participate fully in the cultural changes leading to the modern Pueblo societies, and in addition to having a simpler way of life, they were poorer and not nearly as numerous as the Pueblo peoples.

Then the Athapaskans who left their subarctic homeland began to arrive in the Southwest. For whatever reason, by whatever process, the "left behind" indigenes assimilated with the migrants from the north, learned their language and gave up their own, and gradually became the Navajo.

Is this what happened? The verdict is out, and Brugge has his naysayers. But those who propose alternative theories of Navajo origins will have to explain the nagging and persistent evidence of cross-cultural affinities between Puebloan and Diné cultures. And although oral tradition is a powerful conduit of half-lost truths, the events that gave birth to the Navajo Nation probably occurred too long ago to be lodged in the tribal memories of even the sagest elders. Jimmy Austin, my guide to the Tsegi, could have cast no more light on the question of his people's origins than might the average Anglo graybeard in Florida or Oregon if he was asked whether he was descended from Adam and Eve or from Homo erectus.

Meanwhile, I'll put my faith in scholars who've spent their lives trying to sort out the tangled history of the Southwest. Says Steve Lekson, "I
think Brugge's probably right."

◄◄ ►►

After his return from the Bosque Redondo in 1868, Manuelito tried to lead
a life with one foot each in Anglo America and the newly created Navajo
Reservation. As Barboncito, the eloquent speaker in the final meeting with
General Sherman at Fort Sumner, declined into old age, Manuelito was
recognized by American officials as the "principal chief" on the eastern
part of the reservation. In 1872, a new Indian agent appointed Manuelito
to be head of the fledgling Navajo police force. Four years later, he traveled
to Washington, DC, to consult with President Grant about Navajo land
problems on the reservation.

Yet in 1879, when disaffected Navajos started raiding Zuni Pueblo and
towns along the Rio Grande, and at the same time a summer drought
ruined Navajo crops, Manuelito joined with Ganado Mucho, the "principal chief" of the central sector of the reservation, to take matters into their
own hands. The cause of both problems, the leaders decided, was witch-
craft. In the account of historian J. Lee Correll, "From a list they made of
men suspected of witchery, over forty thieves and suspected witches were
rounded up and killed in cold blood." Among the victims was Muerto de
Hombre, one of the Navajo leaders at the Bosque who had sat in council
with Manuelito and marked his X on the treaty that freed his people to
return to their homeland.

In 1880, Manuelito agreed to try to curb the commerce in whiskey on
his part of the reservation, as more and more of the Diné grew dependent on alcohol obtained from traders. He asked to be appointed Chief of
Scouts, or Chief Detective, with a salary of thirty dollars a month, to carry
out this mission. In retrospect, that appointment pulses with irony, for
within a few years, Manuelito himself would become a serious alcoholic.

The turning point in the Navajo leader's embrace of both worlds came

after 1882, when he sent two of his sons to the Carlisle Indian School in
Pennsylvania. There the boys had their long hair cropped short, were
dressed in the clothes white students wore, and were forbidden to speak
Diné. The school's motto, a purportedly humanitarian slogan of the day,
was "Kill the Indian, save the man."

At Carlisle, both sons contracted tuberculosis. One died in Pennsylvania,
the other only days after returning to the reservation. Navajo sources often
claim that Manuelito's heavy drinking was born of the embitterment he felt
about those deaths. But already by 1882, reservation inspector C. H. Howard was noting in an official report that Manuelito was "an habitual drunk-
ard," and that he "has been accustomed to get liquor and to get drunk at
Fort Wingate. I do not imagine that any commanding officer has connived
at this but I have seen evidence that liquor has been left where the Chief
could find it, though not doled out to him as to other customers."

According to a contemporary quoted by Correll, "Manuelito was very
violent after the death of his son. . . . he said that he didn't care now what
his people did, they might rob and plunder as they pleased." And, according to Correll, "The loss of his son tended to have a sobering effect on
Manuelito." About that time, the Indian agent at Fort Wingate reported
that the chief "actually broke a whiskey bottle which he found in the
hands of one of his band, and spilled the whiskey on the ground."

By the early 1890s, however, Manuelito was losing his battle with the
bottle. His drunken sprees landed him in jail on more than one occasion,
and around Fort Wingate he became the object of ridicule on the part of
the soldiers. The cause of his death in 1893 was recorded as measles complicated with pneumonia, but there is no doubt that drinking contributed
to his demise.

Shortly before he died, Manuelito paid a last visit to his brother K'aayelii,
at the high encampment near the Bears Ears, in the place where both men
had been born early in the nineteenth century. (K'aayelii died in 1896.)
Manuelito was buried in a grave in Coyote Canyon, just east of the town
of Tohatchi in western New Mexico, where he had moved as a young man
when he married Narbona's daughter.

I had read an article in the *Navajo Times* that lamented the grave site as neglected and seldom visited, but when I stopped at Coyote Canyon in September 2019 to see for myself, I found the situation even more doleful than the reporter had indicated six years earlier. The first three Navajos at the chapter house whom I asked about Manuelito's grave said they had no idea where it was. I was about to give up, but the last of those three referred me to Walter, whom I found lying on his back under his pickup in the nearby garage, adding brake fluid to the reservoir. Twenty minutes later he emerged and offered to take me to the site.

Following his pickup in my rental SUV, I meandered north for five miles on a rutted dirt road that followed the dry bed of Coyote Creek, then branched west on secondary tracks. Walter came to a stop. I got out of my car and walked up to his open window. "There it is," said my guide, pointing.

Fifty yards away, atop a low hill, sat a massive white mobile home propped up on cinder blocks. "Right there?" I asked, incredulous. "Yep," said Walter. "Underneath it. If we ever dig up his bones, we'll put up some kind of monument."

I hiked over toward the monstrosity. The trailer looked to be no more than ten or fifteen years old, but it was already derelict. Much of the aluminum siding had broken off; a few pieces lay scattered among the weeds. A four-step staircase yawed crooked away from the locked front door it had once served. The wind whistled through the open spaces between the stacked cinder blocks under the mobile home.

I had never visited a more forlorn or tawdry resting place for the remains of a man who had once been a hero to his people.

Yet thanks to Manuelito's kinship with Mark Maryboy, and to the tide of conservation activism launched by Diné Bikéyah and the Inter-Tribal Coalition, the star-crossed Navajo leader has undergone a kind of spiritual rebirth. Even as Phil Lyman, the Utah congressman who would convert Obama's national monument into leases for oil and gas, decries the "politically motivated outsiders" who agitate for the Bears Ears in Manuelito's name, and even as Robert McPherson, the Mormon historian who has elsewhere championed Diné oral history, reverses his earlier assertion in print and now denies that Manuelito was born anywhere near the twin buttes on Elk Ridge—even as all the opponents of the monument rally to set in stone Trump's evisceration of the matchless tract of federally protected semi-wilderness, the great Naat'aani (Warrior Grabbed Enemy, Holy Boy) lives on.

In 2020, Manuelito has become the totemic apotheosis of what may be the last major struggle in America of its kind: to preserve for eternity the land that was sacred to the indigenous peoples who roamed and settled there before the first white man blundered into the Southwest.

FOUR

SHUMWAY'S SHOVEL

Nobody in Blanding saw it coming.

It was early morning, June 10, 2009. Looking out the window as she made breakfast, Jericca Redd saw men moving up the family's front walk. They were wearing flak jackets, and they had their guns drawn. Jericca barely had time to alert her mother, Jeannie, standing beside her in the kitchen, before she heard the men shout, "Federal agents!"

Once inside the house, one of the agents faced Jeannie and demanded, "Where's the white bird?" Moments later, he clapped handcuffs on the distraught woman, even as he kept badgering her about the "white bird."

Fifteen minutes later, James Redd arrived home. Sixty years old, Dr. Redd had been for three decades the leading personal physician—in the early years, the only doctor—in the close-knit town of some 3,700 residents. He was known for ministering extensively to Native Americans from all over southeast Utah. Fellow Blandingites saluted the man for his "impeccable reputation" and his "irreproachable kindness."

Before Dr. Redd could get out of his car, an agent accosted him at gunpoint and put him under arrest, then handcuffed him as he led the doctor toward the garage. For four hours, the agents relentlessly interrogated the Redds. Inside the garage, one of them pointed at the garden tools and jeered, "Which shovel do you like to dig bodies with?"

Thus was launched the most aggressive crackdown on illegal pothunting ever waged on American soil. The raid, planned in secret for months by the FBI, using undercover informants who bought and sold antiquities from and to Blanding citizens, was code-named Cerberus Action, after the three-headed dog in Greek mythology that guarded the gates of Hell to keep the dead from escaping. In that single day of June 10, twenty-eight suspects were arrested, most of them Blanding residents.

The Redds were driven twenty-five miles north to the regional BLM headquarters in Monticello, then, chained to other defendants, transported another fifty-five miles north to the courthouse in Moab. There a judge charged Jeannie Redd, who was locally known for her passion for digging in ruins, with seven felony counts, and warned her that she faced as many as thirty-five years in federal prison. James Redd was charged only with complicity with his wife in the illegal possession of the "white bird."

The next morning, before dawn, after a sleepless night, Dr. Redd walked through a stand of junipers down to the "south pond," an empty lake bed below the hilltop house, got down on his knees in the mud, and prayed. As the sun rose, he got into his Jeep and drove off. His wife and daughter assumed he was headed for the hospital and his morning rounds. Instead, James Redd drove back to the south pond. There he attached a garden hose to the exhaust pipe and fed the other end through the barely cracked-open driver's side window. He sat inside the Jeep. The engine stayed on.

When his family found him, it was too late.

◀◀ ▶▶

Pothunting is no modern aberration. Throughout human history, the graves and dwellings of the dead have been ransacked by later-comers. The discovery and opening of King Tutankhamun's tomb by Howard Carter in 1922 gained both instant and lasting fame not because the "boy king" was a particularly important pharaoh (he was not), but because almost uniquely among the crypts of the rulers of ancient Egypt, Tut's had not been looted. The thieves on the Giza Plateau and at Luxor who broke through stone walls and coffins to make off with burial treasures were not usually modern pillagers, but rather ancient Egyptians themselves, as one dynasty trashed the monumental legacy of a dynasty that had come before—maybe its own ancestors.

In the United States, the robbing of Native American relics did not become illegal until the passage of the Antiquities Act in 1906. As William Henry Jackson rode through southeast Utah in 1875, scooping up projectile points and pottery and "beads and other trinkets," he had not the slightest qualm that he was doing anything wrong. For that matter, what hiker in our own era, on one of his or her first rambles across a western plateau, has not thrilled to find an intact arrowhead lying in the sand, and hardly thought twice before picking it up and putting it in a pocket to take home, the perfect souvenir of a happy day in the wilderness? I spent my earliest years in Climax, Colorado, at 11,300 feet on the Continental Divide, where my father had established a solar observatory. On late-spring weekends, Dad would drive our family south beyond Leadville to Buena Vista, then up onto the low benches overlooking the Arkansas River, where we spent hours searching for Ute arrowheads. (I wonder if my father knew about the Antiquities Act. I'd guess he didn't, for he was not the sort to flout a law aimed at preserving vanished cultures.)

Fred Blackburn, the man who introduced me to Cedar Mesa, had been a BLM ranger there in the 1970s, and a ranger for Natural Bridges National Monument before that. Yet the idealistic ethic of the Outdoor Museum came to him only gradually over the years. He recently told me about the crucial turning point in his thinking about Anasazi artifacts he found lying on the ground.

"In 1973, I was helping out one of the cattlemen on state land just west of the monument," said Fred. "I always got along with the ranchers, 'cause I'd lend 'em a hand when they needed it. We were pushing cows out of this hole in heavy piñon-juniper. I looked down, and all of a sudden I saw a big red Tucson Polychrome bowl coming out of the ground. And right next to it were the broken pieces of a Dogozhi-style pitcher and a tiny intact Sosi Black-on-White seed jar. It must have been a burial site.

"You can bet I really wanted to keep those pots. It was the first pottery I'd ever seen coming out of the ground. And in those days, there wasn't really an ethic about that stuff. It was all treasure. Anyway, I kept those pots for about two years, before I turned them in to Bridges.

"Meanwhile, I kept arrowheading like mad, every time I got outside. Then in 1976, when I'd started working for the BLM, I was out one day with another ranger named Cindy Simmons. I found an arrowhead and just stuck it in my pocket. But Cindy said, 'You know, we're supposed to be protecting these things. Why are you keeping it?'

"I'd never really thought about that before, the habit was so ingrained. I can't say it turned my thinking around that very moment, but after that I stopped keeping the artifacts I found." Fred paused, a grin on his face. "What I do remember is that after I stopped taking things, I found some of the most beautiful stuff I'd ever seen in my life. Left it all where it was."

No one I know has undergone a more soul-searching transformation with respect to the ethics of collecting antiquities than Winston Hurst. Growing up in Blanding in the 1950s, Winston was steeped in the legacy of his Mormon pioneers: Albert R. Lyman, his great-uncle, had in effect founded Blanding in 1905, as he camped out in a tent with his wife that summer and urged his friends from Bluff to move north twenty-five miles to a fertile plain under the Abajo Mountains that he thought would be ideal for ranching as well as farming.

Winston counted Jim Redd as one of his best friends since childhood. But after he drifted away from his LDS faith and became an archaeologist, the friendship suffered, as the two men quarreled about pothunting, though Redd remained Winston's personal physician. "He couldn't stand my sermonizing and I felt sick every time he showed me his latest collection," Winston told a reporter in 2009. After Redd committed suicide, according to reporter Joe Mozingo, Winston "cascaded into a paralyzing depression." In his anguish (according to Mozingo), he apostrophized his boyhood pal, "Why, Jim, why?" In a Q and A with *Archaeology* magazine about the Blanding shakedown, Winston added, "It's just incomprehensibly tragic that anything to do with artifacts or archaeology should

ever drive someone to suicide, especially someone like Jim. But whenever
there's an outcome like this, there's always a lot more back story than
meets the eye. In this case, the arrest may have been what pushed him
over the edge."

Most archaeologists write the kind of bloodless taxonomic prose, heavily dependent on the passive voice and the triple qualifier, that infests scientific journals but puts lay readers to sleep. Winston, though, whenever
he loosens his scholarly tie, writes a vivid prose that is strong on irony,
whimsical self-deprecation, and a passion for the past and for landscape
that is deeply moral at the core. I've been trying to persuade him for more
than a decade to write his memoir, to no avail: as he e-mailed me in early
2019, "As for memoirs. . . . A life of foolish decisions is not very fun to
reflect on, I'm afraid."

In 2011, in the quirky but invaluable local journal *Blue Mountain Shadows*, Winston published a three-page essay that I consider at once the
canniest insight into the mind of the pothunter and the most trenchant
rationale for the Outdoor Museum that I've ever come across. It's titled,
with Hurstian panache, "Collecting This, Collecting That: Confessions of
a Former, Small-Time Pothunter." The opening is a tour de force of boyhood evocation.

> I was a Blanding kid. I hiked and explored and pushed my Dad's
> '54 ragtop jeep into a lot of places where it didn't need to go, that I
> could easily have walked to. I was always armed, usually with a .22
> Winchester pump, sometimes with a .410 shotgun, occasionally with
> my Dad's 1897 Winchester 12 gauge. . . . I might go without water
> or food, but not without a firearm. If something moved, I shot it.
> If something didn't move, I shot it anyway. I perforated tin cans,
> exploded glass bottles, blew holes in old car bodies, shot up cliff faces
> and left a trail of carnage in dead birds and cottontail rabbits and
> many more deer than any license or tag allowed. . . . I was a country
> boy in America, an idiot wrapped in an adolescent fog. . . .

For a Blanding kid, the next step was inevitable.

> And I was, of course, a collector. . . . I didn't dig in ruins that much,
> compared to some of the kids in town, but I did dig in some, oblivi-
> ous to any legal or ethical reasons not to. Fortunately, my short atten-
> tion span and a lack of immediate success kept me from doing too
> much damage. . . . But by the time I escaped high school, there were
> artifacts on my chest of drawers, on my bookshelves, and scattered
> here and there around the house. And to my Mom's disgust and hor-
> ror, there were human bones in her food storage closet, next to the
> cans of green beans and the mason jars of home-canned peaches.

By the time Winston had graduated from high school, thanks to his
collecting mania, "there were two full, or mostly full, human skeletons
in the fruit closet." With a pair of pals, he had dug them out of an Anasazi ruin in Recapture Canyon, not far from home. After his graduation,
his mother "took advantage of my absence to cleanse her house of dead
people," enlisting a friend to dispose of the skeletons—where and how, she
didn't want to know.

College was not the next step for the Blanding kid. Instead, he set off
on an LDS mission to Ontario and Quebec, and when that was concluded,
joined the army. Through books read in his spare time in the service, he
"discovered archaeology, or rather rediscovered it, since I had first gotten
interested in it as a twelve-year-old kid." But it had never before dawned on
Winston that you could actually get a job as an archaeologist. Deciding that
college was the necessary next step, he enrolled at Brigham Young University in Provo. The classes he took opened his eyes to an uncomfortable
insight: "It had never occurred to me before that there might be anything
wrong with digging ruins or collecting artifacts without documentation of
their discovery context, but as soon as someone said it, I got it."

The short personal essay Winston wrote for *Blue Mountain Shadows* in
2011 modulates from comic evocation of reckless youth to a meditation on

the moral quandary of pothunting and grave-robbing. Unsparing of his younger self, he confesses, "There was a huge element of racism in the whole thing, of course, though we were so embedded in it that we couldn't see it."

> I would never have put a White man's bones in my Mom's closet, and she would never have allowed it. But these were ancient bones, Indian bones, people with no names, not really people, just bones. I imagined myself an insightful detective of the ancient past, and observed in comparative brilliance through my adolescent, mental fog that one was taller and more heavily muscled than the other, and that they were probably an adult male and an adult female.

BYU turned Winston into an archaeologist. The crucial importance of documenting the context of an artifact find or an excavation came home to him with the force of a revelation. Now he could see that pothunting or digging in ruins, as the Blanding boys had always done it, was "an act of erasure, equivalent to cutting letters out of a one-of-a-kind ancient parchment, and putting the rest of it in a blender."

He went home, determined to rectify the wrong he had done with the skeletons in his mother's fruit closet. But the guy who had disposed of the bones wouldn't tell Winston what he had done with them, and by 2011, the disposer's own bones, as Winston put it, were "as deceased as [the skeletons']."

So Winston did the next best thing: he returned to the site he had dug into as a teenager, surveyed it, and prepared an exquisitely detailed map, identifying such still intact features as a "kiva depression" and a "room-block rubble mound." Then he registered the ruin with Utah's archaeological files as Site 42Sa26262. But he did more: he gave the place the official name of "Hurst's Confession Site."

"That's not a lot," he wrote in *Blue Mountain Shadows*, "but it is a beginning, and it is huge compared to nothing. That little settlement, and the two people whose graves I looted, will have a small place in our cultural memory and our growing understanding of ancient patterns of shifting settlement and community organization in that part of San Juan County. At least I've given them that."

The last paragraph of the short essay devolves into Winston's case for the Outdoor Museum. It wasn't easy, he confesses, to break the pothunting habit. But once he did so for good, "I felt like a recovered addict. This need to possess stuff, to take it home and add it to my pile so someone else couldn't, didn't control me anymore, didn't cloud my thinking, or dictate my behavior. I controlled it." During his decades as a professional archaeologist, he has photographed or drawn or imprinted an image in memory of each artifact he found. But

> The arrowhead continued to lie where it had been dropped twelve hundred years before. . . . Since then I have "collected" thousands of artifacts like that, not all intact arrowheads, of course, but quite a few of those, and some pots, and a lot of axe heads, and grinding tools, and tens of thousands of sherds and a whole lot of other neat/cool/interesting stuff that is documented at a basic level and is still (I hope) out there, for the most part, on the ground, in its appropriate place, in the outdoor museum.

I know of no finer mea culpa written by a scholar than Winston's "Collecting This, Collecting That," and no finer forging of an ethical code out of the follies of youth than his. If only every archaeologist in the Southwest, and every local citizen or visitor from afar who picks up an arrowhead and puts it in her pocket, would read the essay, take it to heart, and ponder what a growing number of us believe is the best, the most respectful, and the deepest way of communing with the ancients.

◄◄ ►►

Blanding residents resent the focus on their small town as the nexus of a culture devoted for the last three-quarters of a century to the looting of antiquities. Illegal digging in ruins on federal land has been rampant all over the Southwest for many decades. Yet there is a certain truth to the caricature of Blanding as the Sodom or Gomorrah of pothunting and grave-robbing. Earl Shumway, the most notorious and blatant desecrator of Native American ruins in US history, was born in Blanding, spent most of his life there, and is buried in the town cemetery. (Of Shumway's shameless career, more below.)

The sting that so dramatically hit Blanding on the morning of June 10, 2009, with agents wearing flak jackets and wielding drawn guns, was two years in the making. Operation Cerberus Action was conceived as a joint effort of the FBI, BLM, and National Forest Service, under the leadership of Interior Secretary Ken Salazar, serving in the administration of President Obama early in his first term. In 1986, a raid by armed federal agents had busted sixteen alleged looters in and around Blanding, including two of the three San Juan County commissioners. But the US Attorney for Utah decided not to file criminal charges against any of the suspects. Archaeologists, environmentalists, and Native Americans were outraged, but pothunting in the ruins continued apace.

Meanwhile, during the two decades after the first Blanding bust, a lucrative international market in pots, blankets, pendants, effigy jars, sandals, and other artifacts from the prehistoric Southwest had sprung up. No longer were "collectors" content to mount their goodies in living-room display cases; some of them offered their finds on eBay (often with bogus certificates asserting that they were dug on private land), and others started profiteering from the shady black market in ancient curios. An intact, painted Anasazi or Mimbres pot in good condition could fetch prices of several thousand dollars. Inevitably, in Utah that segment of the pothunting coterie overlapped with meth addicts looking for new ways to fund their habits.

In 2006, Operation Cerberus Action found the ace up its sleeve in the person of one Ted Gardiner. A Mormon from Salt Lake City, a few years shy of fifty, he had a troubled past. According to reporter Joe Mozingo, who has dug into the tangled chronicle of the "Blanding bust" more deeply than any other investigator, Gardiner's interest in Utah's antiquities began as a reverent, idealistic passion. "He felt a mystical connection to the Anasazi," writes Mozingo. "He and his first wife, Debbie, read everything they could find about the culture. They would whisper out of respect when they came across an ancient cliff dwelling or petroglyph; digging in the ruins was sacrilege."

In 1996, however, a severe panic attack started Gardiner's spiral into delusions, heavy drinking, the breakup of his marriage, and the loss of his supermarket business. He moved into a hermit's cabin in the mountains outside Salt Lake City. According to Mozingo, "Desperate for money, he decided to cash in on his expertise. He opened an online business trading in Anasazi items and bought private collections. When he couldn't make ends meet, he started dumping his artifacts on eBay."

BLM agents, already planning Operation Cerberus Action, saw in Gardiner the undercover agent they needed. Though initially reluctant, he signed on in 2006. The BLM paid him $10,000 up front. Soon he was on salary at $7,500 a month plus expenses, and agents fed him envelopes of cash to wheel and deal with known pothunters.

From the start, the sting focused on the Redds, mainly because Jeannie was known to be an insatiable collector, but perhaps also because James Redd was a pillar of Blanding respectability. The BLM put a special agent named Dan Love in charge of the campaign. Though initially ignorant about the black-market trade in antiquities, Love was famed for his aggressiveness in going after lawbreakers. And as the sting gathered momentum, Love's zeal directed its almost sinister design.

To be sure, that zeal was fueled by Love's (and the BLM's) own idealism. As Mozingo concedes, "The task force wanted to send a message: The decades of impunity were over." For more than half a century, environmentalists and archaeologists had looked on in dismay as one pothunter bust after another failed to issue in prison time for the miscreants, or even in prosecutions. As a BLM ranger on Cedar Mesa in the 1970s, Fred Blackburn had surprised more than one looter in flagrante as they dug into ruins, destroying ancient structures in their reckless quest for treasure. But he had no authority to arrest: as Fred recalled in 2019, "If we caught somebody in the act, we had to call the sheriff in Monticello and wait for him to come out to the site." Most of the violators got away with their crimes scot-free; others were taxed only with "small fines paid to the justice of the peace."

Operation Cerberus Action was built around a far more sophisticated modus operandi than the apprehension of a looter caught red-handed by a ranger. Over the course of months, Gardiner got back in touch with the many clients with whom he had bought and sold exotic artifacts during his desperate years of drinking and poverty. Now he let them know that "he was back in business, representing wealthy European clients, including his biggest buyer, 'Sergei from Liechtenstein.' 'My guys are buying like crazy,'" Gardiner told them. "'I've been snatching up anything I can get my hands on.'"

In his meetings with contacts, Gardiner wore a wire and a shirt-button camera. Love and his colleagues needed admissions on tape that the objects Gardiner was buying had been dug illegally on public land (not legally on private land—a loophole that the United States, almost uniquely among countries in the Americas or Europe, opens for grave-robbers and relic-hunters). Relying on tapes and transcripts from the sting, Mozingo captures in vivid detail the ruses by which Gardiner "worked his client list with the duplicitous grace of a drug addict." An example:

At the home of Loran St. Claire, whose wife had died recently, leaving him to raise their two children, Gardiner asked St. Claire whether he was "doing all right." Then he persuaded him to sell two seed jars, one of which his mother had bought many years ago from a Navajo woman.

Gardiner's shirt-button camera recorded it all.

As St. Claire was helping his 4-year-old daughter into her pajamas, Gardiner told her she looked "gorgeous" and, as he left, he called out, "You take care, bro. Holler if you need anything."

Driving away, he took a call from Agent Wilson.

"Yep, that's two felonies," Gardiner said, noting that he and Agent

Cleverly had a bet for dinner at an upscale French restaurant. "So keep track."

As this excerpt suggests, Mozingo's scrupulously researched "A Sting in the Desert" (originally published in the *Los Angeles Times*) is more sympathetic to the Blanding citizens trapped by the undercover agent than to the architects of the crackdown. Mozingo's account of the dawn raid on the Redds' house on June 10, 2009, focuses on the agents' relentless demand, "Where's the white bird?" The object in question was a shell pendant, "smaller than a dime," carved by some Anasazi craftswoman in the shape of a bird, that James Redd had found lying on the ground on a family excursion on the Navajo Reservation, picked up and handed to his wife, who put it in her pocket. Evidently Gardiner had seen the pendant and asked about it on one of his meetings with the Redds in their house. As they ransacked Jeannie Redd's display case on June 10 and seized the family's computers, the agents collected other relics that they suspected had been illegally looted. But they overlooked the white bird.

Along with warning Jeannie about the long prison sentence she would have to serve, the armed intruders taunted James Redd by telling him he would undoubtedly lose his medical license. Although Mozingo admits that Jeannie was an avid collector of rare antiquities, by focusing on the "white bird" he implies that the severity of the raid was out of all proportion to the crime—the thoughtless pocketing of a tiny amulet that lay in plain sight on the ground. Jeannie's passion for antiquities comes across as a relatively harmless aesthetic fancy for pretty pieces of Native American jewelry discarded long ago.

In a draft essay titled "The Pillagers," Utah archaeologist Ralph Burillo amplifies the scene the agents found in Blanding during the raid:

I know a few of the folks who participated in the Cerberus raids. What they saw in many of them turned their stomachs. It was like scenes from the reality television show *Hoarders*. In addition to finding dressers and cabinets filled with exquisite Ancestral Pueblo artifacts, other common finds included mountains of fly-ridden fast food containers, ashtrays of every conceivable construction that were almost always overflowing, plates of rotting food, punch- and kick-holes in walls and doors, dead plants, dead *pets*, and—this part helps explains the rest—crystal methamphetamine paraphernalia.

As word spread of the blitzkrieg sting that descended on Blanding that June day, environmentalists, archaeologists, and those who (like me and my hiking companions in the greater Bears Ears) at first rejoiced. But the Gestapo-style tactics of the federal agents—guns drawn, suspects handcuffed and put in leg chains—provoked a furious backlash. Even Winston Hurst, the Blanding archaeologist who deplored his home town's culture of looting, was appalled by the raid, telling a reporter, "[T]hey . . . came in this time and arrested these guys who have no criminal records and have never entertained a violent thought toward another human being. They go in with half a dozen guys, with automatic weapons, flak jackets, and black FBI suits and not only arrest them, but put them in leg chains and handcuffs. It's nothing but theater."

Dr. Redd became an instant martyr, a hero sacrificed to the overkill of the feds. More than nine hundred people attended his funeral, at which his son Jay, choking back tears, delivered a eulogy: "I know he gave his life for his family. I know that. . . . I love you, Dad. And I'm going to see you."

In subsequent months, as the threatened thirty-five-year prison sentence for Jeannie Redd proved to be a prosecutorial pipe dream, the notion gained currency in Blanding that the physician had taken his own life to foment an uproar that would spare his wife and daughter the draconian punishment the agents hoped to mete out. Longtime Blanding resident Kay Shumway outlined this theory to me in 2019. Shumway had been Dr. Redd's patient for many years, and his wife was the doctor's cousin. "Does the suicide make any sense to you?" I asked Kay. He answered: "Here's how I made it make sense to me. He knew what was coming. They took him to Moab. He said, 'I need to go to the bathroom.' They wouldn't let him go, he had to go in his pants. And that's why he was being treated just like a horrible person. He thought, 'Well my wife and my daughter and I are going to end up in jail for years and years. I better take myself out of this.' And so, I think he thought that he was saving this family from imprisonment by taking his own life. There'd be so much sympathy for his family that they wouldn't be harsh on them."

But others saw a murkier picture. Dr. Redd had been arrested in 1996, along with his wife, when a sheriff's deputy caught them digging on public land. Because human bones were in view at the site, prosecutors charged both Redds not only with misdemeanor trespassing but with a felony charge of desecration of a grave. The judge who presided over the case had been a patient of Dr. Redd, who had performed the delivery of his baby son; now the judge dismissed the felony charge. Jeannie pled "no contest" to the misdemeanor charge and got off with six months' probation. But the outraged prosecutors filed appeal after appeal, and only after five years was the case settled. All charges against James Redd were dropped. Nonetheless, according to Mozingo, "The charges deeply distressed Redd. He was tormented by the thought that he could be seen as a felon. 'You know it's so bizarre,'" he told his assistant, 'I don't even like this stuff.'"

From other folks in and around Blanding I heard vague hints that "something else was going on" in Dr. Redd's life that may have contributed to his decision to take his life. Since suicide is a serious sin in Mormon theology, many friends were further distressed that the man had chosen that way out. There were even suggestions that Dr. Redd might have been addicted to cocaine or some other drug.

Another defendant charged in the sting, a fifty-six-year-old man named Steven Shrader, was a collector based in Albuquerque. Agents had caught him with two other collectors selling a pair of prehistoric sandals and a basket. A week after Dr. Redd's death by carbon monoxide, Shrader visited his mother in a small town in Illinois. Late at night, he drove to the local elementary school, where he shot himself in the chest and died.

Ted Gardiner, the informant at the center of Operation Cerberus Action, was unprepared for the tidal wave of hatred he had unleashed in Blanding and beyond. One ex-con was arrested after he told agent Dan

Love that "he would tie Gardiner to a tree and beat him with a baseball bat." Once the three-year operation was over, Gardiner lost the monthly salary that had fueled his undercover work and given his life a momentary sense of purpose. He started drinking again, lost jobs, had his cabin foreclosed on, and failed to pay his divorced wife child support.

Mozingo spins out the grim denouement in the staccato style of a latter-day Mickey Spillane.

On Feb. 27, 2010, [Gardiner] called Tina Early, his racquetball buddy. "I'm done with this," he cried. "I can't take it anymore."

She rushed to his house to find him holed up in his bedroom, drunk and waving a .38-caliber revolver, crying uncontrollably.

"These people thought I was their friend," he yelled. "I'm such a liar. I pretended to be their friend."

She tried to tell him he had done a good thing fighting the artifact trade, but he bellowed over her.

"I caused two deaths," he said. "I killed two people."

"They thought I was their friend."

She called 911. Police took him to the hospital on a psychiatric hold, but not for long.

Two days later, on March 1, Gardiner's roommates heard a gunshot in his room.When a patrolman arrived, Gardiner pointed the .38 at him.

"You're going to have to do what you're going to do," Gardiner yelled from his bed.

The officer fired. The bullet missed. Gardiner slumped out of sight.

From behind the bed came a single crack, then silence.

Gardiner was dead from a gunshot above his right ear.

In his pocket was an Operation Cerberus Action coin.

The final outcome of the most elaborate and zealously conducted antiquities bust in US history proved deeply anticlimactic. Archaeologist Ralph Burrillo summarizes the result.

Jeannie Redd ended up with three years of probation and a $2,000 fine, mostly because the judge felt sorry for her after the suicide of her husband. Eleven of the other 25 living defendants pleaded guilty to felony charges, eight to misdemeanor charges, and six of them had all charges dropped. Not one of them went to prison for it. What Dr. Redd and Steven Shrader had killed themselves for turned out to be a slap on the wrist.

In Blanding, however, despite the leniency of the sentencing, the bitterness about Operation Cerberus Action lives on. The antipathy focused on Dan Love and the storm-trooper tactics of the raid he directed. Almost a decade later, residents recalled in precise detail instances of what seemed to them the arrogant and insensitive behavior of the special agent.

About a month after Dr. Redd's death, SA Dan Love, BLM agent Brent Range, and an FBI agent returned to the home of James and Jeanne Redd. While there, SA Love noticed a picture of the Latter-day Saint Prophet, Joseph Smith, on the kitchen table and said to Jeanne and Jericca, *"It's good you have his picture there, keep praying to him."* Anyone familiar with Latter-day Saint practices, which includes nearly everyone in southeastern Utah, know [*sic*] that Joseph Smith is not a subject of worship, but is revered as a leader and prophet. Love's mention of "praying to Joseph Smith" appears to have been a sadistic jab at the very tender religious feelings of Jeanne and Jericca.

For his work on Operation Cerberus, Love was named BLM "agent of the year" and given a hefty promotion that put him in charge of all agency campaigns in Utah and Nevada. But in 2017, he was fired for a host of offenses, including corruption involving the Burning Man festival in the Nevada desert, to which he allegedly used his power to wangle special tickets and a security detail for friends and family. Residents of Blanding felt vindicated by Love's comeuppance. As Utah state congressman Phil

Lyman e-mailed me in 2019, "Thanks to the Burning Man escapades and a change in administration, Dan Love was finally revealed as the psychopath that we, in Blanding, already knew him to be."

All but lost in the furor over the Blanding bust was a question at least as important as bringing to justice the looters: what was going to happen to all the artifacts the agents seized? The haul was immense, amounting to some 40,000 objects. In one suspect's home, the raid uncovered no fewer than 5,000 artifacts, which it took fifty agents and archaeologists two full days to catalogue, pack securely, and load into U-Haul trucks. Most of the gigantic collection was transferred to a warehouse on the outskirts of Salt Lake City, where it remains today, under the custodianship of the BLM.

In 2015, a team from *Smithsonian* magazine, including experts in Southwest prehistory, got a look at the vast array of pots, baskets, projectile points, effigy jars, prayer sticks, sandals, and other items that the agents liberated from the looters' homes. Those artifacts were the work not only of the Anasazi, but of their contemporaries the Fremont, Mogollon, Hohokam, and Salado. They ranged in age from 6000 BC to the fifteenth century AD. The warehoused goods amounted to a curator's nightmare, since virtually all of them had been irrevocably separated from their proveniences—the ruins, trash middens, and burial sites from which they had been dug.

Laurie Webster, the leading expert in prehistoric textiles in the Southwest, estimated that about one-quarter of the collection had high research potential. A few of the objects stunned her, like a pair of human effigies made of wood, yucca cordage, and corn stalks, the likes of which she had never seen before. At first she thought they were modern fakes, but gradually came to believe in their authenticity, and ultimately estimated that they dated from between 200 BC and AD 400. If genuine, they would represent, according to Webster, "the earliest example[s] of fertility figure[s] from this region [southwest Utah]." But at present there are no funds available for experts to study the vast assemblage in the Salt Lake City warehouse.

Even more vexingly, the Native American Graves Protection and Repatriation Act of 1990 (NAGPRA) requires museums and institutions to return all "human remains, funerary objects, sacred objects, and objects of cultural patrimony" to the living tribes from whose ancestral sites they were stolen. But with 40,000 unprovenienced artifacts stashed away, and no money to study them or reach out to the scores of tribes that might claim affiliation, this looms as a nearly impossible task.

The consolation for the BLM, for archaeologists, and even potentially for Native Americans is that at least those often sacred objects are neither being squirreled away in display cases and secret storage rooms in homes in Blanding and other towns, nor traded on eBay or the black market in antiquities. But the sterile shelves and drawers and boxes that house the "treasure" Dan Love and his fellow agents seized in 2009 loom as another kind of nightmare. A locked warehouse in Salt Lake City creates a limbo that neither Dr. James Redd nor Laurie Webster and her peers—nor, for that matter, the elders from Hopi, Zuni, a dozen other Pueblos, the Navajo Nation, and the Ute and Paiute tribes—could ever have wished for.

◄◄ ►►

Before the passage of the Antiquities Act in 1906, there was no law in the United States against digging in ruins and extracting not only artifacts but human skeletons and mummies, whether on private or public land. Indeed, in the last decades of the nineteenth century and the first of the twentieth, such bastions of scientific inquiry as the Smithsonian Institution amassed collections anchored by hundreds or even thousands of sets of Native American remains dug up by credentialed savants all over the country, but especially in the West. The unconflicted glee of William Henry Jackson as his party scarfed up "arrow points" and "broken pottery of all kinds" and "beads and other trinkets" in southeast Utah in 1875 was par for the day, and often so little thought was expended on recording the proveniences of those scavenged relics that even if they ended up on the shelves of respected museums, they were robbed of archaeological context almost as completely as the booty in the Salt Lake City warehouse was by the looters from Blanding and beyond.

The Antiquities Act supplied the vital, if perhaps somewhat overdue, thrust in America's nascent concern with preserving and respecting the cultures of the peoples who inhabited the continent long before the first Europeans arrived. So it remains today, buttressing, among other things, the creation of the Bears Ears National Monument by Obama in 2016 and the lawsuits seeking to block Trump's evisceration of the monument a year later. Yet curiously enough, the Antiquities Act was conceived in part as a vindictive strike to forestall a rival in the field by one of the more unpleasant (if hugely influential) characters in the annals of American archaeology. And therein hangs a tale.

My first serious ventures into Grand Gulch, the fifty-two-mile-long, zigzagging centerpiece of Cedar Mesa, came during a pair of eight-day llama-packing trips with my wife, Sharon, in 1992 and 1994. On the first, we entered at Kane Gulch and emerged at Collins Canyon, thirty-six leisurely miles downstream, shuttling vehicles to facilitate a one-way journey. On the second, we entered at Collins, descended all the way to the steep ledges where Grand Gulch pours into the San Juan River, then reversed course and hiked back up and out at Collins—another laid-back jaunt of thirty-six miles. We were dazzled by the unrelenting richness of the canyon in terms of Anasazi ruins and rock art, but on later visits I realized how much we had missed. During both outings, we ran into only a handful of other hikers: from 1992, I remember a pair near the junction of Green House Canyon who were thoroughly lost; two years later, during our first hour, we crossed paths with a group of six or eight who had come up from rafts on the San Juan and were about to emerge at Collins Spring, then saw nobody else during the next seven days.

By 2020, it was hard to have any part of Grand Gulch to yourself for a whole day. Over the years, I'd figured out several shortcuts by which on day hikes I could pop in to Grand Gulch at bends that took backpackers three days to get to, and I took a smug delight in the incredulity with which some of those overburdened plodders greeted my arrival out of nowhere. But now Grand Gulch is "on the map"—worse, it's on the Internet, and such ruins as Turkey Pen, Junction, Split Level, and Bannister can be dialed up with GPS coordinates or pondered via braggart trip reports.

It's worth reminding oneself just how remote Grand Gulch seemed only a few decades ago. The canyon was named in 1879 by scouts for the Mormon Hole-in-the-Rock expedition, but in annoyance rather than admiration, for its tortuous gorges and tributaries threatened to block the massive party on horseback and in wagons from reaching the promised land that would become the town of Bluff. (Of this amazing hegira, more below.)

Of course, Grand Gulch had been a vital landscape to settlers and wanderers long before the Hole-in-the-Rockers came along. In the early 1970s, archaeologists Bill Lipe and R. G. Matson conducted the first (and still the best) deep study of Cedar Mesa prehistory. In a 1975 essay called "Three Days on the Road from Bluff," intended not for specialists but for a general audience, Lipe lyrically evoked those earlier denizens of Grand Gulch:

What the Anasazi called this many-headed and serpentine canyon we don't know, for the last families drifted away sometime in the late 1200s, and the names they called it have as quietly been forgotten. We have some clues that Pueblo people, perhaps descendents of these same families, returned to hunt, trade with the Utes, or visit the old shrines, but they never settled here again. Utes, Paiutes, and a few Navajos must have wandered under its cliffs down the centuries that followed, but they left even fewer traces.

During the 1880s, a few Mormon cowboys may have run cattle into Grand Gulch, although in its whole fifty-two-mile length, there are only two or three entry points that lumbering bovines could negotiate without breaking their necks. The first recorded visits by Anglos into the depths of Grand Gulch—verified in most cases only by the signatures those pioneers scrawled in charcoal or bullet lead on the sandstone walls—came in the early 1890s. Yet according to inscription expert James H. Knipmeyer, those men "had heard stories that untouched prehistoric cliff ruins were to be found in Grand Gulch."

The first such venture was prosecuted by Charles Cary Graham and Charles McLoyd, ranchers from the Durango area who also worked in the silver mines in the San Juan Mountains. In January 1891, the pair entered Grand Gulch via its sizable eastern tributary, Bullet Canyon. Cedar Mesa is so accessible today that it's hard to imagine just how remote it was 130 years ago, or what a monumental effort it must have taken to mount an expedition to explore it from Durango, 140 miles away by the easiest route. As late as 1920, archaeologist Nels C. Nelson could describe Grand Gulch as "one of the least frequented and probably also one of the most inaccessible parts of the United States. A great rift in the earth, tortuous and fantastic, with mushroom or toadstool rocks, monuments of standing, seated, and bust figures, hats atilt, and every conceivable form and shape on which imagination seizes or turns into semblance of life." Even in 1957, historian Frank McNitt would still claim that "Few places in the world are so cut off from civilization as Grand Gulch. In four centuries only a handful of white men have explored its depths."

Graham and McLoyd, of course, were not archaeologists. They were motivated to hunt for "relics" from the "vanished" Indians who had left such striking evidence of their existence in places like Grand Gulch by the hope of selling their treasure to collectors and museums. A dawning fascination with those "Early Americans" would reach a peak in the Chicago World's Fair, or Columbian Exposition, which had been in the planning since 1882, long before McLoyd and Graham set off for Cedar Mesa. Intended to open in 1892 to celebrate the 500th anniversary of Columbus's supposed discovery of America, the Exposition was delayed until May 1893. Still, the country had seen nothing like it. The Anthropology Building, among other dioramas, housed a replica of the habitations of the "Cliff Dwellers" at Battle Rock, in McElmo Canyon a few miles west of Cortez, Colorado.

In my rambles among the canyons of Cedar Mesa, I'd found the signatures of Graham and McLoyd in some half a dozen places, usually on the cliff walls inside crumbling Anasazi dwellings. Yet very little is known about those pioneers. Thanks to the indefatigable sleuthing of Fred Blackburn, a hazy sketch of that first expedition into Grand Gulch can be put together. Along with several cronies, in 1991 Fred located the long-lost diary Graham kept of that bold adventure, in the possession of Graham's grandson. The entries, however, are "agonizingly terse." A sample: "Sunday. We worked in Cliff house no. 1, Graham [Bullet] Canon. found 6–7 bone awls, 1 stone axe, some sandals, one bowl and small jar. Some cloth, one small coil vase with skeleton."

Fred's team was able to reconstruct some of the logistics of the Graham-McLoyd mission. It took the men two days to find a way into Bullet Canyon that their horses could manage, then another four to build a pack trail that they cribbed with logs and dry-stone masonry. Even so, they couldn't trust their horses to carry gear and food down the dangerous ramp, so instead they led the loadless animals down the trail, climbed back out, and in a tiresome bout of relays, hauled all their gear and grub into the canyon on their own backs.

Remarkably, Graham and McLoyd spent almost three months in Bullet Canyon and Grand Gulch, exploring all the way down to the San Juan. All the miseries of winter afflicted them: snow and heavy rain, temperatures below freezing, high winds, as well as the occasional quicksand bog in the streambed. Two months into their toil, in the alcove guarding what would later be named Split Level Ruin, a falling rock smashed McLoyd's feet so badly that he was laid up for almost two weeks. Yet at the end of their toil, the plucky explorers backpacked all their booty up the trail they had built in January. They loaded a makeshift wagon, hitched their horses to it for the haul out to Bluff, then hired a teamster to transport the goods to Durango.

This speculative enterprise in relic-digging paid off when a Baptist minister in Durango paid the men $3,000 for the collection—a lot more than they could have earned from three months' comparable toil in the mines. Fortunately, the minister later sold the collection to the Field Museum in Chicago, where it is curated today. Not all of the early caches of priceless artifacts dug by amateurs in southeast Utah came to such benign resolutions, and the loss of whole collections to the vagaries of ownership underlines the tragedy of those reckless ventures—not only for archaeology, but for the Native American tribes that a century later would be legally authorized to reclaim the patrimony of their ancestors.

McLoyd and Graham were friends with the five Wetherill brothers, ranchers based in Mancos, the small town twenty-seven miles west of Durango. On a cold winter day in 1888, out searching for runaway cattle on a high mesa above the Mancos River—terrain that Anglos had steered clear of, because it was the stronghold of a band of Utes under a headman named Acowitz, who violently opposed the incursions of white men— Richard Wetherill, eldest of the five brothers and their guiding force, and his brother-in-law Charlie Mason made the accidental discovery of Cliff Palace (long thought to be the largest of all cliff dwellings in the Southwest). In a single *dies mirabilis*, the pair of cowboys also discovered and named Spruce Tree House and Square Tower House. All three ruins are protected today as crown jewels of Mesa Verde National Park.

That chance find became a romantic legend of the West, lightly fictionalized in Willa Cather's *The Professor's House*. But in 2000, Fred Blackburn discovered a faint partial inscription in Cliff Palace that predated 1888— the name was unreadable, but the date 1885 stood out clear. And in another Mesa Verde ruin near Cliff Palace, Fred deciphered several inscriptions from 1884. Who those earlier discoverers might have been, and why they never made any public fuss about their great finds, remain mysteries today.

Galvanized by the 1888 discoveries, Richard Wetherill, along with some of his brothers and close friends, explored more of Mesa Verde and Mancos Canyon and dug in scores of ruins through four successive seasons, usually in winter, the only part of the year the men could spare from their duties at the family's Alamo Ranch. In 1891, by a fluke of connection, Richard met a young Swedish nobleman, Baron Gustaf Nordenskiöld, who was touring the West in hopes of finding relief from his tuberculosis (the disease that would kill him at the age of twenty-six). Gustaf was the son of Adolf Erik Nordenskiöld, a Finnish-Swedish explorer who in 1878–79 had led the first successful expedition to navigate the Northeast Passage, the treacherous, ice-choked sea route from Scandinavia across the top of Europe and Siberia and into the Pacific Ocean. In Mancos, the younger Nordenskiöld was instantly smitten by Richard's work on Mesa Verde. Abandoning his health-seeking tour, he was soon hard at work with the Wetherill team in the very side canyon that sheltered Cliff Palace.

Nordenskiöld has been widely credited with turning Richard from a pothunter into a self-taught archaeologist. Trained in geology, he had visited professional excavations in Italy. Early on, he convinced his guide to use a trowel rather than a shovel when uncovering fragile artifacts, and he introduced Richard to the basic but crucial notion of stratigraphy, which when it came to prehistoric ruins meant that unless the ground has been severely disturbed, objects found on the lowest levels underground are older than those found higher up.

After his whirlwind stint in the field, Nordenskiöld returned to Sweden and composed a lavishly illustrated, well-written book about the ancients he and the Wetherill team had unearthed. Published in Stockholm in 1893 and promptly translated into English, *The Cliff Dwellers of the Mesa Verde* was, according to historian Frank McNitt, "the first major record of archaeological work in the United States."

Before he set sail for Europe, however, Nordenskiöld stirred up a hornet's nest. Because he had financed the 1891 diggings in the Mesa Verde canyons, Nordenskiöld evidently thought that all the artifacts and human remains (including four mummies and thirteen skulls) the Wetherill team had unearthed belonged to him. In late August, as the baron took a sightseeing side trip to the Hopi mesas, a group of Durango citizens mobilized their disapproval. Alarmed that the artifacts from the 1891 field season were destined to be spirited not only out of Colorado but out of the country, they persuaded the sheriff to seize the crates in which they were packed, to serve a warrant to Nordenskiöld and to schedule a hearing in Durango in two weeks' time.

But when that showdown unfolded in the local district court, the lawyer assigned to the case had to confess that after a diligent search, he had uncovered no law, local or federal, forbidding the sale or export of antiquities. The twenty-three-year-old Swede was free to head home with his goods, some six hundred "specimens" in all. That he did, and as soon as he got back to Stockholm, sat down to write the monograph that laid out what he knew about the vanished "Cliff Dwellers," based on the relics the team had pried loose from the dirt, mostly in a ruin they named Step House.

The saga has a remarkable sequel. Before his untimely death in 1895, Nordenskiöld sold the collection to a wealthy physician, who later bequeathed it to the National Museum of Finland in Helsinki. There several generations of Europeans admired the exotic baskets and pots and the baron's excellent photographs (and in earlier times, the skeletons and mummies) that anchored a permanent exhibit. But very few Anasazi experts from the United States ever got to see the assemblage, which took on the semi-mythical aura of a virtually lost collection. Then, out of the blue, on October 2, 2019, in the middle of a televised meeting between the presidents of Finland and the United States, during which the American leader mostly railed against the Democrats who were prying into the Ukraine scandal, Trump announced almost parenthetically that an important archaeological collection in Finland would be returned to this country and delivered to the Hopi tribe. (Watching the chaotic performance on live TV, I did a double-take, as I muttered out loud, "Huh? It must be the Nordenskiöld collection!")

In the days that followed, a consortium of Pueblo spokesmen announced plans to rebury the artifacts—especially the human remains—in a secret location at Mesa Verde, during a ceremony closed to Anglos. Clark Tenakhongva, Hopi vice-chairman, expressed the tribe's gratitude to the Finnish government, but then voiced a litany of grievances not only against museum collections in general, but against the very practice of excavating Native American sites, indicting the whole tradition of dirt archaeology in the United States. Said Tenakhongva,

> For me, it's been traumatizing ever since we recognized what happened. In the 1900s, we uncovered the history of how much looting and vandalizing occurred. We're still suffering the consequences of the first contact of non-natives to America, and the history endures

today. This is only to mend the wounds they created here and do so with the best processes we can in putting remains back where they belong.

(Of this Native American backlash against archaeology, more below.)

◄◄ ►►

Not only were McLoyd and Graham friends of the Wetherill brothers, but McLoyd and Graham's older brother Howard had joined John Wetherill in further digging on Mesa Verde only days after Richard's and Charlie Mason's discovery of Cliff Palace. So, three years later, when McLoyd and the younger Graham got back from Grand Gulch with their wagonload of antiquities and their tales of cliff dwellings in nearly every bend of that serpentine gorge, Richard Wetherill was spurred to action.

The expeditions led by Richard in 1893–94 and 1897 were the most ambitious and fruitful of any of the early thrusts into the Anasazi domain by ranchers-turned-amateur archaeologists. On both journeys, the teams explored far beyond Cedar Mesa and Grand Gulch, ranging into northeastern Arizona. On the first trip, Richard's team penetrated the unknown, many-branched Tsegi Canyon system on the Navajo Reservation, making the Anglo discovery of Keet Seel—now acknowledged as the largest of all Southwest cliff dwellings, as well as a consensus choice for the most stunning, complex, and beautiful.

In 1892, two wealthy brothers from New York City visited the Alamo Ranch and were smitten by the Wetherills' discoveries in Mesa Verde. Fred and Talbot Hyde were heirs to the Bab-O soap fortune, and it took little persuasion by Richard for them to sponsor his first foray into Grand Gulch and beyond. The enterprise would be titled the Hyde Exploring Expedition, and it was determined from the start that all the relics retrieved from the far-flung ruins would be donated to the American Museum of Natural History in New York City, arguably the most prestigious institution in the country dealing with prehistoric cultures. On his first trip back East for the Columbian Expedition, Richard had met Frederick W. Putnam, director of Harvard's Peabody Museum, and though Putnam did not formally endorse the Hyde Exploring Expedition, his approval lent an academic cachet to the venture that would ultimately pay dividends.

Whether or not it was Nordenskiöld who had converted Richard from a careless pothunter into a scrupulous excavator, by 1893 the Mancos rancher had absorbed a deep concern for scientific accuracy and for the responsible recording of his finds. Before the first Grand Gulch expedition, he devised a form on which he intended to enter the data concerning each artifact, with spaces for "number of article," "depth" [at which found], "remarks," etc. From that time on, he kept field notes that were the equal of those of many of the professionals of his day. And in a letter to Talbot Hyde, he expressed his worries about how posterity would judge his work: "This whole subject . . . is in its infancy and the work we do must stand the most rigid inspection, and we do not want to do it in such a manner that anyone in the future can pick flaws in it."

Never again would Richard Wetherill sell his collections to private citizens who fancied the curios his teams had gone to such effort to dig and transport back to Durango. All the collections were destined for reputable museums, most of them back East. By the late 1980s, when I first visited Cedar Mesa, the American Museum of Natural History and the National Museum of the American Indian in New York City and the Field Museum in Chicago housed hundreds of irreplaceable objects that Wetherill's teams had dug in Utah and Arizona. But none were on display: instead they languished on shelves and in drawers and archives, where very few professionals had ever bothered to study them.

The germ of my long-term fascination with Cedar Mesa came in 1992 when, acting on a secondhand tip, I proposed an article for *Smithsonian* magazine about a passionate band of what the pros too often dismissed as "avocational archaeologists" who had concocted an enterprise—a mission, really—that they called the Wetherill Grand Gulch Research Project. To pursue it, they were inventing a new technique they called "reverse archaeology." It was thus that I met Fred Blackburn.

By the 1980s, hundreds of artifacts that Richard Wetherill's teams had recovered from Grand Gulch and other canyons were safely housed in the eastern museums. But in effect, they had lost their proveniences. The curators in New York City and Chicago were completely unfamiliar with the landscape of southeast Utah. Wetherill had named the alcoves in which he dug by a simple chronological system: Cave 5, Cave 6, and so on. A finely woven basket or, for that matter, a well-preserved mummy might be tagged in the museum archives as having been discovered in Cave 10, but nobody back East had the slightest idea where Cave 10 was.

With his years of experience as a BLM ranger on Cedar Mesa, Fred knew the alcoves as well as anyone alive. It occurred to him that it might be a great service to Southwestern prehistory to reconnect the objects housed in, say, the American Museum of Natural History with the ruins from which they had been retrieved. In archaeology, context is everything.

A small band of friends, all of them passionate hikers in the Utah canyons, gathered to pursue this quest. They included Winston Hurst, the Blanding archaeologist, but all the rest were nonprofessionals. The key to linking "caves" and artifacts, Fred knew, lay in two sources of fugitive information: the field notes Richard had compiled, still preserved in the museums but meaningless to the curators; and the signatures the diggers had left, scrawled in pencil or charcoal or bullet lead, on the walls of the alcoves in which they had toiled.

At first, the eastern experts looked askance at the amateurs touting the potential of "reverse archaeology." They loomed as hobbyists, dilettantes. But gradually Fred's coalition won over such guardians of the artifacts as the American Museum of Natural History's Anibal Rodriguez. The collaboration that came together between museums and outdoor aficionados justified Fred's vision of a way to rejuvenate "dead" collections by, in effect, rediscovering them in the canyons.

The crowning triumph of the Wetherill–Grand Gulch Project was almost the last of the linkages to be nailed down. In December 1893, in a small alcove that sheltered only a crumbling minor Anasazi roomblock, Richard pursued a hunch and dug deeper than he had before, through a couple of feet of "sterile" soil that lay beneath the usual debris of potsherds and yucca fabric he had found near the surface. Six feet down, he suddenly came upon a jumble of bones, the remains of some ninety skeletons in all, apparently the scene of a massacre or mass execution, for six of the skeletons had projectile points lodged in their bones. Richard noticed several things at once. Arrayed with the dead were baskets but no pots. And the skulls had a fully rounded shape, unlike the flattened backs of the skulls of all the Anasazi he had previously excavated. He thought he had discovered an entirely different race. "Basket People," he called them—a cognomen that soon was regularized as Basketmakers. (We now know that the Basketmakers were the direct ancestors of the later Puebloans—all Anasazi. The flattened skulls were the by-product of hard infant cradleboards introduced sometime after AD 700.)

The problem for "reverse archaeology" was that Richard had identified the shelter where he made his great discovery only as "Cave 7." In Frank McNitt's 1955 biography of Richard Wetherill, a photo someone on the team had taken at Cave 7 appeared, but it was miscaptioned as located in Grand Gulch and shot during Wetherill's second expedition there in 1897. In reality, Cave 7 lay in an obscure canyon nowhere near Grand Gulch. Blackburn knew that McNitt's caption was all wrong. But where was the real Cave 7?

The whole saga of the mission to rediscover Cave 7 undertaken by Fred and his cronies makes for a wonderful story, one I told at length in my first book about the Anasazi, *In Search of the Old Ones*. It's also recounted with zest and specificity in *Cowboys & Cave Dwellers*, the culture history of the Basketmakers crafted by Fred with Ray Williamson. And the "Eureka!" moment of the finding of Cave 7 in Whiskers Draw, twenty-five miles northeast of Grand Gulch, at the end of an exhaustive search spearheaded by Winston Hurst, emerges in Winston and Christy Turner's comprehensive paper, "Rediscovering the 'Great Discovery.'" Besides performing an invaluable service to Southwestern archaeology, the group effort rehabilitated a "cowboy" who had been reviled by generations of rangers at Mesa Verde, who told the tourists that the Wetherill brothers were reckless vandals who had done more damage than good. Richard had also posthumously been accused (on no good evidence) of using dynamite to blow up ruins to get at the "treasure," and even of being a cattle rustler.

The rancher from Mancos would not live to see either the trashing of his legacy by rangers and rivals or the elevation of his life's work in Anasazi sites to a model of early field practice on a par with that of the best professionals of his day. After the 1897 expedition through Grand Gulch and into the Tsegi system, Richard focused on the enigmatic ruins in Chaco Canyon in western New Mexico. By then he had won the imprimatur of Frederick W. Putnam at Harvard's Peabody Museum, at the time perhaps America's most distinguished archaeologist. Putnam delegated a young student named George Pepper to assist Richard's team in the field, and the men went to work excavating Pueblo Bonito, the finest of all the Great Houses at Chaco.

Enter Edgar L. Hewett, who would become Richard Wetherill's nemesis. In 1900, the then president of New Mexico Normal University, in Las Vegas, New Mexico, notified the inspector general of the General Land Office that Wetherill was wantonly destroying Pueblo Bonito. There's no evidence that Hewett had even been to Chaco Canyon, but he was an ambitious man who fancied himself the leading Southwestern expert of his day, and he was so envious of all perceived rivals that he had no scruples about flinging accusations right and left. The upshot was that Richard was forced to suspend his digging at Pueblo Bonito. And though he would stay on at Chaco Canyon, running a trading post adjacent to the great ruin, he would never excavate again. Then in 1910, in a still mysterious encounter fraught with hints of sinister sub-plots, Richard was ambushed, shot, and killed by a Navajo named Chis-chilling-begay, who ended up serving three years in prison for his deed.

Hewett's own legacy is a checkered one. His "reconstruction" of the village of Tyuonyi in Bandelier National Monument is often cited by later archaeologists as such a wretched piece of work that we will never know what the fifteenth-century builders wrought before Hewett took apart the ruins to concoct his own fantasy of a maze-like pueblo. My own dim view of Hewett was reinforced when I came across an anecdote in Douglas R. Givens's biography of Alfred V. Kidder. The founder of the Pecos Conference and of the Pecos System that divides Anasazi chronology into six periods, from Basketmaker II to Pueblo IV, Kidder was a Southwest visionary now widely hailed as one of the most influential and sagacious archaeologists in US history.

In charge of two young grad students from Harvard—Kidder and Sylvanus Morley (who would become America's leading Mayanist)—Hewett practiced a style of supervision he called "push 'em off de pier" (an allusion to a lifeguard on the Chicago waterfront). Hewett put the students to work at Puye, a massive pueblo ancestral to the Santa Clara people, then took off on other business with no instructions how to proceed. When Santa Clarans showed up at the ruin and begged Kidder and Morley to desist, Hewett's parting advice to ignore the qualms of living Indians trumped the two young acolytes' misgivings. (On my own three tours of Puye after 2012, I asked my Santa Clara guides what they thought of Hewett. Their responses ranged from a polite "no comment" to a rage undimmed by more than a century of retrospect.)

And after all the turmoil over his unauthorized excavation, Hewett never published any report of his findings at Puye—the all-too-frequent but unforgiveable sin of many an archaeologist who probes a ruin to divine its secrets, then for one reason or another—laziness? writer's block? crippling insecurity?—fails to commit his discoveries to print.

But one thing that Hewett made happen stands more than a century later as a cardinal triumph of American archaeology: the passage of the Antiquities Act in 1906. Whether or not that law was born of Hewett's vindictive envy of Richard Wetherill, it anchors the ethical mandate, already long overdue by 1906, that what Native Americans built and left behind is in some sense sacred, not to be ransacked for the entertainment or profit of later-arriving Anglos. Neither Cave 7 nor Pueblo Bonito, the act affirms, is an amusement park. The culture of The Old Ones cannot be dug up and owned or sold without inflicting irreversible harm.

◀◀ ▶▶

On our llama trip down lower Grand Gulch in 1994, in an otherwise non-descript alcove, Sharon and I came across a record etched in the rock. WETHERILL 1894, it read. The thrill of the discovery was amplified by realizing that exactly a century had passed since the self-taught archaeologist had spent weeks digging in Grand Gulch, carefully annotating each artifact his team pried out of the rubble of the ages. On later trips on Cedar Mesa, I found other signatures from Wetherill's teams, especially the script of J. L. Ethridge, a cowhand who worked at the Alamo Ranch who had a passion for posting his "Kilroy" wherever the team dug. In the company of Fred Blackburn, I also discovered, to our shared dismay, that several inscriptions from the Wetherill teams we had seen in the early 1990s had been rubbed clean by the mid-2000s, apparently by clueless "environmentalists" who could not distinguish a historic inscription (any of which over fifty years old is protected under the Antiquities Act) from last year's graffito tag.

Yet along with the thrill of discovery of those pioneer inscriptions came the realization of just how accessible Grand Gulch and Cedar Mesa had become by the time I first explored the canyons, compared to the remoteness of the place that posed such challenges to the cowboys from Colorado in the 1890s. In his field notes, Richard Wetherill diverged briefly from dry taxonomy to evoke that wildness:

> Grand Gulch . . . is the most tortuous cañon in the whole of the Southwest, making bends from 200 to 600 yards apart almost its entire length, or for 50 miles; and each bend means a cave or over-hanging cliff. All of these with an exposure to the sun had been occupied by either cliff houses or as burial places.

For his 1897 expedition, with thirteen companions, including his young wife, Marietta, Richard hired no fewer than forty horses to haul gear and provisions. Nine of them died during the expedition. In his field notes, he laconically recorded some of the accidents and mishaps that cost him precious mounts. "One animal fell off of a bridge and broke its neck. Another fell off the trail where it wound about a ledge going into the cañon and was killed instantly. Another fell off of a cliff with the same result. Two gave out completely and were abandoned."

Of course, the "taming" of a once inaccessible wilderness in southeast Utah by decades of settlement and roadbuilding was inevitable. Add to it, by the 1990s, the appeal to adventurers such as myself of ruins and rock art panels not yet turned into packaged scenic attractions by the bureaucracy of national parks and monuments such as Mesa Verde. As early as 1975, after the summers he spent running his field camps out of a spring-fed oasis near the head of Todie Canyon (a short tributary of Grand Gulch), archaeologist Bill Lipe foresaw the spiritual loss of such a transformation. In his lyrical but rueful essay "Three Days on the Road from Bluff," Lipe wrote:

Tent camps are also part of the "romance" of Southwestern archaeology, of an appeal that touches scholar and non-scholar alike. That romantic quality, both a strength and weakness of the field, is compounded from the beauty of the area and its ruins, their remoteness from modern development, and the tantalizing juxtaposition of the complex, well-preserved sites with the mysteries of who lived there and why they left. At its best, this attitude can support an esthetic and humanistic understanding that not only informs but transcends scientific knowledge. If you don't know what I mean, walk Grand Gulch alone some moonlit night, and look up into those black doorways in the ancient walls.

At its worst, however, the romance of the Southwest bears the seeds of its own destruction. It so often finds expression in no more than shallow curiosity, in a destructive rummaging through the sites in search of some treasure, some tangible relic of the past that can adorn a coffee table, or worse, be discarded after a few days or weeks as would another plastic novelty. And even those who come with respect will be frustrated if too many come at once. The sites are fragile, but even more so are the understandings that are sought. For these, there must be time, and quiet—not crowds, or lectures, or guided tours.

Grand Gulch is beginning to be caught in this dilemma. It is still a place where one can visit the ruins alone, and often walk for days without seeing someone else. But it is no longer "three days on the road from Bluff." More come every year, and there has been recent vandalism in some of the sites. . . .

[I]t's clear that even in Grand Gulch, we are moving into an era of managed remoteness, of planned romance. I think that is probably how it has to be if we are to preserve the qualities of the area at all in an increasingly mobile and exploitive society.

"Managed remoteness." "Planned romance." Forty-five years ago in Grand Gulch, Lipe saw it all coming.

Decades have passed since Lipe's field camps, however, without any significant new excavations being undertaken on Cedar Mesa. Indeed, throughout the Southwest, digging up ruins in the name of science has fallen out of favor. Nonintrusive archaeology, undreamed of by the likes of Hewett and Kidder, is the new vogue. Remote sensing techniques such as LIDAR (Light Detection and Ranging) have replaced the time-honored probes by shovel and spade. At Patokwa, a site in northern New Mexico ancestral to the people of Jemez Pueblo, Harvard archaeologist Matt Liebmann enlisted Jemez men as workers in his survey of the important ruin. Over the course of field seasons in 2003 and 2004, the team collected some two thousand potsherds from the surface of the site. Back in the lab, they washed and analyzed the sherds, then, instead of the traditional practice of storing the pieces of broken pots in the drawers of some archive against future study, Liebmann's team returned every single sherd to the exact spot on the ground from which it had been "borrowed." (The diligence of that study seemed almost unfathomable to me, when Liebmann first told me about it.)

Researching *In Search of the Old Ones* in the early 1990s, I was able to visit the American Museum of Natural History and read the original copies of Richard Wetherill's field notes from Grand Gulch. And at my request, a curator went so far as to retrieve a strange mummy Wetherill had dug out of an alcove in 1894, lay it on a table, and let me peruse it. Richard had named the mummy Cut-in-Two Man. I'd never seen anything like it. The body of the adult male had been cut clean through at the hips and abdomen with a stone knife, then sewed back together with twine made of braided human hair. Richard himself had been deeply disturbed by his discovery, writing to Talbot Hyde, "It seems most horrible to me. The face seems to indicate pain." He speculated that the cutting and sewing must have been performed in a desperate bid to save the man's life after he'd suffered some gruesome injury. But the iconoclastic AMNH curator was pretty sure the man could not have survived the "operation." The sewing back together, she guessed, had been done after death—for whatever reason, we will likely never know.

Just a week earlier, Fred Blackburn had guided me to Wetherill's Cave 12/19, from which the rancher had extracted Cut-in-Two Man. Because it required a stiff climb to get up to the alcove, Fred had never been inside it. I was able to clamber up the tricky corner guarding the "cave," then belay Fred into the ruin. To his delight, he quickly located the faint depression in the dirt from which Wetherill had removed the mummy in January 1894.

By about 2010, there was no longer any chance that an independent researcher such as myself would be allowed by the AMNH to see Wetherill's field notes. And the prospect of having a mummy hauled out of storage and laid on a table to slake my curiosity was beyond the pale.

This new rigor was not simply the fruit of institutional squeamishness. It reflected instead a new sensitivity, long overdue, to Native American beliefs. For more than a century, like the Santa Clarans who begged Morley and Kidder to stop digging at Puye, the descendants of the men and women who had built ancient villages had argued that digging in the ruins was desecration. As NAGPRA, the law passed in 1990, started to take effect, museums and universities all over the country began repatriating human remains in their collections to the tribes deemed most likely to have affiliation with the dead. The usual result was a powerful ceremony in which the skeletons and mummies and grave goods were returned to the earth in secret places where even the most avid looters were not likely to find them.

The NAGPRA tide unleashed a backlash among many archaeologists, who saw it as political correctness run amok. The controversy fanned into flames over Kennewick Man, the well-preserved skeleton found eroding out of the bank of the Columbia River in 1996. Radiocarbon tests showed that the man was some 9,000 years old, and the first researchers who studied him thought his features resembled those of Polynesians or even Europeans rather than any Native Americans. Meanwhile local tribes, particularly the Umatilla, demanded the skeleton for reburial. Archaeological eyebrows were raised, for it was thought the Umatilla could not have lived on the Washington-Oregon border throughout the last 9,000 years.

A nine-year court case pitted the archaeologists against the tribes, who were championed at first by the US Army Corps of Engineers. But during that impasse, scientists were able to study the unique skeleton far more thoroughly, and they finally came to the conclusion that Kennewick Man was most closely related, after all, to the Confederated Tribes of the Colville Reservation in northeast Washington (*not* including the Umatilla). In the end, the archaeologists got free rein to study the anomalous skeleton, and the Colville tribes reburied Kennewick Man in 2017.

As I followed the brush fires that were springing up all over the country between Native Americans, armed with NAGPRA, and the archaeologists, I found myself caught on the horns of ambivalence. Ever since I had started to write about the Anasazi in the early 1990s, I had met many of the leading Southwest archaeologists, including such first-rate researchers as Bill Lipe, Jeffrey Dean (the acknowledged master of tree-ring dating), Christy Turner (ditto for prehistoric cannibalism), and my mentor/friends Winston Hurst, Matt Liebmann, and Steve Lekson. But in tours and visits to such Pueblos as Acoma, Jemez, Santa Clara, and Hopi, as well as talks with Navajos and Utes, I found myself leaning hard toward sympathy for the myriad wrongs done to Native Americans in the name of science over the decades.

Even so, when I came across an endnote in Lekson's dazzling and revolutionary new book, *A Study of Southwestern Archaeology*, published in 2018, I was first shocked, then moved by the depths of half-unwelcome empathy the controversy had wrung from the man I considered the most insightful of all the Southwest savants. Lekson wrote,

> I was asked, over and over, first by *ricos* [potential patrons] and then by Indians, why archaeologists do what they do, what good accrues. With *ricos*, I must have answered satisfactorily; we raised lots of money. But with Indians . . . no, I could not justify archaeology in the face of their outrage. I could not defend Southwestern archaeology to Indians and, ultimately, to myself. Maybe the Indians were right: We should pull the plug.

That brave but gloomy statement, which in a sense called into question Lekson's life's work, was leavened only by a single sentence that offered the hope of an escape hatch from the trap of his own scrupulous logic: "This book is, in part, an argument with myself against that conclusion." By 2019, I was wondering whether Steve had won or lost that argument. I think I'm afraid to ask him.

◄◄ ►►

The rehabilitation of "amateurs" such as Richard Wetherill brought with it an overdue scrutiny of the professionals who occupied prestigious museum and university posts in the early twentieth century. The more you looked at the often crude reconstructions and the poorly documented excavations of "experts" such as Edgar Hewett, Byron Cummings (Winston Hurst: "his enthusiasm for artifact collection was not matched by an equal enthusiasm for data collection"), or the blatantly fraudulent Frank Hibben (who planted artifacts at deep levels inside Sandia Cave to claim the impossibly early date of 25,000 BP), the more the boundary between responsible archaeology and outright looting got fuzzy. And there were too many woeful instances of good fieldwork by respectable archaeologists (Earl Morris, Paul Martin, and Joe Ben Wheat, among others) who destroyed prehistoric pueblos forever by failing to publish their findings. In contrast, the truly admirable scholar-excavators such as Alfred Kidder, Samuel Guernsey, Neil Judd, and J. O. Brew stood out as exceptions.

Yet the steady improvement of field techniques among Southwest archaeologists through the twentieth century took place in a universe parallel to that of the ravages of pothunters who never pretended to care about science. It was treasure they sought, and often treasure that could be turned into cash. The Blanding bust of 2009 was only the last and most dramatic clash between grave robbers and federal agents. From the 1870s through the present, the looting and vandalizing of ancient ruins in the Southwest has flourished almost unchecked. It looms today as a tragedy that even NAGPRA has no power to curtail.

The techniques mobilized for Operation Cerberus Action—the planting of informants with secret recording devices, the sting of artifacts bought and sold, and the lightning raid—represented a relatively new approach in the Southwest to combatting the scourge of pothunting and looting. In previous decades, law enforcement focused on trying to catch the culprits red-handed. As a BLM ranger on Cedar Mesa in the 1970s, Fred Blackburn was well acquainted with that approach. Some of his encounters partook of the edgy moments in old Western movies when things start to go wrong:

> We were camping down at the mouth of Grand Gulch. We had this old mule named Red, like 33 years old. One of the last surviving animals of the TY cattle company. We always put the bell on that mule. One night all the mules took off. They went clear up to the head of Bullet Canyon. Red loved it up there, he knew where he was at. When we'd go in to find him, all we'd see is these two red ears sticking up out of the trees. He wouldn't move his neck 'cause the bell would ring and he'd be caught. He was cool.
>
> In Bullet, I noticed human tracks at the water hole below Perfect

Kiva ruin. They were not going up or down canyon so I hollered up into the alcove. Nobody answered. So I walked up in there, and I could see a black hat sticking out over the top of a rock. As I got in there, these two guys rise up. The dust is still rolling out of Perfect Kiva from where they'd been digging. It was this guy and his son. The guy looks at me and says, "What's the goddamn BLM doing here? You trying to outdo the Park Service?"

The guy had a bee up his ass. All I knew was that that was not a good situation to be in. They split up on me so I left and headed back to our camp. We finished the trip and headed out of Grand Gulch. I'm ready to write up the incident, only to find that the guy had filed a complaint with the district manager, claiming that we had left a hot campfire! They got out of their predicament by striking first. They never did get prosecuted.

In the 1970s, at the height of their efforts to catch looters, the BLM deployed helicopters to stake out their territory. Blackburn was then and remains today an enthusiast:

It was the most effective deterrent we ever had. Our patrol method was to fly and clear areas. If we saw something suspicious we sent in a patrol ranger who would wait at the highway to see what we found, and move in to ground-check our observations only when needed. I loved the flying. You could see human footprints leading from vehicles. You could follow vehicles who went off road. You could see the digging in the sites. Even if you missed these people they believed they were seen, and in numerous encounters the rangers sent in to check on these vehicles found screens and shovels abandoned as people dropped everything and ran.

The program was controversial from the beginning. We had numerous threats of being shot down from the sky, by the bad guys, and numerous complaints by the wilderness folks about our intrusion into their experiences. However, it kept everybody honest.

Jim Conklin, Blackburn's colleague as a ranger on Cedar Mesa, had quite the opposite view. During a break in his duties with the BLM, Conklin unloaded his qualms to his friend Jim Stiles, editor of the quirky periodical, the *Canyon Country Zephyr*.

"Stiles," he said, "How would you like it if you were out in the wilderness, miles from any road and feeling like the world is far, far away and suddenly you hear this 'whock, whock' reverberating noise and you look up to see a damn helicopter flying at tree-top level, hovering right over you. And then, if you can believe this, it LANDS in the sagebrush meadow 50 yards in front of you. That is what I'm having to do out at Grand Gulch."

Conklin explained to me that his new job was to do surveillance on hikers in the area and, in effect, to harass them.

"You would not believe the looks we are getting from innocent backpackers. It's crazy! Whatever happened to 'innocent until proven guilty?'"

Whether or not the incident was the cause of his misgivings or merely reinforced them, Conklin had earned his doubts the hard way. In March 1976, on surveillance patrol, the helicopter in which Conklin and ranger Becky Blackburn (Fred's wife) were riding crashed in Butler Wash. According to Stiles's perhaps one-sided later account,

Blackburn sustained a crushed vertebrae [*sic*] and was unable to move. [Pilot Fred] Wardell had severe facial and eye injuries.

Though in severe pain, Conklin stabilized his two friends and moved them clear of the wrecked Hiller, then hiked out seven miles to the main highway and caught a ride to Bluff, where he was able to contact law enforcement. He and Deputy Sheriff Rudy Cook returned to the accident scene, and later Blackburn and Wardell were transported to a hospital.

Jim Conklin was the hero of the day. Later he learned that he'd made the seven mile hike for help with a compression fracture of his vertebrae. And while he worried about his injured friends, he hoped that finally the BLM would put an end to the helicopter surveillance. Instead he got fired.

By 1976, Fred and Becky Blackburn's marriage was in trouble; they divorced shortly thereafter. Despite his lingering enthusiasm for helicopter surveillance as a way to discourage looting, his BLM stint took a psychological toll on Fred. "It was our Vietnam," he told me in 2019. "When I left, I had PTSD from that fucking place."

As fraught as some of the confrontations in the 1970s were between rangers and looters, no one in Utah was prepared for the nightmare of Earl Shumway.

In the late 1980s, poking through the archives of the University of Utah, Winston Hurst made a startling discovery. In 2009, he expanded on his findings in a comprehensive paper, titled "The Professor's Legacy." During the 1920s, Andrew Kerr was a highly regarded assistant professor in the archaeology department, as well as the curator of the museum. He had recently received his PhD from Harvard.

Winston's sleuthing revealed the unhappy truth that Kerr was woefully negligent about publishing the results of his fieldwork.

In a field where documentation and publication are everything, Kerr contributed virtually nothing to our body of archaeological knowledge. He never published a single article regarding his "remarkable work in the field of archaeology," nor is there a single extant map or scrap of notes to show that he ever documented any of his work in any detail. . . . Most of the information he gained from his years of excavation were [sic] kept only in his memory and went with him to the grave.

Even worse, as Winston soon discovered, "Kerr's field work had little to do with archaeology *per se* and everything to do with artifact collecting." In a newspaper clipping of the day, Kerr bragged about keeping the booty in Salt Lake City: "We want the biggest collection of Utah archeological specimens in the world right here in the state of Utah."

From 1924 until his death in 1929, the professor made only desultory ventures into the field. Instead, "Kerr used his annual field budget from the university to finance annual collecting operations in San Juan County. His modus operandi was to hire local Blanding men to dig wherever they felt they could find museum quality artifacts and bring the artifacts to him for payment. His primary digger was Arah E. ('A') Shumway, assisted at various times by Shumway's younger brothers Harris, Lee and Seth, and a changing crew of unidentified other men. . . ."

Winston found further details about this shady arrangement in the transcript of an oral history interview with Lee Shumway, conducted in 1973. "Professor Kerr . . . came down here quite often," Shumway recalled, "and he would get us to show him the country. My brothers A. and Harris used to go with him and we would go out and show him the country. We would do the hard work, the digging for him, and he would take the dishes, the bones, the arrowheads, the beads and anything ancient like that back to the university."

The only record of each artifact retrieved by the Shumway brothers was a perfunctory jotting in the museum catalogue. For example:

#6929 - Tall black & white vase with handle - acq. Mar. 1925 - 1 mi. East of Blanding, San Juan Co. - A. E. Shumway of Blanding working for U. of U. - Very fine specimen. Found on state land (reverted homestead) in a shallow grave.

In other words, the artifacts were every bit as severed from their proveniences as if they had been pothunted. To put it bluntly, Professor Kerr was hiring Blanding locals to do his pothunting for him, all in the name of filling his museum's shelves with remarkable prehistoric relics. Under Kerr's regime, the systematic pillage of southeast Utah's antiquities passed for archaeology.

As a Blanding local himself, Winston could see all too clearly how

Kerr's sanction of grave-robbing fed into the cynical bromide still current among his neighbors today: "The only difference between archaeology and pothunting is a government piece of paper."

This was the culture—both local and familial—into which Earl Shumway was born in 1957. Both Arah ("A") Shumway and Lee Shumway were Earl's great-uncles, and in 1979 Casey Shumway, A's grandson and Earl's cousin, was the first looter prosecuted under the new Archaeological Resource Protection Act (ARPA)—a more stringent law that beefed up the Antiquities Act of 1906. BLM rangers had caught Casey Shumway digging in Turkey Pen ruin in Grand Gulch, one of the richest archaeological sites on Cedar Mesa. (He was fined $700 and put on probation, rather than serving prison time.)

Earl Shumway later claimed that he learned to pothunt from his father, DeLoy. Early in his career, for a documentary film, he echoed the cynical take on the practice nursed by many Blanding citizens: "Around here it's not a crime. It's a way of life."

While others of the Shumway clan enthusiastically looted sites, licensed by Andrew Kerr's benediction, Earl took the avocation to a whole new level. By his mid-twenties he was bragging openly about having dug illegally in "thousands" of sites, of making $5,000 a day selling his plundered goods on the black market, and of using bulldozers to scrape away ruins to get at the treasure. He taunted federal agents by letting them know he was armed with a .44 Magnum he would not hesitate to use, and bragged that the chances of his getting caught were "one in a million."

Along with his pothunting, Shumway dabbled in burglary, breaking into a local business, Lyman Truck Lines, and stealing a safe that allegedly contained $48,000 worth of "valuables." It's hard not to see the man, with his wild shock of red hair, matching mustache, and braggart mouth, as a sociopath, kin perhaps to some of the legendary thieves in Utah history who have been glamorized as the Wild Bunch.

Despite his cockiness, Shumway was busted in the mid-1980s after years of looting a site called House Rock Ruin, in Allen Canyon northwest of Blanding. (Most of Allen Canyon is in the Bears Ears National

Monument that Obama decreed in 2016.) In 1985 Shumway was indicted
by a federal grand jury in Salt Lake City on four felony counts of violating
ARPA, which centered on thirty-four Anasazi baskets Shumway had dug
out of the site. He pleaded guilty, but avoided prison time by helping the
feds retrieve the baskets (some of which he had sold to collectors), and by
turning snitch on a number of Blanding neighbors whom he identified as
fellow looters.

Around Blanding in the 1980s and '90s, Earl Shumway was hated and
feared by many. But he also won a kind of Robin Hood following, as the
local who stood up most defiantly to the federal agents and forces that, in
the town's self-serving melodrama, wanted to take away the basic rights
of peaceful citizens. That attitude was voiced, for instance, by Blanding's
mayor in 1986, after BLM and NFS agents raided several homes, some
of them armed with tips from Shumway's informing on his friends. The
mayor, Mary Shumway (related perhaps to Earl?), railed against "the judge
and his gestapo," the "Nazi inspired BLM and Forest Rangers," and "wilderness terrorists" who supposedly killed "our cattle," as she vowed never
"to kneel to a Socialist government" and to ensure "that not one additional
foot of San Juan County will be designated as wilderness area." That same
chorus of Blanding indignation would emerge in 2016, after Obama created the monument.

If anything, Shumway seemed energized by his narrow escape from
prison in 1985. Six years later (in the narrative reconstructed by prosecutors), in a pool hall somewhere in Utah, Shumway struck up a conversation with a helicopter mechanic. Intrigued by Shumway's honeyed tales of
easy money in the artifact trade, the mechanic put the looter in touch with
a pilot, who quickly bought into the plan. Shumway then posed as a movie
scout, calling the pilot's boss to hire the helicopter to look for backcountry
film locations.

All three men flew to the canyons northwest of Blanding, but when
Shumway couldn't find the ruin he wanted to dig, they changed course
and landed at the mouth of Dop-Ki Cave in Canyonlands National Park.
The mechanic and Shumway started digging in the ruin, but when the

mechanic uncovered a burial, Shumway took over. He unearthed an infant wrapped in a burial blanket, stripped the blanket to take with him, then apparently tore the skeleton apart and flung the bones every which way. When agents later visited the site, the only part of the infant they could find was the skull, perched on top of the dirt pile from the dig.

The signature Shumway regularly left scattered around the sites he pillaged were empty Mountain Dew cans. But this time the agents combing the wreckage found a single cigarette butt, from which they were able to get a DNA sample. When that specimen matched Shumway's DNA, the prosecutors finally felt they had an airtight case.

All this business finally came to trial in 1995. The jurors convicted Shumway on seven felony counts, and the judge, appalled by the looter's treatment of the infant's remains, threw the book at him, fining him $3,500 and sentencing him to six and a half years in prison. The Tenth Circuit Court of Appeals reduced the sentence to five years and three months.

In the van that carried Shumway toward the penitentiary, several fellow prisoners who were Native Americans gave him a severe beating.

To this day, Earl Shumway remains the only person in Utah ever convicted of illegal digging in prehistoric ruins to serve actual time in prison.

◄◄ ►►

On the west side of Blanding stands Edge of the Cedars, one of the finest small archaeological museums in the West. I've made scores of visits there since the early 1990s, and I never tire of even its permanent exhibits. The pièce de résistance of the institution, housed on its second floor, is a glass case housing some nine hundred Anasazi vessels, ranging from big *ollas* to corrugated cooking pots to mugs with intact handles and even effigy jars molded in the shape of semi-mythic humans and animals. A splendid interactive program allows you to pick a single vessel, shine a spotlight on it, and learn more details about it, such as the style of decoration (Mancos Black-on-White, say, or Tularosa White-on-Red) and sometimes the general location in which it was found.

Yet I never spend time in front of that dazzling exhibit without feeling a queasy mixture of pleasure and vexation. For almost all those ceramic objects were illegally looted over the decades from sites ranging beyond Utah into Colorado, New Mexico, and Arizona. That they have been assembled and put on display is the outcome of sensitive negotiations: some are the spoils confiscated from outlaws such as Earl Shumway, some are "on loan" from anonymous Blanding citizens, and some lie in the gray areas in between.

In March 2019 I sat down in the museum to talk with its articulate director, Jonathan Till. Because of the terms under which the pots were acquired, Till had to be vague in answering my questions. "Some of the materials come from law enforcement busts," he said. "Some were donated, and some are on long-term loan."

"So the owners all claim they were dug on private land?" I asked.

"Uhh, no. There is no insistence one way or another. That part of it was never made explicit when they came to Edge of the Cedars. I would bet that a lot of them are from private land. I would bet that a lot of them aren't. I just don't know which is which."

"Did any of those folks keep good records?

"Not that I know of."

I pushed on. "Are some of the pots Earl Shumway's?"

"We have some stuff that Earl Shumway procured, yes," Till answered. I sensed that he could not be more precise.

I knew that Edge of the Cedars, as a monument to responsible science, rubbed certain locals' feelings the wrong way, just as Winston Hurst, returned to Blanding from his graduate school conversion, had been snubbed by former friends he'd known since childhood. I asked Till about those Blanding attitudes.

The question provoked a rich response. "We occupy," Till said, "a really precarious position in the community. There is a lot of conflation here between archaeology and the federal government. One of the basic tasks that we're going to have, probably for the rest of our lives, is to decouple that anti-federal sentiment from people's perception of what archaeology is.

"I do think that a lot of folks in Blanding are interested in archaeology, interested in the deep past. As long as some people feel like that, I feel compelled to work with them. I really want to encourage that interest."

As we shook hands to part, I told myself that I was glad I didn't have Till's dilemma hanging over my thoughts every working day.

In 2000, Earl Shumway was released from prison. Only three years later he died of cancer, at the age of forty-six.

Because he cut such a reckless criminal swath through Blanding and beyond, one unfortunate result is that to outsiders the name Shumway, very common in southeast Utah, can ring synonymous with "pothunter." In 2019 I interviewed Kay Shumway in his Blanding home. At eighty-four, Kay has led a rewarding life as a plant geneticist, and in retirement he avidly pursues his avocation as a nature photographer with a specialty in ruins and rock art—a "hobby" that disguises his professional-level talents. His political leanings are liberal enough that he joined Friends of Cedar Mesa early on, donated photographs to the organization, and volunteered his time for work projects. I asked him about Earl Shumway.

"He was a terrible man," Kay answered without hesitation. "He was mean. People were so scared of him."

The two men were related, even though Kay never met Earl. "His grandfather was my uncle," Kay explained.

Thanks to Earl, Kay amplified, "The Shumways got a really bad reputation for being grave robbers." But Kay's own father taught him and his four brothers a lesson quite at odds with the looter's legacy: "Don't ever dig in the ruins. Those people that are buried there are loved ones of others. Leave them alone."

I had long been curious about the etymology of the name Shumway. Was it Scottish, I asked Kay. He chuckled. "No, it's French. It's an Americanization of *chamois*." I came away beguiled, picturing the clan of Blanding and Monticello Shumways, most of them Mormons, as totemic representatives of the proud beasts I'd seen prowling many a high pasture and crag in the Alps.

In the Blanding cemetery, I looked for Earl Shumway's grave. The directory listed no fewer than fifty-three Shumways buried there, but the coordinates for the plot I was seeking were easy to decipher. The gravestone surprised me. On its gray marble surface, along with Earl's name and birth and death dates, a bucolic scene had been engraved. Four tall evergreens bordered a placid stream winding through high meadows. In the distance, a many-shouldered mountain loomed—perhaps one of the Abajos, which rise north of town. You would think the man buried beneath the grass was a wanderer, a nature lover, perhaps a fisherman. Beneath the scene, a legend read, "We Will Love You Always & Forever."

Somebody loved Earl Shumway, I guess.

FIVE

O PIONEERS!

Despite the assertions of some descendants of pioneer settlers such as Bruce Adams, the first Anglos to settle on land that would eventually fall within or on the edges of the 1.35 million acres of the Bears Ears National Monument were not Mormons. By the late 1870s, gold miners and cattlemen from Colorado had begun to covet the sagebrush plains, the creeks and rivers, the canyons and mesa tops of the southeast Utah wilderness. And the loose band of outlaws orbiting around Butch Cassidy discovered in that same outback not only virtually impenetrable hideouts, but a convenient corridor of escape from rangers hot on their trail after the latest stickup of some bank in a frontier town.

One legendary sanctum for those renegades was Robbers Roost, where the headwaters of several streams tributary to the Dirty Devil River spring from west-facing sandstone cirques that wed concealment with defensibility. That basin lies about thirty miles northwest of the nearest border of Obama's monument. As for American citizens first planting their roots in soil right on the edge of the monument, the nod must go to three families who founded a settlement just south of the La Sal Mountains in 1877, two years before Mormons first attempted to colonize the vast tract that would become San Juan County.

Among those settlers were Tom and Bill McCarty, fortune-seekers originally from Tennessee who drifted to Montana, then to north-central Utah, followed by a stint in Nevada, morphing during the 1870s from businessmen (the patriarch was a surgeon who had served in the Confederate Army) to speculators in horse-and-cattle deals, and eventually, to big-time cattle rustlers. Acting on rumors of unclaimed range land near the La Sals, the three families pushed their wagons through steep-walled canyons and across dangerous rivers to alight in a fertile basin that was, according to historian Charles Kelly, "the answer to every cowman's prayer." There they built cabins and corrals and called their new town La Sal. By 1882 they even had a post office, irregularly serviced by horse and rider on a line that ran 350 miles from Salina, Utah, to Ouray, Colorado. Kelly tantalizingly (and inaccurately) claims, "Only two men had previously penetrated that section—one a Negro, the other a Frenchman."

The Negro was William Granstaff or Grandstaff, known locally as Nigger Bill. The Frenchman was a French-Canadian trapper named Felippe or Felipe Duran. Together they took possession of the old Mormon fort at present-day Moab, built in 1855 and quickly abandoned in the face of Ute attacks. There they raised cattle and planted a small garden. The three families who would found La Sal camped near the Grandstaff-Duran homestead the winter before pushing on to build their own town; presumably they learned much of the lay of the land to the south from "the Negro and the Frenchman."

According to the 1941 Works Progress Administration guidebook to Utah, Nigger Bill Canyon, a short tributary to the Colorado River about three miles northeast of Moab on today's State Highway 128, was named after the "mulatto" who homesteaded near the old Mormon fort. Other sources claim that William Grandstaff had been born a slave in Alabama and may have been part Native American. In 1881, after a bloody battle pitting Paiutes and Navajos against Moab residents, "Nigger Bill" fled up the canyon that would soon bear his name, fearing for his life because the local scuttlebutt had it that he sold whiskey to the Indians. The 1941 guidebook reports his parting words: "The men are gathering up guns to hunt Indians, but I think maybe I'm the Indian they're after."

Sometime in the 1940s or 1950s the name of the man's escape route, which had become one of the favorite short hikes near Moab, was sanitized to Negro Bill Canyon, and in 2017 it was rechristened Grandstaff Canyon (and Campground) by a board made up of representatives from several federal agencies, despite opposition by the Tri-State NAACP. The later career of Grandstaff's partner, the "Frenchman" Duran, nicknamed Frenchie, seems lost to history.

Meanwhile, in their homestead at La Sal, Bill and Tom McCarty, along with the other two pioneer families, were flourishing, with "fine herds of cattle and horses, located on the best range in Utah." But the allure of reckless adventure won out over staid prosperity. In Charles Kelly's judgment, "If they had remained in the stock business they would eventually have become wealthy. But for some reason they sold their holdings at a price reported to be $35,000. Both brothers then turned outlaw."

In the 1930s, Kelly managed to track down the only known copy of Tom McCarty's handwritten autobiography, in the possession of the man's grandson, living in Los Angeles. In only one paragraph does the outlaw account for his conversion from budding ranch baron to serious cattle rustler:

> I was born and raised by as good parents as anyone can boast of, but fortune never seemed to favor me, which I suppose was my own fault. My downfall commenced by gambling. Horse racing was the first, then other gambling games; and as we all know the company one comes into contact with was of the wrong kind for teaching honesty. . . . After losing about all I had I commenced to cast around for something else.

During the next decade, Tom McCarty parted ways with his brother Bill, who made his way to Oregon and settled down to a lawful life. But

Tom ranged from Utah to Arizona, New Mexico, and Colorado, stealing cows and running from posses and sheriffs. Along the way he recruited partners, until he became notorious as the head of the McCarty Gang. One of his accomplices, whom he met in 1884 or 1885, was Matt Warner (*né* Willard Christiansen, a Dane converted to Mormonism). In 1887 the pair graduated from rustling to holding up the Denver & Rio Grande train just east of Grand Junction, Colorado. Two years later they joined Butch Cassidy (*né* Robert LeRoy Parker) in the daring robbery of the San Miguel Valley Bank in Telluride, Colorado, making a clean getaway with $10,500 (some say $21,000) in cash. The bank burned down shortly after the heist, but it was rebuilt as a mercantile outlet in a style replicating the original, and today a plaque on its façade proudly announces the site of Butch Cassidy's first bank robbery.

Matt Warner was one of the most volatile and flamboyant of all the characters in Cassidy's Wild Bunch. He was "stockily built and bubbled over with uncontrolled energy," writes Kelly, who knew the man in his old age. "When in good humor he was a pleasant, likable boy; when in a fit of temper he was a wildcat." Later in life, Warner went straight enough (or put on an act convincing enough) to get elected as justice of the peace for Carbon County, Utah, and he served for years as its deputy sheriff. (A few years ago, as I drove through Buckhorn Wash on the San Rafael Swell, I was beguiled to find Matt Warner's bold signature on the roadside cliff, painted in axle grease in 1920. He'd spelled his first name "Mat," and just to the right of the signature had added a deft portrait of a cow, complete with brand—an "up yours" to some owner whose stock he had stolen?)

Warner also wrote, or rather dictated, a memoir, published posthumously in 1940 as *The Last of the Bandit Raiders*, that captures the romantic frenzy of the Wild Bunch as no other document does. On his frequent excursions from northern and central Utah down to Arizona and Mexico—both for rustling purposes and to escape from the law—Warner rode through the landscape that would become the Bears Ears monument. He had a poet's eye for the natural beauty of the place:

It is a wild country—regular painted-rock desert. The wildest kind of buttes and spires and cliffs rise above the level of the mesas, worn by wind and water into every kind of human and inhuman shape you can imagine, and every color from white through pinks and reds to brown. If you look down into the deep, dizzy canyons on the edges of the mesas, it's wilder and more savage than ever.

Warner's wagon team camped each night in a "closed circle" with armed guards on the lookout. But the rustler's interactions with the natives were simply part of the adventure:

Brooks and me with our field glasses saw just enough of them pesky Utes in the distance to keep the wagon men alarmed all the time, but we got through the Ute country and among friendly Indians without an encounter. We had the time of our lives shooting game and playing hide-and-seek with the Indians and later trading with the friendly tribes. By the time we was through the Indian country, we had turned most of our horses into Navaho blankets and beaten silver and turquoise ornaments the Indians made. . . .

Looking back decades later, Warner remembered the wilderness with an esthete's appreciation of its virtues as an outlaw hideout:

The catch basins was filled with water that dripped or seeped from the sandstone, as springs, and was always dependable. The mesas was dotted with piñons and cedars [junipers], sagebrush, yucca, cactus, wild flowers, and plenty of good bunch grass, which dried and cured and was still fair horse feed after a long drouth. There was only about one chance in a thousand that deputies would discover where any particular hide-out was, and if they did, a few bandits with Winchesters could hold back a whole army and stay there safe as long as their provisions and ammunition held out.

◄◄ ►►

In the mid- to late-1870s, cattlemen from Kansas and Colorado made the first thrusts into the "empty" range land just east of the canyons that would center the Bears Ears monument. While the McCartys and friends were gaining a toehold in La Sal, small-time entrepreneurs ventured into the sagebrush flats east of the Abajo Mountains, some thirty miles south of La Sal. The first of these now-forgotten ranchers were the brothers Pat and Mike O'Donnel (or O'Donnell), of whom little is known beyond the fact that they moved a herd of cattle to a broad mesa later named Dodge Point, at the relatively high altitude of 6,800 feet, just southeast of the valley hollow where Mormons in 1887 would homestead a tiny colony they called Verdure, after the lush vegetation that lined the tiny creek. (Verdant or not, Verdure gave up the ghost almost at once, as the pioneers pulled up stakes and moved six miles north to Monticello, grandly named by other Mormons in homage to Thomas Jefferson's Virginia mansion.)

The O'Donnell boys did well enough on Dodge Point that in 1879 a speculator from far off Trinidad, Colorado, showed up to buy cows for $10 a head that he could turn around and sell back home for $55 a head. The first ranchers from Texas arrived in 1880, and by 1883 no fewer than 15,000 cattle were grazing the benches east of the Abajos, most of them Durhams and Texas Longhorns. The success of those ventures attracted the really big-scale outfits, of which the biggest was the Carlisle company, aristocrat ranchers of English lineage who bought out the smaller herders and began to loom as the monopoly owners of the whole Great Sage Plain.

Two hundred and fifty miles away in Salt Lake City, the elders of the Church of Jesus Christ of Latter-day Saints took note of these incursions and reacted with alarm. Ever since 1847, when Brigham Young led the first expedition of refugees from Midwestern persecution across the Wyoming wilderness and into Utah to found his new Zion, Mormons had regarded the US government as a meddling nuisance at best, a sworn enemy at worst. Nor was that notion a paranoid delusion: the so-called Utah War of

1857–58 saw President James Buchanan ordering the US Army to march in secret against the Mormon "kingdom," and the pitched battles that would have fomented a genuine war were averted only by half-hearted diplomacy compounded by logistical blunders. Young's counterstroke was to expand the Mormon empire in every direction from Salt Lake City, as he sent out "chosen" men to found new towns in valleys and basins where only Native American tribes had previously thrived.

By 1875, that empire had spread far to the south, with the establishment of ranching and farming colonies in Parowan, Panguitch, Cedar City, and a dozen smaller settlements such as Cannonville and Escalante. From 1870 until his death in 1877, Young spent the winter months in his own Mar-a-Lago–style mansion in balmy St. George (founded in 1861). Young coined the epithet "Dixie" for his southern domain, a term still in use today. But the catastrophic failure in 1855 of the Elk Mountain Mission on the future site of Moab had left the Prophet leery of all ventures into the region that, more than a century and a half later, would embrace the Bears Ears monument. That problematic territory had best be left to the "pesky Utes" who had attacked the Elk Mountain fort and sent the demoralized colonists fleeing for their lives.

Now, however, it became obvious that miners, cattlemen, and outlaws had no such misgivings about planting their stakes in southeast Utah. The knee-jerk Mormon response was to forestall those interlopers by sending forth an expedition to build a San Juan Mission a good hundred miles south of the crumbling ruins of the Elk Mountain fortress. In 1879 John A. Taylor, the church president who succeeded Brigham Young, announced this bold enterprise by selecting men to lead it, almost all of them from southern towns ranging between Panguitch and St. George.

Thus was born the migration that, under the name of the Hole-in-the-Rock expedition, would become almost as legendary as Young's original thrust into the Utah wilderness. In 1879, the church was not eager to admit that its new migration was designed to nudge out the Gentiles. Instead, the official line decreed that the grand effort had as its principal aim making peace with the Indians.

The definitive account of the Hole-in-the-Rock expedition is a book titled simply *Hole-in-the-Rock*, by the distinguished historian David E. Miller. Though for the most part scrupulously even-handed, Miller's narrative uncritically repeats the cover story from 1879 of an altruistic mission to establish a truce with the natives. Writing in 1959, a decade before scholarly iconoclasm would begin to scrutinize the canon of heroic LDS deeds, Miller insists that the expedition embodied "the highest type of pioneer endeavor that broke the wilderness and brought civilization to the West." The book is dedicated to "the men and women of the San Juan Mission whose valiant efforts brought American culture to one of the remotest regions of the United States." And Miller slips into the lazy period hyperbole of asserting that, despite the centuries and even millennia during which Native Americans had flourished in the region, southeast Utah in 1879 was "almost completely unknown and unexplored country."

Make no mistake: the Hole-in-the-Rock expedition, through sheer hardship and danger, brought out the very best in the families that signed on for the hegira. A journey that was supposed to take six weeks ended up spanning almost six months, through the winter of 1879–80. Ravenous hunger, debilitating cold, and toil that could easily have led to crippling accidents defined the day-by-day ordeal. The oft-quoted summary, that 250 men, women, and children with eighty-three wagons pulled off a trek with few parallels in nineteenth-century Western history without the loss of a single life or the wreckage of a single wagon, is a fair measure of the pluck and tenacity of the emigrants. Indeed, their number increased by three, after the births of infants en route.

For sheer technical genius, the blazing of a "road" down the 1,800-foot escarpment to the Colorado River through the eponymous notch in the cliff at the eastern end of the Escalante desert, and the jerry-building of a boat to ferry passengers and wagons across the swift current of the biggest waterway in the canyon country, have few rivals in the annals of the Anglo exploration of the West. The unmapped country proved far more tortuous than even the most pessimistic among the travelers foresaw. Four scouts sent ahead to find a feasible route were gone for twenty-four days, after planning a foray they provisioned for only eight, and much of the time those pathfinders had to admit they were lost. The temptation for the whole party to give up and straggle back to the safety of their home villages was trumped by what can only be called blind faith in the importance of their mission.

It's not my intention here to retell the Hole-in-the-Rock saga in all its drama of privation and perseverance. Miller's book does an excellent job of cobbling journal entries and pioneer reminiscences into a coherent and sometimes thrilling story. The legend that the journey became obscures, however, the fact that the very conception of the trip was based on a colossal mistake. The plunge of ill-prepared pilgrims into a labyrinthine wilderness through the dark months of winter could easily have spiraled into a tragedy on the scale of the Donner Party's collapse in the Sierra Nevada in 1846–47. Instead it figures today—and not only among Mormons—as an epic of fortitude, ingenuity, and teamwork. A pertinent analogy might be made between the Hole-in-the-Rock journey and Sir Ernest Shackleton's star-crossed third Antarctic expedition. The cult of Shackleton, never stronger than it is today, tends to overlook the fact that that enterprise was a complete failure. Shackleton hoped to traverse the whole continent between 1914 and 1917; instead, after the *Endurance* froze solid in the ice pack, then sank, the team never even reached the shores of Antarctica. Survival became the goal of the twenty-eight men marooned on the ice, rather than discovery, and survival, when it is pulled off against such odds as Shackleton and Frank Worsley and their teammates faced, makes for a better tale than success.

In brief: from the southern Utah towns, a reconnaissance expedition blazed a route between April and July 1879 that took twenty-six men, two women, and eight children southeastward through the Navajo reservation, across the Colorado at Lees Ferry, and back up northeast to the middle San Juan River. The leaders of that team chose the spot for the intended mission in the open valley where Montezuma Creek flows into the San Juan from the north. But having found long gaps between reliable water sources on the reservation, and having slipped through edgy encounters with hostile Navajos, the leaders decided not to recommend their route for the upcoming mission expedition itself. Rather than return by the way they had ventured out, the recon party swung far to the north, joining and following the Spanish Trail pioneered by Antonio Armijo in 1829–30. That uneventful homeward journey occupied a mere four weeks from August into September 1879.

Had the main expedition set out in November to pursue the northern route, it might well have accomplished a comparably routine voyage. Instead, the leaders of the second trek opted for a "short-cut," determined to cross the gap between Panguitch and Montezuma Creek in an almost straight line, despite the fact that no one among the party had more than a hazy idea of what the terrain they hoped to traverse looked like. The plan looked good on paper: a *direttissima* of only 200 miles, in preference to the meandering northern route of 450.

For the team, the last outpost of civilization was the hamlet of Escalante, settled in 1875 and home to a mere 600 Mormon citizens four years later. Escalante was also the last place to buy supplies and food. The advance guard of the team passed through that settlement on November 15–16, as families in wagons, men on horseback, and a thousand head of cattle and oxen ventured out into the badlands that Escalante ranchers called simply the Desert. On that stark plain beneath the soaring cliffs of Fifty-Mile Mountain (the near edge of Kaiparowits Plateau), the pioneers found a dire shortage of forage for the animals and of firewood for their camps. Only forty miles out from Escalante, full of uncertainty, the team stalled, even as more wagons and families piled into the makeshift headquarters sustained by one of the few reliable springs to be found in that outback. From this camp the four scouts headed out on what was supposed to be their eight-day reconnaissance. When three weeks passed with no word from those men, the leaders at Forty-Mile began to wonder whether the scouts were lost or dead.

I've spent many days on the Escalante Desert, hiking down the canyons tributary to the Escalante River or climbing up onto the otherworldly mesa of Fifty-Mile Mountain. To me, it's one of the most beautiful places in the

Southwest. Not so for the pioneers of 1879. In his diary, Platte D. Lyman, the de facto leader of the expedition, wrote, "It is certainly the worst country I ever saw. . . . There is no us[e] of this company undertaking to get through to San Juan this way." Already provisions were running short. Couriers regularly rode back to Escalante to buy more food, at wildly inflated prices. Elizabeth M. Decker lamented to her journal, "We have just sent our last five dollars to Escalante to get some pork and Molasses."

A mile and a half away from Forty-Mile Spring stands a curious sandstone dome the team named Dance Hall Rock. On the south side of this outcrop, buttressing wings enfold a natural amphitheater. The pioneers, forced to halt while men rode back to Escalante for more provisions and while the scouts plunged onward into the unknown east, turned that flat bedrock floor into a dance hall, as they whiled away several evenings with quadrilles and reels to the beat and screech of three prairie fiddlers. I've spent hours exploring Dance Hall Rock, which is covered with old inscriptions, initials, and dates, although as far as I know no record from the 1879 layover adorns the sandstone.

Some fifteen miles farther on, in mid-December, the team at last came to grips with the obstacle that would lend the expedition its name. The Hole-in-the-Rock was a narrow slit in the cliff overlooking the Colorado, widening out forty feet down to a boulder-choked couloir, which in turn gentled into a talus fan spilling into the great river. At first glance, it must have promised a hopeless passage. No one is sure just how wide the topmost cleft was in 1879, but most accounts picture it as too narrow for a man to slip through, let alone a horse or a wagon. The leaders, however, saw in this precipice only an engineering challenge. Blowing the bedrock to pieces with dynamite, dangling men over the edge on ropes to chip away at the debris, the team constructed a foot trail within only a few days. In the couloir itself, great holes between the boulders had to be filled with sand and smaller stones. Toward the bottom, the engineers confronted a fifty-foot cliff. Under the direction of Benjamin Perkins, the canny workers carved a diagonal ramp that circumvented the cliff, built cribwork on the downhill side, and filled the bed with brush and gravel. The ingenious detour was celebrated as Uncle Ben's Dugway. By January 26, 1880, after more than five weeks of toil, the Hole-in-the-Rock was at last ready for the first wagon.

The process of getting the wagons down to the river sounds today like something out of a John Ford movie. The wheels were wrapped with chains and ropes to serve as brakes. As many as twenty men and boys pulled on ropes tied to the wagon to retard the inexorable pull of gravity. The men tried hitching a horse to the rear of the wagon and whipping the beast uphill against the dead weight, but that expedient proved disastrous when several horses were dragged down the rocky incline and badly injured. Incredibly, all eighty-three wagons reached the banks of the Colorado, essentially undamaged, in only two days.

In 1998, and again a decade later, I spent a number of days exploring the far eastern end of the Escalante Desert, as I researched first a long article, then a book, about Everett Ruess, the vagabond artist and diarist who vanished there in 1934, at the age of twenty. Four months after Everett passed through Escalante, a search party discovered his last camp, along with his pair of emaciated burros, deep inside Davis Gulch, the last southern tributary of the Escalante River before the Desert abrupts in the cliff above the Colorado.

As I prowled through that still-wild outback, I marveled at the passage the Mormon pioneers had gouged through the Hole-in-the-Rock in January 1880. Two or three times I hiked—"scrambled" would be the apter word—down the couloir and fan that delivered 250 men, women, and children, eighty-three wagons, several hundred horses, and a thousand head of cattle and oxen to the Colorado River. The fill between the boulders had washed out and rock-slid in the more than a century that had passed, leaving dangerous holes in the "road." I realized that you could no longer lead a horse down that vertiginous trail; it would make for a perilous jaunt even for a sure-footed dog. By 1998 the waters of Lake Powell had flooded the lower four hundred or five hundred feet of the passage, drowning Uncle Ben's Dugway.

The top of the notch, where the pioneers had dynamited open a slot to accommodate the wagons, was covered with inscriptions carved in the bedrock walls. I spent hours deciphering those runes, shading them from the sun or shining my headlamp sideways to bring out the hard-earned names. There were scores of Kilroys from the late nineteenth and early twentieth centuries, but I found only a single inscription from the trailblazers: a faint, laconic "DEckER 1880." There were no fewer than twenty-five Deckers in the Hole-in-the-Rock party, all from five inter-related families hailing from Parowan—including a baby named Lena Deseret Decker, born at the last camp before the cleft only three weeks before the cavalcade of humans, horses, and cattle made the improbable descent to the river.

Having assembled, after so much toil and drama, on the west bank of the Colorado, the huge team needed now to cross it. This was a challenge the leaders had long anticipated. While the emigrants piled up at Forty-Mile Spring in November and December, Charles Hall, who must have been something of a genius as a carpenter, was put in charge of building a boat that could transport both wagons and people across the 350-foot-wide river. Since no trees suitable for the task grew anywhere near the east end of the Desert, Hall and his two grown sons retreated to the Escalante Mountains, twenty miles west of the town of the same name. There they spent weeks cutting down trees and hewing the wood into boards, as they manufactured a prefab boat. In pieces the vessel was carried by wagon all the way out to the Hole-in-the-Rock, then hand-carried board-by-board down to the river, since the boat needed to be ready by the time the team arrived. On the west bank of the Colorado, the Halls built a kiln in which they cooked "pitch pine wood" to excrete a sap to caulk the boards and make the craft waterproof.

Once assembled, the boat measured eighteen feet long by sixteen feet wide—big enough to carry two wagons and a man steering with paddles from the stern. So well did the ferry work that all eighty-three wagons and two hundred and fifty passengers made it across the river in just a few days. One young lad, nudged overboard by a restive ox, took an acci-dental swim, but he spluttered ashore without harm. During the ferry, a bitter late-January cold snap arrived. Ice formed near the banks that had to be cut away by hand. Only a day or two after the last load completed the passage, the river froze over. The party looked on bemused as beavers and otters gamboled across the ice, recognizing that the fragile skin would never have supported the weight of even an unloaded wagon.

Arrived on the east bank, the team might well have thought they had solved the two major obstacles in their "short-cut" pilgrimage to the San Juan. It was not to be so. The country ahead would prove even more difficult to traverse than the sixty-odd miles of desert, cliff, and river the pioneers had taken two full months to negotiate.

The account of that second half of the monumental journey, patched together by David Miller from diaries and reminiscences, reads like an anthology of hardships, dead-end stabs, and engineering challenges that taxed the pioneers to the limit. With the provisions running out, hunger became a way of life. There was still the occasional heaven-sent delivery of supplies from the towns left far behind to the west. Around February 10, for example, a party rode in from Panguitch, some 160 miles away, carrying 200 pounds of pork and forty pounds of cheese. The team promptly named that lay-over Cheese Camp. Yet even that windfall did not go far to slake the craving of 250 emigrants. Near the end of the journey, C. I. Decker bemoaned his family's larder: "[O]ur meat and everything else had give out on us. My dear wife and my poor little boys had to eat dry bread for their supper. This is where I thought my heart would break." There was always the cattle herd to turn to for beef, but the emigrants had hoped to keep alive most of their cows to stock the colony they planned to build on the San Juan. As it was, scores of cattle had to be left behind to be rounded up months later. Some of them went feral. And horses often wandered off and got temporarily lost.

The spotty record of the second half of the trek is replete with disgusted accounts of ankle-deep mud and deeper snow; with stretches of "road" that had to be carved out of bedrock and leveled and filled to make a bed that wagons could ride; and with even worse cold than the team had borne in December and January. On March 15 Platte Lyman complained to his diary, "Last night was the coldest night I ever experienced, it was impossible to be comfortable in bed or anywhere else."

After three months on the trail, beset with uncertainty and privation, with the outcome entirely in doubt, the emigrants inevitably began to quarrel among themselves. The most serious breach occurred after a small contingent of men decided to push the herd of horses far ahead of the main body of the team, which was occupied with the day-by-day drudgery of building the "road." Some among the rear guard suspected that the horse-drivers hoped to take advantage of the grass and other forage along the way before the whole team of oxen and cattle could graze it to stubble.

According to Miller, in a strangely oblique summary, "Accounts of this incident indicate that near bloodshed resulted before the controversy was settled. For a time wagon owners rode with rifles slung across their saddles, threatening to stop the movement by force if necessary. However, no violence resulted."

By early March the main team had reached the western edge of the piñon-juniper country that would be incorporated in the Bears Ears monument 136 years later. There they confronted the serpentine canyon athwart Cedar Mesa that the Hole-in-the-Rockers had already named Grand Gulch. The label was apparently bestowed in late December by the four scouts. The only surviving account of that reconnaissance is a reminiscence by George Hobbs dictated almost forty years after the event. In Hobbs's telling the Gulch is a fearsome obstacle that camouflages what he calls "the Cliff Dwellers' trail"—an abyss, he reported, "between perpendicular walls from one to two thousand feet high." (The deepest stretches of Grand Gulch actually range no more than 900 feet below the rim.)

Crossing the same terrain around March 8, Platte Lyman noted, "We found gulches with perpendicular banks 1000 feet high running from the extreme north 30 miles into the San Juan on the south, but by going around the head of these we can make a passable road by following an old indian trail."

I've often wondered whether the "gulch" in Grand Gulch conveyed the emigrants' distaste for the place. All of the other defiles that cross Cedar

Mesa, and that furnished such vital homes for the Anasazi, are called "canyons" today: Slickhorn, Johns, Fish, Owl, Road, Lime, et al. Only Grand Gulch is a gulch. It's hard to think of a major cliff-hung valley anywhere in the United States that doesn't bear the name "canyon," as in the Grand Canyon, the Black Canyon of the Gunnison, Glen Canyon ("the place no one knew"), Snake River Canyon, and others. A "gulch" is an ugly, useless thing. Only "ravine" rivals it for gloomy innuendo. Even "gorge" has favorable overtones, as in the Royal Gorge of the Arkansas River.

It is understandable that the Hole-in-the-Rock emigrants took no pleasure in discovering Grand Gulch. The damn thing—all fifty-two zigzagging miles of it—was in the way. When you're struggling day after day for months to craft a route across a tortured landscape, it's hard to see the beauty in it. Elizabeth Decker, who back in January had spent her last five dollars on pork and molasses out of Escalante, summed up the second half of the trek in a pithy vignette: "It's the roughest country you or anybody else ever seen; it's nothing in the world but rocks and holes, hills and hollows. The mountains are just one solid rock as smooth as an apple."

It's curious that the main body of the expedition, led by Platte Lyman, seems to have benefited little from the scouts' reconnaissance of the same terrain two and a half months before. Instead they had to rediscover the "Indian trail" that circumvents Grand Gulch on the north. At the nadir of their earlier thrust into the wilderness east of the Colorado River, effectively lost, George Hobbs and his three fellow scouts had scrambled up a tiny hill, from which they saw and recognized the Abajo Mountains to the north and knew they had solved the challenge of a route to the San Juan. Salvation Knoll, cut off by a Route 95 roadcut today, is celebrated in a pullout plaque that hails the topographic bump as the key to the whole puzzle.

Long stretches of the Mormon route across Cedar Mesa survive today as rugged four-wheel-drive roads. In recent years, those stretches have been adorned with handsome trail markers, black upright posts each topped with a white omega in the shape of a stylized covered wagon.

After the emigrants got past the head of Grand Gulch, they pushed a route southeast across the spine of Cedar Mesa, threading a passage between Fish and Road Canyons. The crux of that passage remains today a gnarly Jeep track looping like the figure "S," which the pioneers later named The Twist. By the end of March, the team was camped in Comb Wash. "The water is very bad and feed pretty good," wrote Platte Lyman in his journal. The whole party sensed how near their promised land— Montezuma Creek on the San Juan River—lay. But right in front of them loomed the nearly vertical, unbroken escarpment of Comb Ridge. The four scouts in late December had been able to use an old Navajo trail to surmount the Comb (along the route of today's Route 163, dynamited through the cliff in the 1970s), but there was no way wagons could make such a crossing. So near the finish line, the pioneers faced their most daunting topographic obstacle of all, a barrier even more intractable than the Hole-in-the-Rock itself.

In 1977, Fred Blackburn joined Lynn Lyman (a descendant of the pioneers) to retrace most of the Hole-in-the-Rock route east of the Colorado River, as they traveled by Jeep, on horseback, and on foot. Early on Lyman discovered the scattered remains of a wrecked wagon that he thought had likely been part of the 1880 exodus. On a second trip a few years later, in the midst of a brutal snowstorm, Fred found bullet casings and an ox shoe that probably derived from the pioneer journey. He turned these "artifacts" over to the Edge of the Cedars Museum in Blanding. "To my knowledge," Fred wrote me in 2019, "these are the only known relics, along with the wagon, ever recovered, or at least preserved in museums, from the Hole-in-the-Rock expedition."

The laboriously carved "road" from 1880 had virtually disappeared by 1977. But along the track through The Twist, Lyman and Blackburn found further traces of the pioneers: wagon ruts in the soil and bedrock, tree stumps from logs most likely felled to use as trail cribbing, and tall cairns that might have dated from 1880.

Nowadays on the Internet, you can find all kinds of trip reports from latter-day adventurers proud to claim they've ridden the Hole-in-the-Rock Trail. But these blogs tend to glorify the slickrock antics of twenty-first-century cowboys in Jeeps, on motorcycles, or atop ATVs, rather than history sleuths in the mold of Blackburn and Lyman.

In only one place along the 200-mile road did the Hole-in-the-Rockers make anything like a concerted effort to record their passing. About a mile up Cottonwood Creek, the shallow draw the team climbed after ferrying across the Colorado River, their track led between twin prongs of sandstone. On the face of the northern wall, at least thirteen men etched initials, names, and dates. As he retraced the emigrants' route in 1954, David Miller named this gateway Register Rocks. The signees included Edward Lyman (Platte Lyman's brother), Cornelius Decker (whose wife Elizabeth had lamented the loss of her last five dollars), and Joseph Barton (who would lend his name to the benches west of Bluff as the preeminent cattleman from 1880 to 1905). Old photographs are today the only documents that preserve that record, for, like so many other memorable features of the landscape, Register Rocks now lies beneath the waters of Lake Powell.

In early April 1880, facing the quandary of Comb Ridge, the emigrants under Platte Lyman's leadership opted for what at first loomed as a desperate solution. They followed Comb Wash south to where it spilled its trickle into the San Juan River. There was no hope of sneaking past the butt-end of this northern segment of the hundred-mile-long monocline that is Comb Ridge, for the cliffs shelve abruptly some five hundred feet down to the lapping shore of the river. So once more the pioneers, near exhaustion, pooled their talents to build a "road" up the incline, which they named San Juan Hill. Facing the prospect, Lyman laconically noted in his journal, "We cannot follow up the river, so we have to do some work to get up over the bench."

It took three days to complete the job. Charles Redd, the son of one of the emigrants who tackled San Juan Hill, left a far more vivid account than Lyman's of the last-ditch effort it took to forge that wagonway.

Here again seven span of horses were used, so that when some of the horses were on their knees, fighting to get up to find a foothold, the still-erect horses could plunge upward against the sharp grade. On the worst slopes the men were forced to beat their jaded animals into giving all they had. After several pulls, rests, and pulls, many of the horses took to spasms and near-convulsions, so exhausted were they. By the time most of the outfits were across, the worst stretches could easily be identified by the dried blood and matted hair from the forelegs of the struggling teams.

In 2004, on the twelfth day of our traverse of the whole length of Comb Ridge, Greg Child, Vaughn Hadenfeldt, and I backpacked up San Juan Hill in ninety-degree heat. The dried blood of the emigrants' horses had of course long since been washed off the jagged bedrock, but we were awed to find vestiges of the cribwork the builders had deployed to shore up the road, as well as the faint ruts the wagons had left 124 years before.

Having solved San Juan Hill, the team limped eastward along the north shore of the river. Montezuma Creek still lay some twenty miles beyond, but no one in the party had the will left to close the gap. Six miles east of Comb Ridge, at a broad basin framed by Cottonwood Creek on the west, Cow Canyon on the east, with bold cliffs standing sentinel to the north, the Hole-in-the-Rockers called a halt to their monumental trek. They were simply played out. They would build San Juan Mission here rather than at Montezuma Creek.

On Sunday, April 25, Platte Lyman noted in his journal, "Today we held meeting and by unanimous consent named our town Bluff City."

◄◄ ►►

For several years during the mid-2000s, I researched a book (published in 2008 as *Devil's Gate*) about the Mormon handcart tragedy of 1856. That year some nine hundred converts to the LDS faith, most of them from Great Britain and Europe, set out too late in the summer from Iowa City to travel overland 1,300 miles to Salt Lake City. Unlike their predecessors in some 150 teams between 1847 and 1855, the emigrants in the Willie and

Martin companies, the last to hit the trail in 1856, traveled not in covered wagons but with handcarts—glorified wooden wheelbarrows loaded with all the pilgrims' worldly goods, which they pushed and pulled across the plains and mountains.

In western Wyoming, the two companies were caught in early snowstorms. Belated rescue missions out of Salt Lake were of minimal avail. Of the nine hundred Saints toiling with their handcarts, more than two hundred died.

To me, as a non-believer, the greatest disaster in the annals of westward migration in the United States was an entirely preventable catastrophe, compounded by Brigham Young's obsession with cutting costs and his inadequate response to all the signs of the impending tragedy. I expected Mormon apologists in the twenty-first century to find a silver lining in all the suffering—"They came to know God" was a favorite bromide both in 1856 and 2006. But I was unprepared for the way in which having had an ancestor in the Willie or Martin companies had become an ultimate badge of authenticity in LDS circles. I coined the phrase "the Mormon Mayflower" for this romanticization of the terrible ordeal the emigrants underwent.

My savvy research assistant, Ardis Parshall, herself a devout Mormon, concurred. "Most of us secretly feel," she told me, "that having ancestors who came by wagon is better than having ancestors who came by train. It's even better when your ancestors came by handcart. And of course you're practically royalty if you can claim someone in the Martin or Willie companies."

It's clear that a kindred baptism in the crucible of survival gilded the Hole-in-the-Rock expedition of 1879–80. Although no emigrant died during the six-month trek between Escalante and Bluff, the challenges the team overcame and the suffering its members endured fostered a legacy for the settlers of southeastern Utah that no other pedigree could rival. Even in the twenty-first century, if you are a Lyman or a Redd or a Decker who can trace the family tree back to one of the stalwarts on the Hole-in-the-Rock trail, you enjoy a "natural" aristocracy like that of Cabots and Lowells in Boston.

What I suspect is that the validating myth of the 250 pioneers who tamed the wilderness "to bring civilization to the West" transmutes into a certain entitlement that some of today's citizens of Blanding and Monticello feel: the notion that "nobody had really settled here before [my ancestors]." And of course that Plymouth Rock–style affirmation of priority rubs especially raw the feelings of Native Americans whose ancestors really were there before anyone else. All too often, the struggle over the Bears Ears today pits Mormons against Navajos, locals against the feds, farmers and ranchers against "wacko environmentalists."

◄◄ ►►

With their characteristic industriousness, the pioneers set to work on their third day in Bluff surveying lots and digging irrigation ditches. Although at first they lived in their wagon boxes or in hastily erected brush shelters, eventually they were building solid houses. The homes of seven Hole-in-the-Rock emigrants, two-story edifices in the standard Mormon style, with sturdy walls made of thick, heavy bricks of native brown sandstone, still stand: Jens Nielson, Hyrum Perkins, Kumen Jones, Willard Butt, James Decker, Lemuel Redd, and Platte Lyman.

Nielson was an extraordinary man. A Danish farmer converted to the faith by missionaries in 1852, he had the misfortune to heed the call to Zion by joining the Willie Company on the fateful handcart trek of 1856. He was thirty-six that summer. On Rocky Ridge, a long incline of snow-covered swales in western Wyoming, the team struggled through bitter winds and subfreezing temperatures in late October. Nielson would have died had his wife, Elsie, not carried him several miles in their handcart. As it was, their six-year-old son froze to death during the crossing. Jens suffered severe frostbite, and though he later submitted to no amputations, for the rest of his life he walked awkwardly—shuffled, really—with one foot at right angles to the other.

Within two years of his arrival in Salt Lake City, Nielson was assigned by Brigham Young to move to the southern town of Parowan. From there he joined a small band to found the settlement of Panguitch, thirty miles to the east, across the high Markagunt Plateau. In subsequent relocations, the family moved to Circleville before ending up in relatively prosperous Cedar City. Along the way Jens acquired a second wife, Kirsten, also a Dane from the same Baltic island of Lolland.

Incredibly, at age fifty-nine, Nielson accepted the call to join the Hole-in-the-Rock expedition, crippled foot or no. Having studied for the priesthood in Utah, he was made chaplain of the large party hoping to establish the San Juan Mission. And once the emigrants had arrived at Bluff, Nielson became the new ward's first bishop, a post he held for the next twenty-six years until his death at the age of eighty-six.

It's a pity that Nielson kept no diary of the arduous journey through the unmapped country on which the emigrants embarked, for he played a leading role in that trek. It was he who early on recognized the need to send four scouts ahead to reconnoiter the route. In early December, when doubts about the feasibility of the journey threatened to derail the expedition, and a general meeting was convened for all the Saints to voice their pros and cons, Nielson argued that the company must "go on whether we can or not." He had coined a term for the Mormon resilience that he believed would win the day: "stickie-ta-tudy."

With Jens on the long peregrination came his second wife, Kirsten, and their six children. In September 1880, only seven months after the team's momentous arrival in Bluff, Jens traveled back to Cedar City to bring his first wife, Elsie, to the colony. When Elsie finally reconciled herself to her final home in 1885, Jens built a log cabin for her, to keep the ménages of his two marriages discreetly separate. (Other polygamous pioneers in Bluff housed both their wives in a single home, sometimes with separate balconies and exterior staircases—a configuration that titillates visitors even today.)

As a traveler, even at age fifty-nine, Jens Nielson must have been a wonder. It's a measure of Mormon perspicacity that once the Hole-in-the-Rock trail had been blazed, it became for a short while a workable road for pioneers making journeys *back* to their former homes in southwest Utah. But it's a tribute to Jens's hardiness that he made the trip from Bluff back to Escalante in September 1880 in only two weeks!

Industrious the pioneers' start on building the town of Bluff and the San Juan Mission may have been, but almost at once the solidarity of the emigrant band fell apart. Somehow the scale of the riverside terrace on which the surveyors were laying out streets and lots proved smaller than anyone realized. Basing each lot size on the grid that had laid out Panguitch, the surveyors soon realized that they had room for only forty of the sixty-two families who hoped to establish their homesteads. Rather than reduce lot size and cramp the settlers, the leaders came up with the dubious plan of drawing lots for the lots. Sixty-two paper squares were deposited in a receptacle, forty with numbers on them, twenty-two blank. Among the unfortunates who literally drew a blank was Platte Lyman. (As if that were not insult enough, Lyman managed to fall into disfavor with the church authorities in Salt Lake City, and in 1884 he was "released" from his leadership of the San Juan colony.)

Now greed and selfishness came to the fore, as a proposal to share all sixty-two lots got voted down, and the lucky numbered families bluntly urged the losers to move on and find their homes somewhere else. As Jens Nielson's biographer David S. Carpenter puts it, "Self-interest had almost destroyed in days the union they had forged through six months of shared hardship." In the end, a grudging compromise saved the day, with a grid of fifty-nine cramped lots redrawn over the original forty.

Lot size was only the beginning of the pioneers' troubles. There was a drastic shortage of timber available for building—mainly a few clumps of cottonwoods distributed along the river. The first town hall was not erected until the autumn of 1880. Until then, civic meetings were held in the shade of a stately cottonwood that gained the affectionate nickname "the Old Swing Tree." The sandy banks of the San Juan were ill-suited for dredging irrigation ditches that would hold their shape. One barometer of the schism that divided Bluff was that sixty-one of the 250 men, women, and children who had arrived after their six-month emigrant ordeal were gone for good before June 1880, moving on to Montezuma

Creek, or to other clusters of habitation eastward into Colorado, or even returning, defeated, to the southwest Utah towns they had left the previous November.

On top of these vicissitudes, the storms along the San Juan could be sudden and violent, taking a brutal toll on the homes struggling to be built. In David Carpenter's vivid evocation,

> Many of the homes had doorways without doors, and windows without glass that first year. Women sprinkled the floors to persuade the dust to settle, and when it rained the permissive roofs did it for them. . . . Whatever combination of willow boughs, dirt, sand, and weeds they tried, these roofs "never turned away the rain, which dropped dismally long after the sky cleared." And when the wind blew, nothing could keep the sand out, either. It found its way into everyone's clothing, bedding and food.

The pioneers were vaguely aware that the site of Bluff lay exactly on the "seam" that marked the edges of the domains of three native tribes that sometimes allied with, but more often raided against, one another: the Navajos, the Utes, and the Paiutes. During the whole first year, and to a lesser extent thereafter, the citizens of Bluff lived in constant fear of Indian attack. To defend against that menace, they built a fort in the shape of a square 400 feet per side, with the houses inside separated by picket walls.

From the distance of 140 years, it's hard to gauge just how real that threat was. One mirror image of it emerges from the voluminous writings of Albert R. Lyman.

In January 1880, as Platte Lyman was directing the blasting, filling, and cribbing to construct a road down the Hole-in-the-Rock cleft, his wife, Adelia, gave birth to a son in Fillmore, a town roughly halfway between Salt Lake City and St. George. Soon after the founding of Bluff, mother and son emigrated to the new colony. But in 1884, when Platte, in disgrace with church elders, was "released" from the San Juan Mission, the family moved to Scipio, a small town just north of Fillmore. In 1891, with the father enjoying a partial rehabilitation, the Lymans moved back to Bluff where they lived, as Albert later recalled, "in a very small log cabin with a mud roof."

In that hardscrabble existence, with Platte Lyman reduced from his leadership of the Hole-in-the-Rock expedition to the lot of a poor colonist struggling to make ends meet, Albert, baptized into the church at the age of eight, lost his faith and became an atheist, convinced that "this is just a world of meaningless, merciless chance." While still a teenager, however, he had a "miraculous" conversion after a prayer on the banks of the Colorado River convinced him that a Mormon God was, after all, in charge of creation.

Albert Lyman grew up in Bluff and elsewhere as a voracious seeker after truths of all kinds. Marrying at age twenty-two (he and Mary Ellen would have fifteen children), even as he toiled gamely to make a living as a farmer and shoemaker, Albert discovered that he had a gift for writing. He would eventually publish dozens of books ranging from local history and biography to novels that dramatized the struggle of the Saints in southeast Utah, as he became a kind of Mormon Zane Grey. In addition, he compiled seventy volumes of stray *aperçus* that he called "Thots," and he kept a diary all his life from the age of nineteen onward in the pages of forty-one leather-bound volumes. Once an immensely popular author, he is still avidly read in Blanding and Monticello, even though nearly all of his books have long been out of print.

Lyman's thumbnail sketches of the three Native American tribes in fear of which the settlers of Bluff built their fort can be read today as representative of the attitudes of those pioneers at the turn of the twentieth century.

The Navajo or Piute not skilled in the essential art of theft, was regarded by his people as slow and stupid. The loss of shoes, knives and forks, dishes, clothing, ropes, axes, or any of the limited supplies and utensils carried away from the camps, amounted to little as compared with the disappearance of teams, cattle, and the dear old cow on which the children depended for their most precious item of food.

... Yet within rifle range across the river from Bluff was the Navajo reservation with its fifteen thousand or more impoverished savages, eking a scanty living from the sterile sand hills, or stealing it from the outside. To the east and north and west of Bluff roamed the surly Piutes with crisp contempt for white man's law, or for all other law.

Albert Lyman remains a paradoxical figure. At the same time as he was indulging in his condescending stereotypes, he was establishing schools for Indian children who lived in and around Blanding. Yet his lifelong antipathy for the Paiutes, in particular, never waned.

There is no reason to doubt the sincerity of Saints called on missions who believed they were devoted to making peace with the natives, with the secondary goal of "civilizing" them at the same time. One of Brigham Young's favorite mottos vis-à-vis the Indians was, "It is cheaper to feed them than to fight them." This somewhat cynical but ultimately pragmatic formula nonetheless embodies the bedrock conviction of Mormon superiority to the "savages." In Monticello and Blanding today, that condescension persists. In 2018, when for the first time in history, two of the three elected San Juan County commissioners were Navajo, the latent racism crept out of the woodwork in all kinds of snide aspersions against these councilmen.

Indeed, the racist treatment of Native Americans is built into the Mormon faith, in the form of the Doctrine of the Lamanites. In the Book of Mormon, founder-prophet Joseph Smith divined a history of the ancient peopling of North America that had the New World settled by Lehi, a patriarch who built a ship in the Holy Land and sailed with his followers across the Atlantic around 600 BC. Two of the sons of Lehi were Laman (pronounced "LAY-man") and Nephi (pronounced "NEE-pheye"). During the next several centuries they split into hostile factions, and in 231 BC they began a war that lasted 150 years. The Lamanites, who rejected Christ (himself an emigrant to the New World, during an interval between his resurrection and his ascent into heaven), ended up victorious over the righteous Nephites. The last Nephite, Moroni (pronounced "More-OWN-eye"), buried the golden plates that Joseph Smith would dig up in New York state in 1823 and decipher to produce the Book of Mormon.

For their crimes, God cursed the Lamanites with dark skin, and in his revealed truth Smith explicitly equated their descendants with American Indians, as well as implicitly with Negroes. Jews, though white-skinned, were also beyond redemption. However, these wretched souls were not excluded from all hope of salvation. If they forswore their heresies and converted to the Church of Jesus Christ of Latter-day Saints, they would be blessed in the next life as "a white and delightsome people." Jews who came around to Christ could also enjoy a rebirth as a "delightsome" folk.

In 1981, bowing to intense pressure, the church revised the crucial verse to read "a pure and delightsome people," as Mormon scholars claimed this reading was actually Smith's original intention. And in 1978, the church reversed its policy of almost a century and a half, allowing Blacks and Indians to become eligible for the priesthood.

As dogmatic and wrong-headed as this belief system seems today, there's little doubt that the more devout emigrants who settled Bluff in 1880 indeed saw the Navajos, Utes, and Paiutes as Lamanites. Even those "bloodthirsty" thieves and raiders, against whom the settlers took refuge in their fort, could be saved—though only after conversion, and only in the next life.

◄◄ ►►

In the end, it was not hostile Indians that doomed the fledgling colony, but the San Juan River. As they had scouted Montezuma Creek in 1879, then opted for Bluff in 1880, the emigrants had taken for granted that the river more or less kept its orderly course from one season to the next. The very idea of a farming community laid out in rectangular plots on the banks of that river depended on that unquestioned assumption. Yet the irrigation ditches the men started digging upon their arrival in April 1880 never worked well, thanks to sandy soil and sparse vegetation.

As early as 1881 the Bluff citizens decided to funnel all their irrigation efforts into a canal whose head lay four miles upstream. To confine the diverted water into a manageable course, the laborers built a massive riprap channel, laying rocks, brush, sand, and logs (an estimated one thousand cottonwoods felled along the banks of the San Juan). Yet almost as soon as the ditch was completed, the settlers saw it fail, as the waters sieved through gaps in the barrier and ate new holes in it. For two years in a row, the crops mostly failed as well. Then came the great flood of 1884.

All February and March it rained. By mid-March, the San Juan had risen seven feet above its normal level. Even the diminutive tributary of Cottonwood Creek, bone dry through weeks in a normal year, raged beyond its shallow banks and flooded the western half of Bluff, filling cellars and houses ten inches deep in mud and sand. The plucky farmers planted crops in April, but the rains continued into May. The riprap channel was utterly destroyed, and in the splinter settlement at Montezuma Creek, all but one house was swept away. By June the vast majority of the 250-odd denizens of Bluff were ready to give up. It was only a question of where to move, and how to build another town from scratch, that delayed the wholesale abandonment of the San Juan Mission.

It would take another twenty years for the colonists to choose the site on which the town would be reborn. That decision came after Albert Lyman camped in a tent with his family through the summer of 1905 on a broad shelf 6,100 feet above sea level (versus Bluff's 4,300) on the southern skirts of the Abajo Mountains. With it came the hard-won realization that a lasting Mormon stronghold in southeast Utah would have to be built not on farming as a way of life, but on ranching. Lyman's homestead planted the seed of Grayson, soon renamed Blanding, after an eastern benefactor who donated a thousand books to the town library in exchange for the maiden name of his wife.

Bluff never completely gave up the ghost, but through the early decades

of the twentieth century, it was more derelict than flourishing. The 1941
WPA guide to Utah recorded the population of the town as seventy (versus Blanding's 555). Bluff "consists of a score of dusty red brick houses,
built of the soil on which they stand." The sole business worth noting was
an Indian trading post. Historian David Lavender remembered Bluff in
the early 1940s:

> An occasional automobile kicks up a plume of red dust on the nar-
> row road which leads to the railway a hundred miles north. There
> are a few bright patches of alfalfa, a few milk cows, a few saddle
> horses standing droop-headed in the shade. That is all. That is the
> metropolis of southeastern Utah.

Only in the 1970s did Bluff begin to rebound. Gradually it attracted not
Mormons, but artists and writers, outdoor enthusiasts, and counterculture
vagabonds of all stripes—including my friends Jim and Luanne Hook,
who to this day manage Recapture Lodge, one of my favorite hostelries in
the world; and Vaughn and Marcia Hadenfeldt, whose Far Out Expeditions guides seekers into the mysteries of Cedar Mesa. From my first days
in Bluff in the early 1990s onward, I felt the comfort and congeniality of
that traveler's cliché, a home away from home.

All of us who discovered Bluff in its new incarnation marveled at the
natural setting of the town, between the cliffs overlooking it on the north,
including the surreal pinnacles called Twin Rocks, to the gentle banks of
the San Juan, now tamed by the Navajo Dam far upstream. How could
the Hole-in-the-Rockers have ever thought that dreary Montezuma Creek
made a better place to build a colony than Bluff? How could Bluff have
been only their exhausted second choice?

In contrast to thoroughly Mormon Blanding, twenty-five miles to the
north, Bluff in recent decades has styled itself as "the most non-Mormon
town in Utah." It's no accident that in the recent controversy over the Bears
Ears, Bluff is the headquarters for the passionately partisan Friends of
Cedar Mesa. The tensions that swirl around Obama's monument and

Trump's dismantling of it ride the tarmac on the half-hour drive up High-way 191 from Bluff to Blanding, passing, not coincidentally, through the small quadrangle of the White Mesa Ute Reservation.

The century and a half during which that cultural cavalcade has rolled out makes for a saga full of contradictions, characters, and conflicts. It springs from no simple legacy—not that of the Hole-in-the-Rock expedition, nor even that of the Navajo, Ute, and Paiute actors who crisscrossed its stage. It's quite a story, but one that can best be told in jagged fragments.

SIX

COWBOYS AND CHARACTERS

The first cattlemen to exploit the fertile terrain around the Bears Ears were relatively small-time operators such as the McCarty brothers out of La Sal. By 1880, much bigger outfits based in Kansas, Colorado, New Mexico, and Texas were drifting into Utah in search of new range land. The first of these entrepreneurs were the ranchers making up the L. C. Company, who built a headquarters on Verdure Creek in 1880, seven years before Mormons fed up with Bluff and the untamable San Juan would gain a foothold along the same stream. (Little remains of that stab of colonization except for a handsome three-story Pennsylvania-Dutch–style barn, its wooden roof still mostly intact.)

Three years after the L. C. Company arrived, the Carlisle outfit moved in. British-born aristocrats operating out of Kansas and New Mexico, the Carlisles bought up the herds of several Mormon ranchers in and around Bluff. Soon they were running 10,000 cows on the Great Sage Plain east and south of the Abajos, and not soon thereafter the range began to be grazed out. So the Carlisles expanded operations into the tortured canyon country to the west.

Most of the Carlisle hands were Texans, and thus an imperishable antipathy between Utah citizens and Texas cowboys was born. In the vignette of historian James Sheire,

Texas cowboys from the big outfits became famous for upsetting peaceful dances at Bluff or Monticello. On more than one occasion a wild bunch from the Carlisle headquarters rode into town and shot it up in good Hollywood fashion. There were also a number of murders.

Into this volatile frontier mix one day in 1891 rode an eighteen-year-old adventurer from Salina, Utah, called J. A. (Al) Scorup. As Scorup's nephew Grant Bayles, born in Bluff and raised in Blanding, recalled in 1971:

> When he was just a kid . . . , he came to San Juan and he came the hard way. He came alone and he crossed the Colorado River with a pack horse. Not very many fellows would do that, but I guess he was coming over to see his sweetheart. She had come to Bluff in the Eighties with a group who came through the Hole-in-the-Rock.

Grant Bayles's recollection raises some problems. Al Scorup would marry in 1895, when he took Emma Theodora Bayles as his bride. She is not listed on the roster of Hole-in-the-Rockers, though her brother Hanson Bayles is. On his first visit to Bluff, Al spent a night at Bayles's rooming house, where he met Emma, who was cooking for the boarders. (Presumably she had emigrated to the outpost on the San Juan sometime after 1880.) It was love at first sight, at least on Emma's part, if family history can be trusted. "He was very attractive," Emma later told her sister-in-law. "All the eligible girls wanted him, but I said to myself, 'that nice-looking Mormon cowboy was meant for me and I mean to get him.'"

On that first jaunt out of his hometown of Salina, Al Scorup forded the Colorado at Dandy Crossing, a relatively broad, shallow stretch of river first used by ranchers and miners in the late 1870s (and by Indians before them). Today's derelict Hite Marina, where State Highway 95 crosses the Colorado, spans the old ford. As soon as he reached the eastern bank, Scorup smelled opportunity. "He saw lots of grass," Grant Bayles remembered, "lots of grass and not very many stock. He got the idea then that that's where he wanted to go into business. It was grass that makes meat."

By 1891 there were quite a few cattle running loose in the canyons between the Colorado River and Bluff, but left untended, they wandered off into obscure slots and slickrock corners. Owning not a single cow himself, Scorup made a deal with Claude Sanford, a rancher and neighbor from Salina, some of whose longhorns had gone feral in that far-off wilderness. If Scorup "could find the cattle in the maze of cracks, washes, and cliffs that split and hedged the country," he could keep a third of the calves.

Grant Bayles conjures up the dogged discipline his uncle applied to the job.

> The way they would catch those wild cattle was just simply the hard way, by roping them and tying them up, and then leading them into a country where they could handle them. In that rough country where the cattle were, they couldn't just drive them. He caught several hundred of those wild cattle. . . .
>
> He'd take a sack of flour and a sack of beans and sow belly and he'd go out and stay for months with those cattle alone. He kept them on the feed and on the water and they increased.

But at the end of that successful first season, Scorup ran into a band of Texas cowboys camping on the rim of White Canyon. Several of them were playing cards with three "runnygade" Utes, as Anglos characterized the "bad hombres" who, three decades hence, would prosecute Posey's War—of which, more below. In the camp, five other armed Texans accosted Scorup, telling him that "there was no room for him around White Canyon anymore and that he would be much better off where he came from." Tail between his legs, Scorup recrossed the Colorado and headed home to Salina.

Even at the age of nineteen, however, Al Scorup was not the sort of fellow to give up easily. He talked his older brother Jim into returning to the canyons in 1892, and this time he brought 300 cows leased from Salina neighbors. Historian and memoirist David Lavender, who knew both Scorups later in life, compared them in a deft sketch: "Jim was a hard-twisted youngster with a more volatile nature than Al's—freer to fight, freer to laugh, and lacking Al's pigheadedness when it came to butting his head against a stone wall."

Al had bargained with those neighbors by conveniently omitting any mention of trouble with the Texans. After months alone in the wilderness the year before, he had seen firsthand how the Texans' modus operandi— simply turning the cows loose in the canyons, then hoping to round them up later—was doomed to failure. His confidence was infectious, for he talked Claude Sanford into upping the offer: this year, if he could retrieve the cattle, Al could keep half the calves. "I really wanted to go back," he told his sister many years later.

To make the journey even more lucrative, Scorup persuaded his father and two other Salina ranchers to trust him with their own cattle on a drive southeast into the fertile but little-known canyon country. When they set out in late autumn, Al and Jim were in charge of a herd of 300 cows.

The journey of some 200 miles from Salina to Dandy Crossing— around the Wasatch Mountains and through the San Rafael Swell with its fiendish slot canyons—was a challenge in its own right. When they got to the Colorado, it was well into December.

Historian Neal Lambert conjures up the struggle of two men trying to coax 300 bovines across the powerful river in early winter:

> The cows mill around on the edge, snorting suspiciously at the chocolate water. The boys cut big willows to drive with and start the herd toward the river. The leaders splash into the cold water, then panic and turn back. In go the two cowboys to head off the turning cattle. The buoyant cows outmaneuver the heavier horses and swim toward the bank. The calves howl; the men shout. Cows begin to chill; their

struggles slow down and they drift farther and farther downstream. All around cattle churn in the water and scramble up the bank. Al and Jim splash out of the water, round up the herd, and try again.

It is Western history's loss that Al Scorup, who died in 1959 at age eighty-seven, never wrote a memoir. The closest thing to a biography is the affectionate and hagiographical portrait self-published in 1945 by Al's sister Stena, as *J. A. Scorup, A Utah Cattleman*. By Stena's own admission, she had "not even attempted to present his life objectively."

It was only after the brothers left Salina that Jim found out about the bothersome Texans. "One can only guess at his reaction," comments Lambert. Since the Texans ran their herds all the way up to the south rim of White Canyon, Al and Jim decided to avoid confrontations by turning their own cows loose only on the benches beyond the north rim, and in such tributary canyons as Gravel, Cheesebox, and Hideout.

White Canyon itself is a canyoneer's paradise, with several major pouroffs and a number of technical slots, but it was a tough and scary place in which to run cattle. Al Scorup did not make the Anglo discovery of White Canyon: he was preceded in 1883 by prospector Cass Hite. On an exploratory jaunt looking for gold, Hite made his way up White from his base camp on the Colorado. Thirty miles out, he discovered the three great natural bridges that would be incorporated by President Teddy Roosevelt as a national monument in 1908. Hite named the bridges President, Senator, and Congressman. In 1903, Jim Scorup and a cowboy colleague (not Al) unabashedly renamed the two largest bridges after their wives, Augustine and Caroline, and three years later an army colonel appropriated the smallest bridge as Edwin, slapping his own first name on it. It would take a government ethnologist with a longer view to grace the sandstone spans with the Hopi names they bear today: Kachina, Sipapu, and Owachomo.

Because of its pouroffs and sheer cliffs, White Canyon could stymie a cattleman in cruel ways. As Lambert elucidates, "[A] cow just a few hundred yards away on the other side of White Canyon wash might just as well be in the next state. The ride was just about as long to one place as to the other."

No matter how familiar a cattleman—or in more recent times, a hiker—got with White Canyon, the dangers it posed could never be underestimated. Jacob Adams was a later partner of Al Scorup, and in his own day one of the ranchers best acquainted with the wilderness that the Scorup brothers had first opened up. Longtime Blanding rancher Dereese Nielson (Jens Nielson's great-grandson) remembered Adams as "a big man who was uncomfortable and had stomach trouble," but also as a kind elder who would "always pay special attention to the younger boys or the new hands." His fatal flaw was a congenital stubbornness. One day in 1940,

> A friend of mine and another young boy about my age were with Jacob. They packed up their horses that morning when this flood came down [White Canyon]. . . . Jacob said to Clyde Lyman, "Clyde, take your horse and go across, and see how deep the water is." Clyde's horse wouldn't go, so Jacob said to Mark Goodmanson, "Mark, that mule will go into the water; kick him out in there." But the mule wouldn't go. Jacob was riding a great big blue horse they called Sam. I can just hear him saying what he said, "Oh hell, boy, what's the matter with you?" as he put the spurs to his horse and led him into the water. He'd had it right then. . . . The boys saw him go around the bend and ran down there on their horses, but they never saw him again.
>
> The horse came out about four or five hundred yards down the creek. No, the horse wasn't hurt.

After a futile search, the shocked young men got to the Kigalia ranger station to call for volunteers from Blanding, including Dereese Nielson himself. At the end of the long day, one of the volunteers found Adams's body five miles downstream. The man "had washed off to the side and was facedown," Nielson remembered. "His Levis and his chaps were hanging down on his boots. Evidently he had tried to get his clothes off so he could swim."

Jacobs Chair, the striking butte that rises 1,700 feet from its base between Long and Gravel Canyons, is named after Adams.

In 1892, from the eastern edge of the White Canyon plateau, Al and Jim Scorup spotted a pair of lofty cliffhung mesas far in the distance. They named them Woodenshoe Buttes. As Al told Stena many years later,

> We saw a mountain ahead of us that looked like the wooden shoes grandmother used to wear, so we called it the Wooden Shoe and made that mountain our stopping place. . . . We were the first white men to venture into this jumbled wilderness, which proved to be a paradise for cattle with its long grass and plenty of water.

Pushing their cows up to and beyond the buttes, the Scorups discovered a deep canyon running south to north. Seven miles beyond the buttes, it joined an even larger canyon running west, merging at last in a single torrent that dumped its flow into the Colorado River at the lower end of Cataract Canyon. The whole network of chasms carved between towering cliffs and forests ranging beyond piñon and juniper up into ponderosa pine and Douglas fir is known today as Woodenshoe and Dark Canyons. Still remote country, this outback was protected until 2016 as the Dark Canyon Wilderness. With Obama's proclamation, it became a key component of the Bears Ears National Monument.

In 2014, with four friends, I leased llamas to execute a leisurely sevenday loop down Woodenshoe Canyon and up Dark. I wasn't thinking about Al Scorup at the time, but as I look back at the photos I shot, I can see how the lush vegetation and generous springs made for "a paradise for cattle." I can also see that the numerous short side draws must have served as fiendish traps for stray cows. That tangled quality, of course, had only appealed to the Anasazi. A mile up Poison Canyon, a short upper branch of Woodenshoe, we found an assemblage of cramped granaries and dwellings fit only for a small family, erected on skimpy ledges over a lethal void.

All his long life, Al Scorup would return to the Woodenshoe-Dark

Canyon wilds. A cabin he built in the 1930s in Rig Canyon, a tributary of Dark, was later dismantled, moved piece-by-piece, and reassembled a few miles up Horse Pasture Canyon, another Dark Canyon branch. Still in a state of exquisite preservation, it serves today as an emergency shelter but also as a kind of museum of the cowboy life.

That spring of 1892, the Scorup brothers faced a serious obstacle to grazing the cattle they had driven all the way from Salina. Over the years, hundreds of horses gone feral had found their way into the canyons Al and Jim were the first Anglos to explore. Those steeds depleted the browse available for the cows. Harve Williams, a protégé of Al Scorup, later swore that the brothers "would spend whole days shooting horses—700 at a time." There was also a wolf, nicknamed "Ol' Big Foot," with a fiendish propensity for killing calves, as many as 150 in one season, according to Al.

Ol' Big Foot evaded all efforts by the Scorups to hunt him down. According to Grant Bayles, the legendary wolf, by then tagged with a thousand-dollar reward, finally succumbed to a pair of trappers who trailed the animal for two days, as the animal fled despite having a leg caught in a strong trap, itself attached to a second trap to slow the beast down. The trappers at last found Ol' Big Foot dangling off a cliff, the second trap caught in a bush on the rim. The wolf had died in that mid-air agony.

As Bayles remembered, "[The trappers] took him into Bluff and hung him in one of those big trees. I can remember seeing it just as plain as anything, a big gray fellow."

Despite their tireless toil throughout the 1892 campaign, Al and Jim barely broke even. Historian Neal Lambert evokes the struggle:

> By living in caves and shanties; eating sourdough, beans, dried fruit, and venison when they had time; by riding as long as daylight would let them see and often longer; looking for grassy pockets and drifting their herd along to each one; the boys kept their cattle alive. The first year the number dwindled, but the next year the cattle wintered well. By the summer of 1893, Al and Jim had good reason for hope.

Meanwhile the big cattle companies, after nearly a decade of easy profit, saw a turndown in the market coming. Cutting their losses, the Texans pulled out of White Canyon altogether, leaving it to Jim and Al Scorup. Always uneasy with Gentiles as rivals, a group of Mormon settlers organized as the Bluff Pool and bought 1,300 cows and 300 horses from the Texans. The Scorups had gotten through two mild winters in their remote "paradise," but they were hard hit by heavy snows all through the winter of 1894–95. The Bluff Pool was all but wiped out, as 700 of their 1,300 cows died. The partners in Bluff threw in the towel. Al Scorup was no neighbor of theirs, but at least he was a fellow Mormon, and his reputation as a savvy cattleman had spread. The Pool hired him to drive what remained of their herd to market.

Still, the downturn in the market for beef on the hoof severely undercut the Scorups' profit margins even as it drove their rivals out of the canyon country. During their first six years of backbreaking toil, still "commuting" annually from Salina, the brothers had little to show for their struggle. In the words of historian James Sheire, "At the end of the 1897 roundup . . . , the Scorups discovered that they barely had sufficient cash to buy supplies. Their herd consisted of a grand total of 40 cows and a few calves. The range was theirs, but they had nothing to put on it."

During these years, more than once Jim Scorup wanted to give up, only to be talked out of quitting by the "pigheaded" brother with a knack for butting his head against a stone wall. The first big break came after the Bluff Pool, having given up their own ambitions to maintain a herd deep in the canyon country, hired Jim and Al to round up as many stray cows as they could in an especially dense wooded region to the west of Bluff. In Lambert's words, "Unmolested now for years, generations of wild longhorns had grown up in this jungle-like juniper forest without ever seeing a human being." No doubt many of those cows had originally belonged to the Texas outfits, but the Bluff Pool claimed them all as their own feral runaways.

Al made a bargain: figuring the cows were worth ten dollars a head, he offered to extricate them from the wilds for a fee of five dollars each. With a small crew of Bluff men whom he taught as they rode, he spent months on the roundup.

It was hellacious work. A contemporary of Al Scorup, John D. Rogers, left a vivid account of what it took to round up wild cows in such terrain:

> You couldn't lay that rope on in any fancy way like those trick ropers in the rodeos because of the thick trees. Oh, they wasn't so thick but what you could get your breath, but too thick for ridin'. Here is where a good fast tree horse earned his money. He'd get you right up there trompin' on the steer's heels where you could lean over and lay your loop right over his horns easy like. Then you'd bust him. And when his head whipped around behind him and his belly went into the air, if you hurried you could get him hogtied before he even tried to get up. . . .
>
> Older cows and steers had long, sharp horns, which were wicked and vicious, and a bull's strength and quickness could give you a scare. Many a horse has been horned, and some of them gutted and killed by angry critters that got up before the hogtie was completed. But a good horse would keep the rope taught and the animal stretched out. Without that perhaps you'd just as well not try.

At the end of those months of work, Scorup and his partners had rescued more than 2,000 cows from the wild. Al took his payment of $10,000 and deposited it in the bank. For the first time in his life, he felt flush—indeed, almost prosperous.

After 1897, the Scorup saga reads like the latter half of the classic Horatio Alger story. During the coming decades, he would buy up other ranches all over southeast Utah, until he became the most powerful rancher in the state. By 1928, his domain stretched across 1,800,000 acres, embracing not only the existing Natural Bridges National Monument but the future Canyonlands National Park. The most important acquisition came in 1918, when he bought the Indian Creek Cattle Company, whose headquarters at Dugout Ranch, in a blissful setting at the junction of Cottonwood and Indian Creeks, would become a legendary symbol of the supposedly idyllic homesteading life. The ranch, still in charge of Heidi Redd, another pioneer of Utah's cattle country, was sold to the Nature Conservancy in 1997, which operates it today as an experimental research station conjoined with a working ranch. Before that sale, Heidi Redd fended off bids by the likes of Ralph Lauren and Christie Brinkley.

If indeed the Al Scorup story verges on mythic status, all the romance of it adheres to the desperate years from 1891 to 1897. Living in the wilds with the cattle, often alone for months, Scorup got to know the country in a way few Utahns ever have. To the end of his long life, he remained a hard-bitten but unpretentious fellow (Lambert: "Al would have no 'nonsense' from his cowboys"), a man of few words, a workaholic, a perfectionist. In 2016, he became one of the first two inductees into the Utah Cowboy Hall of Fame. But by now, more than sixty years after his death, those who guard his legacy fear that Al Scorup is in danger of slipping into the limbo of forgotten heroes.

Not that he would have cared.

◄◄ ►►

More than half a century after Scorup plunged into canyon country, a mineral boom exploded all over Utah and its neighboring states. Unlike the earlier gold rushes along the Colorado and San Juan Rivers, this one was born not out of fortune-seeking on the man-by-man level so much as in response to a national crisis.

The mineral was uranium. After Hiroshima and Nagasaki, as the Cold War spawned an arms race that saw the United States and the Soviet Union frantically building up their nuclear arsenals, the demand for the crucial component in all such weapons skyrocketed. As Raye C. Ringholz writes in *Uranium Frenzy*, the definitive account of how the quest for uranium seized the West,

It was the first and only mineral rush triggered by the U.S. government. America, on the threshold of the nuclear age, was desperate for a domestic source of uranium. The Atomic Energy Commission was the only buyer of the ore. But it was ordinary citizens who engaged in a massive treasure hunt to satisfy the nation's needs.

Ringholz covers the story on a personal level, detailing fortunes won and squandered, lives saved and ruined, without losing sight of the unique role the uranium frenzy played in America's history: "It was a vivid and sometimes crazy time, perhaps the last time that an ordinary individual could wrest riches from the earth with his own two hands."

The lethal dangers of exposures to crude uranium, in the form of "radon daughters" (see below), were suspected long before 1950. But when men and women were willing to bet their lives on a golden goose laying radioactive eggs deep in the ground all over the canyon country, the warnings of dentists and pulmonologists fell on deaf jaws and lungs.

Ringholz builds her narrative around Charlie Steen, whose Mi Vida mine, a few miles south of the town of La Sal (and thus just off the edge of the future Bears Ears monument) would yield the richest deposit of uranium ever found during the decade of the boom. Steen was a twenty-nine-year-old carpenter out of small-town Texas, struggling to make ends meet with a wife, three young kids, and another on the way. With a college degree in geology and a father who'd made and blown a fortune before the age of twenty-two in wildcat oil drilling, Steen had the right genes for a career in high-stakes prospecting. He also had a short fuse, having been fired for insubordination in a brief stint as a field worker for Standard Oil.

Steen figured he could read the half-deciphered language of sandstone tectonics better than the experts, which is what led him to Big Indian Wash in the Lisbon Valley, a region dismissed as barren by uranium gurus. But he was close to flat broke. The family had recently moved to Cisco, a forlorn former railroad stop on the D&RG line, a ghost town today and not far from one in the early 1950s. The tarpaper shack that housed the

Steens had neither running water nor a flush toilet. Charlie was so poor he couldn't even afford to buy a Geiger counter.

On July 6, 1952, Steen's drill bit broke off 197 feet underground in his Mi Vida shaft. Disgusted, he took a hunk of the mucky black core he pulled out of the shaft back to Cisco. The core sat in the back of his Jeep for almost two weeks. On July 18 he stopped at Buddy Cowger's filling station in Cisco. Confined to a wheelchair after an accident with a cyanide gun, Cowger still prowled the country on the lookout for uranium prospects. The two men traded hard luck stories. Steen told his friend about the broken drill bit: he'd hoped to hit ore 250 feet down, not 197. To cheer him up, Cowger showed off his brand-new Geiger counter. The men tried it on a core Cowger had recently drilled. The counter gave a feeble response.

As Ringholz tells the story:

Charlie reached into the jeep and pulled out his ugly black rock. "Hell, I've got better stuff than that," he joked.

"Well, put her under," Cowger laughed.

Charlie jabbed the sample under the counter. The instrument swung clear off the scale.

The men stopped laughing.

"Try it again," Cowger said.

The needle pegged. The counter chattered like static.

"My God!" he shouted. "You've hit it!"

It took a while for Steen to find backers, so skeptical were investors that this maverick from Texas knew what he was doing; some even suspected him of "salting" the mine. But soon the assays proved the case. The Mi Vida uranium, in the form of pure pitchblende, was some of the richest ever found in the United States.

In 1953 Steen moved to Moab. On a cliff rim overlooking the town from the east, he used his overnight fortune to build a mansion complete with a swimming pool, a greenhouse, and servants' quarters. (The mansion survives today as the Sunset Grill, with a wall devoted to period photos and clippings about the Uranium King. A big clock with frozen hands is captioned "It's always 5:05 at Charlie's"—Steen's inalterable cocktail time. Patrons complain about slow service and mediocre food, but unfailingly hail "the best view in Moab.")

Steen also spent lavishly on quirky whims such as flying his private plane to Salt Lake City to take rhumba lessons. He became famous for his quips: "Poverty and I have been friends for a long time, but I'd just as soon keep other company." His charitable giving and the parties he threw for the whole town in an airplane hangar made him a beloved figure in Moab. He ran for US Senate and won in 1958, but got fed up with politics, resigned in 1961, and moved to Nevada.

Like many a loose-fisted dreamer who strikes it rich, Steen managed his money poorly. In 1968 he had to declare bankruptcy after the IRS came down hard on him for failing to pay back taxes. But he's still revered in Moab as the man who turned a sleepy burg into "The Richest Town in America," and for planting the seed of the tourist mecca Moab is today. After he died of Alzheimer's disease in 2006, his ashes were scattered over the Mi Vida mine.

Most of San Juan County felt the surge unleashed by the uranium boom. Claims were staked and shafts blasted through the bedrock on mesas all over the future Bears Ears monument. Between 1949 and 1959, in fact, no fewer than 309,380 uranium claims were filed in southeast Utah. Though no single mine produced uranium of the purity and in the quantity of Mi Vida, there were some big-time strikes that made their owners wealthy and that substantially raised the standard of living in such towns as Blanding and Monticello.

The most lucrative of all these mines was the Happy Jack. But the story behind its success is the polar opposite of the Mi Vida saga. Charlie Steen set out in 1950 with the single-minded determination to find the richest lode of uranium in the West, no matter what it took to get at it. The three men who developed the Happy Jack struck pay dirt almost by accident.

Way back in 1899, several gold prospectors whose names are lost to history gouged an adit (a horizontal shaft) into a steep hillside overlooking White Canyon. Originally called the Blue Dike, the mine never turned much profit, and it changed hands several times before it was abandoned. Somewhere along the way, the Blue Dike became the Happy Jack, although the origins of that felicitous name are likewise lost to history.

In 1946, a road contractor from Monticello named Joe Cooper bought the derelict Happy Jack for $500. With his father-in-law, Fletcher Bronson, and Fletcher's son Grant, Cooper hoped to probe the underground for copper rather than gold—all because he had heard a rumor of copper ore being mined somewhere along the White Canyon corridor. The shoestring enterprise set up business under the august title of the Bronson and Cooper Mining Company.

The Happy Jack, about fifteen miles up White Canyon from the Colorado River, was a hard place to get to in 1946. The only road was a dirt track barely negotiable by Jeeps, and the mine itself hung 500 vertical feet above the south rim of White Canyon, reachable only by tortured switchbacks on a road the men bulldozed themselves. With little more gear than a jack hammer, a small compressor, a wheelbarrow, and several shovels, the trio extracted a hefty first load of what they hoped was high-grade copper ore. Today State Highway 95 runs from below the Happy Jack to Blanding, offering an easy sixty-mile cruise on blacktop. In 1946, the Bronsons and Cooper had to creep along the Jeep road to Natural Bridges, then climb up and over Elk Ridge and down another winding dirt road to Blanding. From there, the men drove their cargo 109 miles north on the state road to Crescent Junction, where the D&RG tracks crossed Utah from east to west. At the junction, the men transferred the ore to a rail car parked on a siding. A train then carried the load, "along with our hopes and dreams," as Grant Bronson remembered years later, to a smelting and refining company in Salt Lake City.

Two weeks later the Bronsons and Cooper got the bad news. The copper assayed at 11 percent, barely enough for a small profit, but unfortunately the ore was contaminated with some radioactive mineral. Because there was no viable process to separate the copper from the contaminant,

the smelting company refused to accept any more ore. "So our grand mining venture at the Happy Jack," Grant recalled, "was put on hold while we
tried to figure out what to do."

After several stabs at interesting other companies in the ore, the three
men decided to sell the Happy Jack to cut their losses. When no potential buyers pricked up their ears, the Bronsons and Cooper were on the
verge of dumping the mine for back taxes. But at that very moment the
Atomic Energy Commission announced that it was buying uranium. The
boom was on.

During the early 1950s, Cooper and the Bronsons were besieged with
offers to buy the Happy Jack at figures far beyond the men's once-modest
dreams. By the time the trio sold the Happy Jack in 1959, the diggings
above White Canyon had earned them $25 million—$221 million in
today's dollars.

The wild success of the Happy Jack and of several other uranium ventures transformed the economies of Monticello and Blanding. According to local historian Buckley Jensen, before 1950 San Juan County was
"a primitive backwater, inhabited mostly by Native Americans and the
descendants of Mormon pioneers who scratched out their daily bread
from dry farms and cattle operations that were often marginal at best."
New trailer parks, motels, grocery stores, and restaurants sprang up overnight. The assessed valuation of the county soared from just over $1 mil-
lion in the 1940s to $132 million in 1959. In both towns libraries, sports
centers, new roads, and new schools grew like dandelions, and for the first
time the residents were able to enjoy adequate sewer and water systems.
Because the big uranium (and oil) companies paid 94 percent of the property taxes during the 1950s, the county's residents got the lowest assess-
ment in Utah.

During the boom years, then, life in San Juan County seemed unchar-
acteristically rosy, especially if you made your fortune from the mines.
Once he became a millionaire, Charlie Steen transformed himself from a
hardscrabble prospector into a jet-setting party boy with a predilection for
breeding Arabian horses. But Joe Cooper, Fletcher Bronson, and Grant

Bronson were proud to show that fame and affluence had done nothing to corrupt their values. As Buckley Jensen summarizes, "With that kind of money, Fletch, Grant and Joe could have gone anywhere and done anything. However, they all stayed in Monticello for the rest of their lives. They built beautiful homes for the times, but nothing that would raise eyebrows today." Grant Bronson became a local benefactor, supporting the Blue Mountain ski area, donating money for the Monticello swimming pool, and buying a grand piano for the town's concert association.

Not that getting the uranium to the market had ever been easy. As Jensen writes, "Finding radioactive rock along the outcroppings of the [S]hinarump formations was easy. Finding the money to build roads, drill shafts and haul that 'hot' gold to the mills in Moab, Monticello or Mexican Hat was simply impossible for most of the poorly capitalized prospectors and miners." (The Shinarump member of the Chinle formation is the geologists' label for a late Triassic mix of coarse-grained sandstone and pebble conglomerate. It serves as a reliable "tell" for prospectors looking for hidden beds of the "yellow cake" that signals a uranium strike.)

Especially during the winter, a trip hauling ore or equipment from Happy Jack to Blanding could border on a survival epic. In 1970, Cleone Bronson Cooper Hansen, Joe Cooper's wife and Grant Bronson's sister, recalled her vigil in Monticello one night as her husband, brother, and father struggled to get home through a snowstorm.

I recall one January the first, when I was expecting them home for New Years, I sat up all night that night waiting, and we had an old Chevrolet coupe. They decided to try the old Mormon Trail; they knew they couldn't get over the Elk Mountain, and some distance out it broke down. They had to abandon the car there and walk about, it must have been 15 or 20 miles to the highway, and Dad even at that age was the one that kept their courage up, I think. How to break trail, "Sure we can make it." And we never went back for the old car.

Dorothy Rossignol spent many months at the Happy Jack between 1959 and 1963, after the operation had gone big-time. Looking back in 2005, she had vivid memories of the hard life at the mine, where she stayed for as long as three months at a stretch, often as the only woman in the camp.

Water was hauled from Fry Canyon, about 12–15 miles from the spring. You did not waste water. You didn't wash your car. We had laundry facilities, a wash house. Each woman had 2 hours (they worked 10 on and 4 off) twice in that 10 days to do your laundry. Wash it, get it outside on lines to dry or whatever when all the people were there.

Supplying the camp with food was a trial in its own right.

Fry Canyon had a store about like Dave's Corner Market, very small, where you could get milk and just a few things. Not much meat, but anything that wasn't frozen. You could survive. Beer, of course; you had to go twelve miles to get that. Your big shopping was either in Monticello, Cortez, or Moab. . . . In the wintertime, you didn't travel a lot. . . . We didn't come out; we would stay in three months at a time. Some of those die-hard guys that had four-wheel drive and big vehicles we'd send our grocery list and a check with them and they'd bring our groceries back.

The company made us a recreation hall. It was just a building and we used to have movies once a week. . . . Every movie night usually two families or two women would make popcorn so we could have popcorn with our movie. . . .

[I]t was always BYOC, bring your own chair. You had to bring your own chair because they didn't have any furniture. We had several fellows who played banjo, accordion, different instruments and we'd have music and dancing. When there weren't many women in camp, the men used to have to dance together. . . . We were just one big happy family.

Even as early as 1950, there were reasons to suspect that mining uranium could be hazardous to a worker's health. Studies of silver miners in the *Erzgebirge* ("Ore Mountains") of Germany documented an alarmingly high death toll dating all the way back to the 1500s. We now know that the danger from radioactive minerals centers on radon, an inert noble gas released into the atmosphere when rock is blasted open. Radon is part of the sequence of steps by which uranium decays to stable lead. But it's actually the isotopes given off by radon—the so-called "radon daughters" or "radon progeny"—that cause all the human harm.

Even many of the best scientists were slow to acknowledge the fatal consequences of handling radium and uranium. Marie Curie, the great scientist who first isolated radium and who pioneered the medical use of X-rays (she coined the term "radioactivity"), ultimately died from its side effects. Well into the twentieth century roadside "spas" touted radium cures for everything from rheumatism to cancer to even insanity.

A government-authorized study to assess the risks of uranium mining, launched in early 1950, suffered from woeful underfunding and widespread indifference. The miners themselves, blinded by the prospect of top wages, pooh-poohed the risks. Raye Ringholz quotes a Colorado mine inspector's exasperation over the resistance of workers themselves to taking the hazards seriously.

Most of the miners thought they were all right. The radon gas was something you couldn't see, taste or smell. . . . It was hard to teach these people that something was wrong. We'd tell them they needed more ventilation and they'd say, 'I catch pneumonia when I come into the mines now. There's a draft coming through here all the time.' You'd inspect a mine and find it high in radon and order them to keep out of the mine until such time that better ventilation was provided. You'd turn your back and they'd go back in and work.

As mentioned in chapter 3, the father of Mark Maryboy, the Navajo activist who got the snowball rolling that would become Obama's Bears Ears National Monument, died of lung cancer almost certainly contracted from years of work in the uranium mines. Calvin Black, who served for twenty-two years as the right-wing San Juan County commissioner and became the scourge of environmentalists of all stripes, locked horns for decades with the writer Edward Abbey. In Abbey's comic-novel-cum-manifesto *The Monkey Wrench Gang*, Black was transmogrified into the villain Bishop Love. (The bishop, serving as a volunteer for the search-and-rescue squad, is given to such utterances as this, while he hunts down the "hairy little hoodlum" who has monkey-wrenched a government vehicle: "Well first I'll take my needle-nosed pliers and remove a couple of his toenails. Then his back teeth. Then I'm gonna ask him where Seldom Seen is, and that Dr. Sarvis and that little whore of a girl they transport around with 'em. We might get them all on the Mann Act, come to think of it—crossing the state line for immoral purposes.")

As late as 1970, Black minimized the dangers of uranium mining, telling an interviewer,

> Dr. Saccomono in Grand Junction makes the statement that there's more hazard of lung cancer from smoking cigarettes than there is in mining uranium. . . . Now why do they get concerned and pass national health standards for less than two thousand uranium miners—and they don't worry anything about fifty million smokers? But why should they tell them that they can't work in uranium mines? . . . One thing about it, [a miner's] going to die sometime anyway. If that's the way he wants to die, he ought to be able to do it.

Be careful what you wish for. In 1990, at the age of sixty-one, Calvin Black died of inoperable lung cancer, which by then even he granted was caused by his work in the uranium mines in the 1950s. When he learned that his old antagonist was suffering from a terminal disease, Abbey, who had less than a year to live himself, wrote Black a remarkable note:

Dear Cal,

I hear rumors that you've come down with a serious illness. If true, I hope you beat it. Although you and I probably disagree about almost everything, you should know that I have never felt the slightest ill will toward you as a person. Furthermore, you still owe me an airplane ride. Good luck and best wishes.

◄◄ ►►

In 1959 Cooper and the Bronsons sold the Happy Jack to a consortium called the Texas Zinc Minerals Corporation. Once the new owners had decided to establish a processing mill (which later became a toxic dump) at Halchita, just across the San Juan River from Mexican Hat and not incidentally on the Navajo Reservation, the company decided it was imperative to build a new direct road from White Canyon south across Cedar Mesa, then down the 1,100-foot cliff to the bench that slopes south and east toward the San Juan. Thus was born the Moki Dugway, one of the marvels of road engineering anywhere in the West.

All of us who set out today from Bluff to hike and camp on Cedar Mesa usually drive twenty-eight miles west on Routes 163 and 261, zigzag up the Dugway, and vector north on 261, the road built by Texas Zinc. The canyons that contain the wonders of the Anasazi lifeway during the two centuries before the great abandonment of AD 1300 spill east and west off Highway 261. By now I've driven that route a least a hundred times: Vaughn Hadenfeldt, perhaps a thousand times. It was during our first trips together in the 1990s that Vaughn shared with me the lore of the Dugway.

Near the top, just beyond the scenic turnout where tourists snap photos of Monument Valley and Comb Ridge in the distance, lies the wreckage of two vehicles that tumbled off the edge and cratered among the boulders fifty feet below. The upper vehicle, its fading yellow paint still proclaiming its sorry demise, belonged, according to Vaughn, to a Navajo woodcutter who'd spent the day on Cedar Mesa sawing and chopping logs. With his brother, who drove a separate pickup, the fellow headed down the Dugway after dark. At the first bend he cranked the steering wheel left, only to have his truck sail straight off the edge. Later he figured out that his load made the truck so rear-heavy that on the turn his front wheels weren't touching the road. Coming second, his brother watched the fall in horror. Remarkably, the first woodcutter survived the plunge with only cuts, bruises, and a broken leg.

The other wreck, one bend farther east, is a smashed black upside-down truck that launched into space for a forty-foot vertical drop, but miraculously came to a grinding stop at the edge of a much bigger precipice. The story has it that the driver—let's call him Pete—was coming last in a caravan of Texas Zinc trucks hauling uranium ore to Halchita in the early 1960s. At that bend, his truck lost its brakes. It's hard to believe that Pete could have survived the crash—Vaughn thinks he must have jumped out before the vehicle barreled into space. Battered and scared, Pete managed to crawl back up to the highway, where he sat and waited.

Meanwhile the caravan, oblivious, puttered on down the Dugway switchbacks, motored south through Mexican Hat, crossed the old bridge over the San Juan, and arrived at Halchita. Only then did someone ask, "Where's Pete?" Someone else answered, "Dunno. He was right behind me." A rescue posse, expecting to find only a corpse, if anything, drove back up the Dugway to the top, where they came upon a thoroughly disgusted Pete, who griped, "Why the hell didn't you stop and look for me?"

Shortly thereafter, Pete quit his job with Texas Zinc and moved to the Midwest. Not long after that, he was killed when his truck collided with a moving train.

There's a third truck carcass halfway down the Dugway, a square black chassis parked on a bench eighty feet below the road. I noticed it only after many trips up and down the Dugway. To my surprise, the wreck had never caught Vaughn's eye. What story lies behind that vehicular disaster, nobody whom I know knows.

Years ago, driving down the 1,100-foot roller coaster of a road, I looked out the side window and saw for the first time that a number of tire tracks actually departed from the road at the narrowest bend on the whole route, only to reappear five or six feet farther on. Incredulous that drivers could actually have veered off the road above a vertical wall and somehow recovered, I pointed out the tracks to Vaughn, who instantly deciphered the markings. They were tracks from trucks hauling trailers uphill. Each driver must have handled the bend just fine, while failing to realize that the dead weight he was dragging behind him had a mind of its own. It seemed to me that dangling your trailer, however briefly, off the edge was an invitation to calamity, as the trailer hanging in space might well pull the truck back into the void. But neither Vaughn nor I have ever heard of a fatal accident occurring at that treacherous bend. Apparently the scenario recurs every other week or so, for I've never failed to find tracks there flirting with the abyss, and I love to show them to friends on their first rides up the Dugway, just to watch the shudder the sight provokes.

One way to appreciate what an unlikely feat of roadbuilding the Moki Dugway embodies is to survey the cliff bands as you wend your way up or down. It's indisputable that before the road was dynamited through the bands, a hiker could never have ascended the mesa from bottom to top on the buttress that Texas Zinc chose to assault. In fact, given the overhangs that festoon two of the bands, along with the absence of vertical cracks in the sandstone, it's doubtful that a rock climber could have solved the precipice without resorting to expansion bolts and direct aid.

The road is so well designed that there's no point in its three-mile course where a car headed up and a truck headed down can't easily pass each other without scraping a side wall or inching near the edge. And thanks to the hard, gravelly surface of the dirt, the Dugway is drivable even in rain. For motorists with a modicum of experience on mountain roads, the Dugway is a piece of cake.

Nevertheless, the erstwhile uranium haul road terrifies all kinds of soi-disant adventurers. In 2017, for the *New York Times*, one Max Read recounted his daring battle with the Dugway, with a wife in the passenger seat who was quite sure both of them would die before reaching the summit. The road, muses Read, "looks like the accidental record of a cartographer's sudden stroke." The ascent, he adds, will induce "a coronary event or two." Read concludes that the Dugway "is a test of your nerves, your skill, your transmission and, if you're with a partner, as I was, your relationship."

Another intrepid driver, having solved the challenge in 1994, testified, "Make no mistake, serious acrophobes should not take the Moki Dugway switchbacks. It never occurred to me to ask my friends about their fears— I simply hauled everyone up there—until one hapless passenger begged to make the trip with a bag over her head."

Other accounts over the years make Max Read's taming of the highway sound cavalier. Several correspondents ponder whether the Dugway is "the most dangerous road in the U.S." A survivor posts a testimonial to "the scariest drive of my life" on Tripadvisor. An online journal called *living magazine* ranks the Dugway among "The Most Dangerous Roads in the World."

My favorite Moki Dugway saga is one Vaughn told me years ago. Long before Vaughn moved to Bluff, an old-timer named Melvin Gaines was driving his bulldozer up the switchbacks to work on the road. Mel had been part of the crew that built the Dugway, and for years thereafter he served on the highway crew. On this trip, halfway up, he came upon a woman standing next to a car parked in the middle of the road. Melvin asked her if anything was the matter. She said, "I'm too scared to drive either up or down. Could you drive my car up for me?"

"Lady," said Mel, "I'm on the job here. I've got work to do"—only to have the addled woman burst into tears, "Oh, all right," he said, opening the driver-side door. "Get in."

"Oh, no," answered the woman. "I'm too scared to ride. I'll walk up. Just leave the keys in the car."

Exasperated, his day's mission on back burner, Melvin steered the auto gently up the Dugway until he reached the rim of Cedar Mesa. But as he got out of the car, he realized that the seat of his trousers was soaking wet. The poor woman had been so frightened by the time she got halfway up the Dugway, she had peed her pants as she sat there awaiting a rescue.

SEVEN

POSEY'S TRAIL

n Bluff, the pioneers from the Hole-in-the-Rock expedition struggled after 1880 with the perceived Indian threat, with crops that failed too often, and above all with disastrous floods unleashed by the San Juan River. Some of those founders were gone within months after their momentous arrival that April, disenchanted with the schisms that split the new settlement. But most of the leaders of the great hegira stayed on, determined to see the San Juan Mission survive and even flourish. Inevitably, though, old age began to take its toll among those stalwarts.

The first of the leaders of the Hole-in-the-Rock expedition to die in Bluff was Platte Lyman. As recounted in chapter 5, Lyman had effectively taken charge of the strung-out procession of emigrants, and he more than any other principal was responsible for its success without the loss of a single life. He also kept a diary during the journey, which forms today the best primary source for the details of the six-month odyssey. In Bluff he built the sturdy two-story house that stands today, and he figured as one of its leading citizens, until the still murky episode in 1884 that caused him to be "released" from the San Juan Mission by church authorities in Salt Lake City, which prompted his exile from the town he had done so much to found.

Back in favor in 1891, Lyman returned to Bluff, where he lived out the rest of his days. In September 1901 he was chosen as president of the San

Juan Stake. But within a week he developed a large, painful tumor under his arm. Surgeons in Salt Lake City removed the tumor, but left the cancer uncured. Back in Bluff, he declined rapidly. The town rallied around its president, with Bishop Nielson declaring a fast and summoning a doctor from Cortez, but Lyman was in constant pain.

The end was gruesome. Writes David Carpenter, "Platte Lyman's agony became awful in his final days. His cries could be heard through much of the town; his family and neighbors were 'horrified at his torture.'" Faithful to the church that had once scorned him, he uttered his last words on November 13: "O pray the Lord to let me go."

By early 1905, Bishop Nielson, now eighty-four, was in declining health himself. His hearing was poor enough to require an ear trumpet, he suffered from dropsy, and by the end of the year he was virtually confined to a rocking chair in the house he had built for his first wife, Elsie. Realizing that he could no longer perform his duties, he tendered his resignation after twenty-five years as the bishop of Bluff. His mind stayed sharp to the end, and his fidelity to the church never wavered. He told his friends that he had never regretted leaving his native Denmark to pursue the faith to which the missionaries had opened his eyes at age thirty-two. One of the last hopes he voiced was to have been a good enough man "to see the Prophet Joseph Smith . . . on the other side." He died on April 20, 1906, five days short of his eighty-sixth birthday.

With the passing of its spiritual leader, Bluff itself seemed to give up the ghost. The Old Swing Tree, center of the fledgling colony, was swept away by a flood in 1907. Only five months after Nielson was buried in the cemetery on the hill behind town, the new bishop and the new stake president met with church president Joseph F. Smith, great-nephew of the founding prophet, in Salt Lake City. The dry verdict on Bluff they reached: "It was decided to abandon that place."

Yet Bluff never became a true ghost town. From a population of 193 in 1900, Bluff declined to seventy residents in both 1930 and 1940, before experiencing a modest growth at the onset of the uranium boom in 1950. (Pending the 2020 census, the estimated population of the town today is a little over 250.) During the more than 110 years since the church decided to "abandon" Bluff, the demographics of the settlement have shifted, until the town is now predominantly non-Mormon.

Glimpses of life in that sleepy but special hamlet between the sandstone cliffs and the San Juan River during the fallow decades come from a variety of sources. Zane Grey's most popular novel, *Riders of the Purple Sage*, published in 1912, centers around the Mormon town of Cottonwoods, a thinly disguised Bluff. Its heroine, Jane Withersteen, is the beautiful young, unmarried daughter of the town's founder. She has inherited the ranch that encloses Amber Spring, "the water which gave verdure and beauty to the village," runs a thousand head of cattle, and owns "the swiftest horses of the sage." Though born and bred a Mormon, she has fallen into disfavor with the town leaders because of her friendship with various Gentiles, including the two loner-cowboy heroes of the novel, Bern Venters and the single-named Lassiter. A legendary gunslinger but a man ill-suited for social life, Lassiter has dedicated his days to wiping out Mormons, because of a personal vendetta whose roots are only gradually revealed in the pages of the book.

Grey was a fierce critic of the LDS church, and *Riders of the Purple Sage* is the locus classicus of his enmity. As the scholar and historian Gary Topping writes, the novel "fairly drips with anti-Mormon rhetoric, and one could search for some time in Western literature before finding more despicable villains than the Mormon leaders Tull and Dyer." Elder Tull is a hypocritical polygamist who, despite already having three wives, is bent on making Jane his fourth. On only the third page of the novel, Tull arrives at the ranch shortly after Venters has departed. The elder, alert to Jane's feelings for the cowboy, fumes, "I'm sick of seeing this fellow Venters hang around you. I'm going to put a stop to it." To do so, he later arrests Venters and throws him in jail on spurious charges.

Bishop Dyer, who bears no resemblance to the real Bishop Nielson, is a manipulative coward who masterminds the kidnapping of Jane's adopted daughter. In a Hollywood denouement, Lassiter guns down the bishop against long odds, one man outshooting not only his antagonist but the bishop's cordon of bodyguards. As the bishop slumps to the floor, Lassiter spews a taunt: "*Proselyter*, I reckon you'd better call quick on thet God who reveals Hisself to you on earth, because He won't be visitin' the place you're goin' to!"

The climax of the novel takes place far from Cottonwoods, in a wilderness enclave north of Navajo Mountain, on the Utah-Arizona border, called Surprise Valley. The book ends with Jane and Lassiter safely ensconced in Surprise Valley, having toppled the Balancing Rock to seal off its entrance against Elder Tull's pursuing posse.

Surprise Valley is a real place. In fact, it was named by Zane Grey on a long pack trip he took to Rainbow Bridge, guided by John Wetherill (Richard's brother), who established trading posts on the Navajo Reservation at Oljato and Kayenta and came to know that backcountry better than any other Anglo. Ironically, though, Grey's journey took place in 1913, the year after *Riders of the Purple Sage* was published. It seems that Grey transferred his own name for the imagined Elysium of the novel to a remote clearing surrounded by soaring cliffs that took on the power of a real Elysium in the writer-adventurer's life. In two later novels, *The Rainbow Trail* and *The Vanishing American*, Grey returned to Surprise Valley.

On three trips between 1994 and 2003, I backpacked into Surprise Valley and camped in a corner of that stronghold, making it my base for day trips to explore the short, technical canyons threading north toward Lake Powell. About that oasis in the slickrock, I feel as Zane Grey did: I know of no more enchanted place anywhere in the Southwest. I'd give anything to make one more trip into Surprise Valley, but I know that now, post-cancer, it's beyond my powers.

Grey's Cottonwoods, on the other hand, is a fictive invention. By 1912, Bluff was already less of a Mormon stronghold than either Blanding or Monticello. With the 1930s came the first inklings that Bluff might someday serve as a tourist destination, as a few visitors arrived, lured by the appeal of vestiges of the Anasazi. The cliffs encircling the town are rich in rock art panels, especially at Sand Island, just three miles west along the north bank of the San Juan. Across the river just east of town, a spacious alcove cradles the ruin called 16 Room House.

From the 1930s through the present day, Blanding has remained a staunchly dry town, in which you can't buy a single can of 3.2 percent beer in either a restaurant or a convenience store. Monticello has a minuscule liquor store not much bigger than a phone booth, but nothing remotely resembling a bar. But Bluff has had a series of bars and saloons over the years. None survives today, but three of the four restaurants serve beer and wine (the fourth dry not because of Mormon tenets, but because its owner is a Muslim).

Perhaps the most colorful and undoubtedly the most infamous of the Bluff bars was a wooden-shack emporium on Main Street called the Navajo Trail, which a Swedish immigrant named John A. Johnson ran in the 1950s. Interviewed in 1972, Johnson recalled some of the livelier episodes he witnessed as bartender. Most of the customers were Indians, said Johnson, and liquor brought out the age-old antagonisms between Utes and Navajos. Johnson's take on the Utes from the White Mesa reservation was not exactly politically correct: "If they keep on drinking like they're doing, there won't be anybody left up there. They drink everything they can get a hold of: shaving lotion, rum, vanilla [extract]."

Johnson had witnessed a bloody scene in another Bluff bar a couple of years before.

They were all drinking there. Finally they threw a man out, but they left the man's squaw in there—his wife. Of course, that boy outside figured something would happen to his wife inside there. He was jealous. He got in his pick-up, got a .30-.30, and shot through the wall three or four times. The bullet holes are still there. . . . Five of them got hurt in there. They got shrapnel in the legs, and one got shrapnel in the stomach which cut one of his intestines in two. That fellow was sent to Salt Lake City.

Later, as bartender in the Navajo Trail, Johnson wielded what he called his "persuader" (some kind of cattle prod) to keep order.

I tell you the truth, I made them afraid of me. I'm a tough son of a gun. . . . After they started drinking, I could see when they were going to start a fight. I used to walk around the bar and open the door and say, "Everybody out! And you can fight all you want out there. I don't care if you kill each other, but out!"

Pointing to his cattle prod, Johnson told his interviewer, "That's my persuader right there. You hit anybody like that, and it will give you such a shock that you will fall down. . . . I bought this one from Montgomery Ward just for my purpose. If you didn't mind, you went around the bar and they took off through the door."

By 1972, Johnson was witnessing a cultural transformation in Bluff. His views about the younger residents flocking to the town were no more enlightened than his take on the Indians he had served in the Navajo Trail. "I don't like the new fellows who have come in here lately," he told his interviewer. "They're a bunch of longhairs, and I don't like them. They don't do anything."

In 1959, a geologist named Gene Foushee moved to town. He had visited Bluff with his father in the late 1940s, and had come away with a lasting impression of a moribund settlement on the road to nowhere. After he built the motel that would play a large part in transforming Bluff, Foushee kept a favorite quotation mounted under glass on the office counter. It was from Ernie Pyle, the legendary journalist, who had come through town in 1939. "Bluff was dead, and well it knew it," Pyle wrote. "Dust was deep in the streets; no one moved very fast. No one new ever came to Bluff."

Even in 1959, Bluff was barely alive. The town had gotten electricity only two years earlier, the telephone in 1958—but at first, a single phone served the whole community. Still, something caught Foushee's eye. "It seemed to me that Bluff was a beautiful place," he recalled in 1972. "What attracted me here? For one thing, the big old cottonwood trees. . . ." On the 1940s visit with his father, "Suddenly we came out of the desert with a broken axle in hand and that place looked like an oasis with beautiful, red-rock cliffs all the way along each side."

During the 1959 visit, the idea of building a tourist lodge lighted a bulb in Foushee's head, but convincing his wife, Mary, was a tall order: "I came home from Nevada after a three-week trip and said, 'Let's move to Bluff and build a motel.' She cried for six months after we moved down here, but it wasn't quite that bad."

At the time, Foushee had a solid job with Union Carbide, working out of the uranium boom town of Uravan, just across the border in western Colorado. "Looking back," he remembered thirteen years later, "it was a drastic decision. . . . If you would ask an economist or a financier about the return on our investment . . . , they'd say, 'You've got rocks in your head.'" But Gene and Mary bought a tired corn field, started building their tourist lodge, and eventually raised two children in the little town.

Foushee designed the motel himself, and directed the workers who put it together "a few rooms at a time." He named it Recapture Lodge, after Recapture Creek, a tributary of the San Juan a few miles east of Bluff, which in turn got its name from the Hayden Survey, after the team recovered horses stolen along that creek by Utes in 1875. Aware of the spiritual tenets embodied in the Navajo hogan, Foushee built the motel so that the door of each unit faced east, with a porch in front. In the prime seasons of spring and fall, that means that guests can sit basking in sunlight in the cool mornings, sheltered in shade through the blazing afternoons. After Foushee's death in 2017, Colorado journalist Andrew Gulliford evoked the man as a construction boss: "He always pointed a stubby pencil at two-by-fours, friends, neighbors, anyone who would listen. He taught young Navajos the basics of carpentry. . . . Foushee knew how to straighten nails, re-use lumber, work hard and encourage others. He lived by the Depression adage: 'Use it up, wear it out, make it do or do without.'" Jim Hook, who with his wife, Luanne, bought Recapture Lodge in 1989, affectionately reminisced, "It was exhausting to work with him. He had so many ideas about what to do. Everyone who ever met him had a list given to him by Gene. I still haven't done everything on the first list he gave me and that was over thirty years ago."

Starting in the early 1990s, I got to know Gene and Mary Foushee.

They were the kindest and most unpretentious of elders. Gene had become a skillful small-plane pilot, and in 1994 he gave Jon Krakauer and me a ride I'll never forget, as we first flew low over Cedar Mesa, when I was just beginning to learn the labyrinth of its canyons, then over a virtually unknown slot canyon on the north side of Navajo Mountain that Jon and I hoped to descend.

Gene loved the wilderness as keenly as anyone I've ever met. The last time I saw him, when he was well into his eighties, he was way out near the end of the dirt road that leads from the town of Escalante across the Desert (as the locals call it) toward the Hole-in-the-Rock. Hobbling along, wielding a pair of ski poles like canes, unsteady on his feet, he was determined to prowl into the headwaters of Davis Gulch, where Everett Ruess had disappeared in 1934.

Gene died at age eighty-eight in the summer of 2017, Mary, also at age eighty-eight, only nine days later. It would be hard to overstate their role in rejuvenating the dead town of Bluff. As Gulliford wrote in his memorial salutation,

> Gene would get a project started, move it along, then pass it on for someone else to finish, and he'd begin a different project. He lobbied for better roads. He planted shrubs, river privets, currents [*sic*], lilacs and dozens of trees, including Carolina poplars, pecans, mulberries and fruit trees, whose shade today's residents enjoy. He found funds for a small airplane strip at Bluff, and he built a hangar for visiting aircraft. He created the town's first water system from shallow wells and an artesian well. And one by one, he restored the town's historic stone houses built in the 1890s and early 1900s by successful Mormon ranchers and merchants.

Luanne Hook, tearfully recalling both Gene and Mary, said, "They were like our second parents. They were a unit together. Jim and I have patterned our own marriage and our partnership after them. He was the face of the community, but she was behind the scenes, the bookkeeper.

The Bears Ears buttes themselves. *Photograph by David Roberts.*

Grand Gulch from the air.
Photograph by David Roberts.

The hidden ruin in the book's opening scene. *Photograph by David Roberts.*

Fred Blackburn, the author's first Bears Ears mentor.
Photograph by David Roberts.

The author with longtime pal Vaughn Hadenfeldt (right). *Photograph by David Roberts.*

Greg Child, partner in countless outings. *Photograph by David Roberts.*

Starting the home stretch on the Comb Ridge traverse.
Photograph by Greg Child.

Manuelito, the great Navajo leader, in his late fifties.
National Anthropological Archives, Smithsonian Institution.

An old Navajo hogan
on Cedar Mesa.
Photograph by David Roberts.

Manuelito's grave, either under
or near the derelict mobile home.
Photograph by David Roberts.

The gravestone of America's
most notorious pothunter.
Photograph by David Roberts.

The Hole-in-the-Rock cleft from the air. *University of Utah Marriott Library, Special Collections.*

Bluff City in 1895. *Utah State Historical Society.*

Bluff's first "meeting house," where townsfolk gathered beneath the cottonwood.
Utah State Historical Society.

Albert Lyman, pioneer Mormon chronicler.

San Juan County Historical Society.

Signpost irony in Bluff—prehistoric and historic.
Photograph by David Roberts.

Ed Ward at Moon House. *Photograph by David Roberts.*

The Citadel. *Photograph by David Roberts.*

Anasazi pot discovered
by the author in 1993.

Photograph by David Roberts.

Charlie Steen, king of the
self-taught uranium hunters.
Wikiwand.

The author at Big Man Panel, 1992. *Photograph by David Roberts.*

Detail of pictographs at the Green Mask site. *Photograph by David Roberts.*

Sharon Roberts studies ravens at the Great Gallery, Grand Gulch. *Photograph by David Roberts.*

Detail from the Procession Panel. *Photograph by David Roberts.*

Atlatl Man. *Photograph by David Roberts.*

Matt Hale in Beef Basin. *Photograph by David Roberts.*

Freestanding ruin in Beef Basin. *Photograph by David Roberts.*

Jim Mike, Paiute:
visionary, guide, shaman.
Photograph by Fred Blackburn.

Tse-ne-gat: murderer or martyr?
San Juan County Historical Society.

Posey, Paiute leader, 1921.
Utah State Historical Society.

After his death in 1923, members of the "posse" dug up Posey's body and posed with it. *Utah State Historical Society.*

One of the wildly defensive ruins on Cedar Mesa. *Photograph by Greg Child.*

Sarah Keyes and Emmett Lyman at Muley Point, sunset. *Photograph by David Roberts.*

She was actually the nuts and bolts, the welcoming face at the front desk. They were the saviors of Bluff."

The Foushees were my link to the Bluff I knew only from reading memoirs and historical tracts reaching back to the Hole-in-the-Rock expedition of 1880. Ever since 1992, whenever I make Bluff my base for yet another excursion onto Comb Ridge or Cedar Mesa, I stay at Recapture Lodge or in the Adams House, one of the red-stone pioneer homes that Gene restored. I could never live in a town of only 250-odd souls, no matter how simpatico—without a morning newspaper or a wine bar or a bookstore within a hundred miles. But I thank "whatever gods may be" that Bluff is there.

From 1995 to 2004, a team under the leadership of University of Colorado archaeologist Catherine Cameron excavated an Anasazi site on the bench just above town on the north, only a few paces from the cemetery containing the graves of Bluff pioneers such as Jens Nielson and Platte Lyman. The dig morphed into a major discovery: not only did the site contain fifty to sixty rooms, four regular kivas, and a great kiva, but it proved to be a Chacoan great house, linked by the enigmatic Chacoan road system to the greatest Anasazi center of all, Chaco Canyon in western New Mexico, the hub of a virtual empire that flourished from AD 1000 to 1150. Among the more than 150 Chacoan outliers yet identified, the Bluff great house is one of the most northern and among the farthest from the center.

During the last decade, the counterculture vibes of Bluff have embraced the Cameron team's discovery of the place as a major Anasazi site. A wry pairing of signs on Mulberry Avenue points the way to "Cemetery" and to "Chacoan Great House Built in 1200's." With the controversy over the Bears Ears monument, that embrace has only grown tighter. A few blocks west of Recapture Lodge on Main Street stands the Bears Ears Education Center, which opened in 2018. Signs on the edge of town proclaim "Proud Gateway to Bears Ears," just as placards in front yards exhort "Rescind Trump." In most Utah towns, the obligatory sign on the highway as you cross the city limits reads, for example, "Welcome to Blanding. Founded 1905. Elevation 6,000'." The sign as you enter Bluff announces, "BLUFF. Est. 650 AD."

◄◄ ►►

As mentioned in chapter 5, the avowed goal of the Hole-in-the-Rock expedition was to make peace with the natives, while "civilizing" them at the same time. In the fondest dream of its missionaries, civilizing Indians would have meant converting them to the LDS faith.

During the two decades after 1880, however, relations with the Navajo were so explosive that conversion was out of the question. In the annals of the early settlers of Bluff, it's hard to find even a hint of the idea that the land on the north bank of the San Juan, laid out in lots and streets by the pioneers, "belonged" to anyone except the Saints themselves. In a tradition that persists today, the settlers argued that the Navajo ought to stay within the confines of the reservation granted them in 1868 and expanded in 1884. The northern border of that purported homeland was the San Juan River. Navajos venturing outside the reservation, therefore, were "trespassing."

That any of the land the Hole-in-the-Rockers claimed in 1880 might have had historic significance for the Diné, much less a sacred numen, was beyond the ken of Bishop Nielson or Platte Lyman. Yet the most striking landmark within the Bluff town limits, the astonishing pair of freestanding pinnacles called the Navajo Twins, figured in just that way in the Diné cosmology. In the creation myth, they symbolize the Hero Twins, Monster Slayer and Born for Water. In the words of historian Robert S. McPherson, the towers are "a reminder that these two deities with their extraordinary power are still available as Holy People to bless and protect the Navajo from evil influence, as guardians of the traditional way, as role models of bravery, and examples of the potency of prayer." The pinnacles, with their striking multicolored strata, also represent prayer sticks left by Monster Slayer, and even today traditional Navajos leave offerings at the base or pray in the echoing alcove just around the corner.

Over the years, the towers have been called other names by Anglos, including Twin Bottle Rocks, Punch and Judy, and Idol Rocks. The last appellation was bestowed by a government surveyor in 1911 who deduced that the pinnacles were actually idols constructed by the Aztecs. In June 2019, on a trip to Languedoc in southwest France, I was reading E.-A. Martel's classic *La France Ignorée*, his evocation of exploratory wonders from Normandy to Provence, published in 1928. I was astonished to come across a page bearing a lithograph of the Navajo Twins, which Martel (who never visited Utah) compared to various bizarre geologic formations in his native land.

If Bluff occupied terrain familiar and important to the Navajos, it was even more significant to the Paiutes and Utes who had flourished for centuries across the region now claimed by the Saints. In the first decades of the twentieth century, the clash between those tribes and white settlers would spiral into the tragedy that has often been called the last Indian war in the United States. A strange foreshadowing of that conflict emerges in the person of a single Paiute called by the Mormons Jim Mike.

Born near Agathla, the volcanic plug on the south edge of Monument Valley, around 1870, Jim Mike lived for more than a century. It is possible that when still a child he was baptised, along with his father, "Big Mouth" Maik, by Mormons in Tuba City, Arizona, in the early 1880s. By then the family had camped and hunted often along the San Juan near Bluff. Late in life, on the White Mesa Ute Reservation between Bluff and Blanding, having by then become a member of the LDS church, he startled an interviewer by suddenly saying, "I saw Jesus, and he called me by my Secret Ute Name." The full record of this epiphanic event—which seems to hint at early efforts around Bluff to convert Paiutes and Utes to the faith—is contained in a twenty-three-page manifesto that I consider the most outlandish document I came across in all my research about the Bears Ears. Published in 1999, it bears the cabalistic title *The Ute Spiritual Cross of the San Juan Mission*, and is the work of one Stanley Warren Bronson, who claims to be the tribal historian of the White Mesa Avikan Utes. On the first page, resorting to all caps, Bronson announces that he will present "AN ACCOUNT OF THE APPEARANCE OF JESUS CHRIST TO FOUR AVIKAN UTE INDIAN MEN NEAR THE 'MORMON' COMMUNITY OF BLUFF, UTAH, IN ABOUT THE YEAR 1920."

Avikan, which means "a house (or home) of rest" in Ute, signifying a semi-mythic homeland, is identified with Allen Canyon northwest of Blanding, a tributary of Cottonwood Creek, just east of the edge of the proposed Bears Ears monument. Portions of Allen Canyon are Ute land today. Why Jim Mike, a Paiute born far to the south, should be identified as an "Avikan Ute" is unclear, though in later life he ran cattle in Allen Canyon.

Bronson heard only that single utterance about meeting Jesus from Jim Mike when he interviewed the man in 1970. In 1977 Jim Mike died, age at least 105. Nine years later, through an interpreter, Bronson interviewed the Paiute's daughter Pochief, with Jim Mike's son Billy sitting in and concurring. Pochief delivered the full story of the meeting with Jesus. Her father, Pochief's husband and her brother, and another brother whose name neither sibling could recall, were making the short ride on horseback from Sand Island to Bluff in August, sometime around 1920, to buy watermelons.

Just before they came to Cottonwood Wash, they met a man walking toward them in the sandy roadway. The man had long, un-braided hair, and a beard. He wore a robe with un-hemmed sleeves, and his feet were bare.

The man spoke, calling Jim by his secret Ute name. Jim answered, "You must be Jesus!" The man smiled, and pointed to himself. Jim and the other men dismounted from their horses and started asking Jesus questions. They asked, "Where do you live? Where do you sleep?" Jesus pointed to the sky. . . . They asked, "Do you like watermelon and corn?" Jesus then spoke in the Ute language and said, "Yes, I do."

The men were fascinated by the feet of Jesus, because they were very smooth and clean, like pearly white, even though he was walking barefoot in the sandy roadway. They asked, "Doesn't this hot sand burn your bare feet?" Jesus said, "It is not hot to me."

Jesus talked about other things, and then he held his hands out toward the men and showed them his crucifixion scars and said, "I want you to know—you would not have done this to me here."

Jesus then went on his way. The men mounted their horses and rode on toward Bluff. As they crossed Cottonwood Wash they met a Model T Ford, traveling in the same direction as Jesus.

What to make of this story? Assuming that Bronson didn't simply make it up, or fudge the details to fit his beliefs, the appearance of a barefoot Jesus on the road near Bluff may betoken a real vision that Jim Mike was granted one day, at about the age of fifty, long after he was baptised by Mormons as a child. Renowned all his life among his people as a shaman, Jim Mike was a man to whom visions of all kinds bridged the gulf between the "real" world and the cosmos of gods and spirits.

But what about the other three witnesses, Pochief's brothers and her husband? Were they still alive in 1986? (A website for Bronson listed in the self-published *Ute Spiritual Cross* was defunct when I searched for it in 2019.)

Alas, the vision of Jesus that Bronson records fits all too conveniently into the reductionist portfolio of a True Believer. As he comments, "This writer believes that Christ's appearance and testimonial to the Ute Holy Man Jim Mike, and to his sons [*sic*], naturally serves as a powerful confirmation to Native American people everywhere of the important role that the Children of Lehi play in the fulfillment of the work of the Great Gift of the Priesthood, which gift is yet to be received by Lehi, as a nation." In other words: *You poor benighted Lamanites, cursed with dark skin for wiping out the virtuous Nephites way back when, get your act together and listen to Christ's message. Come around to the true faith and in the next life you can indeed become a white and delightsome people.*

Whatever the substance of Bronson's tendentious screed, based on the by now unverifiable account by Pochief of her father's encounter with Jesus on the road to Bluff, Jim Mike was a remarkable man. About a decade before that encounter, in 1909, known then as Mike's Boy (presumably in reference to his father, "Big Mouth" Maik), he guided a party led by John Wetherill, the archaeologist Byron Cummings, and the surveyor-anthropologist William Douglass along a difficult slickrock route north of Navajo Mountain to make what the team hailed as the discovery of Rainbow Bridge. For decades thereafter, all the credit for guiding the party was granted to the other canny Paiute who showed them where to go, Nasja Begay, before Mike's Boy/Jim Mike was granted his due. (For that matter, it's now clear that other, less famous Anglos—among them gold prospectors on the Colorado River—had seen the great arch before 1909. And as Neil Judd, a member of the 1909 party who would later become a preeminent Southwest archaeologist, wrote in 1927, "Who actually discovered Nonnezoshe [the Navajo name]? Some Indian way back in that pre-Columbian past when man romped and roamed widely over this continent of ours but left no written record to prove it.")

Jim Mike was also a close friend and ally of another Pauite, known to Anglos as Posey or William Posey, whose antagonism to the Mormons would culminate in the dramatic denouement of "Posey's War"— that tragicomic campaign, more than eight years in the making, that has earned the dubious laurel of our country's last Indian war. And it would be Jim Mike who supplied a key to the puzzle of Posey's last stand west of Comb Ridge in 1923, with a claim that, like the vision of Jesus on the road to Bluff, now lies forever beyond the reach of proof or disproof.

Neighbors and enemies for centuries, the Navajo on one hand, the Utes and Paiutes on the other, claimed ancestral rights to much of southeast Utah, with the San Juan River as a rough boundary between their nonetheless overlapping domains. They belong, however, to completely different ethnic and linguistic groups. As detailed in chapter 3, the Navajos are an Athapaskan people, related by language, customs, and religion to the Apaches in the Southwest, but also to numerous tribes such as the Chipewyan and Gwich'in in subarctic Canada and Alaska. The Utes and

Paiutes are Numic peoples, speaking a subset of the great Uto-Aztecan language family, connected in that respect to the Shoshone, Comanche, Bannock, Mono, Chemeheuvi, and other tribes. Ethnographers believe that from a homeland in the Great Basin of Nevada, large numbers of Utes and Paiutes migrated toward the Four Corners, perhaps as early as AD 1300, just about the time that the Anasazi were abandoning the Colorado Plateau. Other scholars would move the date of that influx to much later, even as late as AD 1600. As with the Navajo, but perhaps even more frustratingly, archaeological vestiges of Ute and Paiute presence on the ground (tent rings, lithic points and flakes) are hard to find and harder to date.

Distinctions between the Paiutes and the Utes are strong and long-lasting enough to warrant classifying them as separate peoples, even though their languages are generally mutually intelligible. Early Anglo explorers in western Utah and Nevada, observing the Paiute dependence on roots and tiny animals for subsistence, gave them the pejorative label "Digger Indians," and it is a commonplace in their reports to pity (or despise) the Paiutes as the most wretched of all Western tribes. The San Juan Paiute tribe, of which Posey and Jim Mike were members, have never had a lasting reservation, their homeland having been folded into the Navajo Reservation, and not until 1980 were they even officially recognized as a tribe.

The origins of Posey's War can be traced to a single incident in May 1914. According to one version of the story, Juan Chacón, a Hispanic herder from New Mexico, was on his way home from a season of well-paid work in Utah. He made the mistake of stopping to play cards with a group of Utes and Paiutes in a camp near the Utah-Colorado border, and he won most of the pots. As he rode on south the next day, he was trailed by one of the losers, who ambushed Chacón, shot him three times, and hurriedly buried him in a wash not far from the "toe" of Sleeping Ute Mountain, southwest of today's town of Cortez.

A few days later, five Utes reported the murder to the government agent at nearby Navajo Springs, headquarters of the Weeminuche Ute reservation established in 1896. After visiting the scene of the crime and disinterring Chacón, the agent sent out word asking for the alleged murderer to turn himself in. That man was Tse-ne-gat ("Silver Earrings"), a twenty-six-year-old already making a name for himself as a rebel against white authority, or, in Anglo terms, as a "troublemaker."

It's here that the record becomes murky. It's not even clear whether Tse-ne-gat (also known to Anglos as Everett Hatch) was a Ute or a Paiute. Historian Robert McPherson asserts the former without hesitation; other sources just as firmly peg the young man as a Paiute. Intermarriage between the tribes was so frequent that the distinction sometimes became almost meaningless. But one source quotes, without attribution, a taunt that Tse-ne-gat supposedly uttered while still an adolescent: "Me no Paiute. Paiutes scared of dark." (I'll assume, then, that Tse-ne-gat was indeed a Ute.)

What is clear is that by 1914, Tse-ne-gat and his father, Narraguinip ("Polk" to Anglos, or "Poke" or "Old Poke") were feared even by the men they rode with. The formal deposition of one of the Utes who reported the murder of Chacón complains that "we were afraid of this Indian and his father, as they were known as bad men, the father, Polk, having killed a number of Indians . . . , and we now fear that he will try to kill us for having told this." An 1884 account in a local periodical, sounding the alarm about dangerous Indians, stated that "The Narraguinip band is composed of renegades from Uncompahgre [Ute], Paiutes, Navajos, and other tribes, and is not recognized at any agency."

In May 1914 Tse-ne-gat and his father apparently came close to turning themselves in, but instead rode past the Navajo Springs agency all the way back to their habitual range in Allen Canyon, underneath Elk Ridge and the Bears Ears buttes. McPherson quotes a woman named Stella Eyetoo who knew Narraguinip (also referred to as Billy Hatch), who swore that the man "was believed to hold supernatural power that made him bulletproof." In May 1914 the commissioner at Navajo Springs passed on the rumor that Narraguinip's band "were coming to the agency in force and if an attempt was made to arrest young Hatch [Tse-ne-gat] and take him away they will kill anyone making the attempt."

Thus began an impasse that would last for ten months, surge into an armed battle that would cost lives on both sides, put all of Utah into an uproar, and make national headlines. If Tse-ne-gat was innocent of the killing of Juan Chacón, as he always insisted he was, his refusal to turn himself in at Navajo Springs can be attributed to the distrust of white authority he and his father had long harbored. If the Utes who reported the Hispanic herder's murder pinned it falsely on Tse-ne-gat, they might well have viewed the deed as a convenient way to get rid of a volatile young warrior they already deeply feared.

In September 1914, Deputy Marshal David Thomas had a chance to arrest Tse-ne-gat when the man made a brief visit to a store in Bluff. But the lawman backed off, fearing that the townsfolk of Bluff were so terrified of retribution at the hands of Tse-ne-gat and Polk that they would offer no support for the arrest. Instead, Thomas feebly won Tse-ne-gat's pledge to surrender the following day—a pledge he predictably ignored.

Through autumn and into winter, the impasse festered. The killing of a single itinerant herder from New Mexico—not even an "American," as the newspapers defined him, but a "Mexican"—hardly seemed pretext enough for the campaign that mounted through the cold months, as federal marshals, officers in the Department of Indian Affairs, and the governor of Utah mulled plans for the capture of Tse-ne-gat. The band of loyalists his father commanded hardly numbered more than twenty-five, but the same newspapers inflated it to a horde of as many as 150 "Bronco" Indians.

By 1915, it had been twenty-nine years since the last tribe to wage war against the US government—the Chiricahua Apaches under Geronimo—had surrendered. It had been twenty-five years since the army had wildly overreacted to the Ghost Dance revival among the Lakota in South Dakota and massacred more than 250 men, women, and children. The romanticization of the Indian, as a doomed but noble antagonist clinging to a migratory lifestyle and a superstitious religion, was well under way. By 1914, in a sense the newspapers reflected a public hunger for yet one more Indian war, even as colonists turned their old paranoia about the "redskins" into a clamor for severe justice.

The winter of 1914–15 was a harsh one, with snows said to be the heaviest in twenty years. Facing lean rations and even the threat of starvation, Polk's band, along with Posey and his followers, left the icebox of Allen Canyon and set up quarters along the San Juan between Sand Island and Bluff. In Allen Canyon, the ground lay under four feet of snow, but in wickiups and tents on south-facing sand dunes the Utes and Paiutes made the most of the wan sun and the thin snow cover.

Meanwhile, in February, Marshal Aquila Nebeker started organizing a major campaign to capture Tse-ne-gat without engaging in an all-out battle with the Polk-Posey forces. Operating out of Cortez, Nebeker hoped to sign up recruits and move his "troops" toward Bluff in secret, but the newspapers eagerly broadcast the developments. The citizens of Bluff felt caught in the impending squeeze. The temper of the day burst into headlines on February 22. "Bluff at Mercy of Hostile Redskins," announced the *Salt Lake Tribune*. Other journalists regarded the marshal's volunteer army with jaundiced eyes. "Nebeker made the mistake," wrote one, "of gathering a posse of men composed chiefly of the rougher element of the cowpunchers. These proceeded to tank up in anticipation of the coming fun with the Indians." Another journalist summed up the posse as "booze fighters, gamblers, and bootleggers" who approached the upcoming skirmish "as if they were going rabbit hunting."

The real battle erupted on February 22. Nebeker had hoped to surprise the Indians by encircling them with attackers from both west and east, trying to move the men into position before the Indians would notice. But a barking dog gave away the plot. Despite having stayed up all night playing cards, Polk and Tse-ne-gat, along with their twenty-five–odd warrior allies, flung themselves into position, using the sand dunes as cover. The first casualty was a member of the posse named Joseph Akin, who raised his head over a ridge of earth to get a bead on the target below, only to fall dead with a bullet to the forehead. Years later, Polk bragged to a local trader about how he had wielded his ancient .35 Winchester rifle to pull off the perfect shot. He had "used all of his sights and the bullet landed on line about twenty-five yards short. The next time he shot he used the end of his barrel for a sight and shot the man right between the eyes."

Posey, on the west side of the encampment, recorded the next coup, shooting an attacker named José Cordova through the torso. Nebeker's forces numbered some seventy-five men, while the defenders included women, children, and elderly men. The posse eventually killed four Utes and Paiutes, one of them an unarmed man who was a friend to many Bluff residents, another as he ran out to save his six-year-old daughter from gunfire on both sides. Six men who wanted no part of the fight surrendered. They were sequestered on the second floor of the San Juan Co-op in Bluff. One of them, a son-in-law of Polk, managed to pull off his handcuffs and jumped out the window of the Co-op, only to be shot point-blank by a guard. He died three days later in excruciating pain.

The defenders succeeded in depriving four posse members of their horses and guns. Those four were feared dead until they showed up sheepishly in Bluff, having walked to town bereft of their arms and mounts.

Nebeker's grand plan had been to encircle the renegade Indians, but with the outcome of the battle still uncertain, the headline of the *Salt Lake Herald-Republican* screamed, "Indians Surround Marshal's Posse: Whites Taken by Surprise; Bluff in Danger." By February 23, all the warriors in the Polk-Posey band had fled, escaping down the San Juan River. Most of their family members escaped with them. The great attack had ended without the loss of a single Ute or Paiute combatant.

If the news out of Utah had reached ears all over the United States before February 22, now it took on truly national import. President Woodrow Wilson decided that the "uprising" deserved the full attention of the US Army, so he dispatched chief of staff Brigadier General Hugh Scott to try to resolve the impasse. In 1890 Scott had been in charge of the suppression of the Ghost Dance in South Dakota, and the massacre at Wounded Knee would stand as his lasting legacy, an atrocity almost without parallel in American history. But a quarter century later, Scott's views about Indians had dramatically changed, and in the outcome of the Polk-Posey-Tse-ne-gat debacle, he would play an enlightened and benevolent role.

By now the furor over the renegade band had far outgrown the murder
of a Hispanic herder ten months before. At the core of the disturbance
was the old assumption, which had bedeviled the country's relations with
Native Americans for most of the previous century, that Indians should
stay on the reservations the government had provided for them. But Polk,
Tse-ne-gat, and Posey wanted nothing to do with the Weeminuche Ute
Reservation over in Colorado: that was not their homeland. Moreover, no
lasting reservation had ever been allotted to the San Juan Paiutes.

By the beginning of March, the Polk-Posey band had retreated to the
area around Douglas Mesa on the Navajo Reservation, a good forty miles
as the crow flies west of Bluff, across roadless terrain unfamiliar to Anglos.
All kinds of official machinations took place between the shootout near
Bluff and General Scott's arrival in Bluff on March 10. But almost at once,
an unlikely resolution arrived, seemingly out of nowhere.

We will never know precisely how General Scott was able to talk
Polk, Posey, and Tse-ne-gat into surrendering. A crucial first step was
to send Nebeker and his ragtag posse packing. The intervention of two
go-betweens—a Navajo named Bizhóshi, whom Scott had arrested and
befriended the year before; and Louisa Wetherill, John Wetherill's wife,
who from their trader's outpost at Kayenta had mastered the Diné tongue
and won the trust of more Navajos than any other Anglo up to that
time—was crucial. A potent additional factor was the wretched condition
of the refugees on Douglas Mesa. It was still winter up there, at 5,700 feet,
with freezing rain and snow in deep drifts. Some of the ponies died. The
thirty-five refugees, including women and children, who had completed
the flight from the San Juan were short on bedding, clothing, and food.

From a new base in Mexican Hat, Scott sent out his emissaries. Louisa
Wetherill wrung a promise from the general that he would not allow the
three main perpetrators of the "rebellion" to be hanged. On March 18,
Posey and four of his followers showed up in Mexican Hat. Before any
bargaining could take place, Scott gave the Indians flour, coffee, and a
butchered cow, as well as blankets for the families warily camped in hiding outside of town on the other side of the San Juan. The next day Polk,

Tse-ne-gat, and ten other followers arrived. In the parley that ensued, according to one source, Posey spoke for the group in his broken English. "Pony die," he complained, and "Allatime papoose cry." "Squaw mad," "Hand cold" (he held his hands over an imaginary fire), "Allatime belly heap flat." Then the clinching pledge: "Indians no make war."

Scott earnestly insisted that he wanted no harm to come to his "Indian friends." But he hoped to convince four of them—Tse-ne-gat, Polk, Posey, and his son, Jess Posey—to go to Salt Lake City, where the last three would be tried for their role in the February 22 battle. Tse-ne-gat, who had been indicted in Denver for Juan Chacón's murder, would then make the long trip to the Colorado capital for his own trial. Scott promised that he would travel to Salt Lake City with his wards, if they agreed to go. To the general's delight, they answered, "We are going to do just what you tell us to do."

It is at this point that the drama of outlaw Indians brought to justice begins to turn to farce. Or perhaps vaudeville. The four captives traveled from Bluff to Moab on horseback and mail wagon. There they were surrounded by onlookers who, unlike the frightened residents of Bluff, regarded them more as curiosities than as dangerous outlaws, offering them cigarettes and asking them to pose for photographs. Scott had already proclaimed his belief in his captors' innocence: "These Indians are poor ignorant grown-up children who have had no advantages and no knowledge of our laws and customs. They are victims of mutual misunderstanding between two well meaning races."

At Thompson Springs, north of Moab, the four boarded the train for Salt Lake City. Everything about the iron horse was a novelty, and the prisoners were treated like royalty. They were delighted to be served breakfast in a comfortable dining car on a moving train. The railroad superintendent offered each of the four a pricey twenty-five-cent cigar, a form of tobacco none of the Indians had previously encountered. All four men smoked eight cigars each, back-to-back. In Salt Lake a crowd of 5,000 greeted the entourage. Taken to the county jail, the captives were overjoyed to reunite with four of their brethren who had surrendered in Bluff.

In the courtroom, Scott himself took on the role of defense lawyer.

He hammered away at how Nebeker had launched the battle near Bluff, pointing out that the posse had made no attempt to identify themselves, had presented no arrest warrant, and had not even explained a reason for attacking. He made short shrift of the pusillanimous district attorney. "Did the posse wear uniforms so that they could be identified as marshals and not a mob?" he stabbed.

"Well, no," answered the attorney.

"Then where is your case?"

"I guess we haven't got one."

The trial ended with the seven captives' pledge to return to the Weeminuche reservation and live there as law-abiding wards of the government. Polk even offered an abject plea of guilt: He "put his hand on his heart and declared he now saw clearly that he had been blind before, that his heart was bad, but that now he knew his duty and would do it."

Before they left Salt Lake, the acquitted Indians were treated to rides in electric trolleys and automobiles, demonstrations of the miracle of the telephone, and matinees at the movies. In the end, the seven never did return to the Weeminuche reservation, but simply headed back to Bluff and Allen Canyon and took up again the life they had led before the one-day "war" broke out.

In Denver General Scott was not present to defend Tse-ne-gat, but a pair of lawyers competently pleaded his case. By now the Indian Rights Association had taken a keen interest in the trial, and local representatives lent their indignation to the courtroom drama. Even the prosecuting attorney sensed the odds against conviction; in McPherson's paraphrase, "He recognized that the murder victim had been a Mexican, that Scott was a hero who supported Tse-ne-gat, [and] that the Ute people were afraid of Polk." The newspapers had a field day, saluting "the most thrilling criminal trial ever held in Denver," and their headlines milked a public sympathy for the Indian in the dock: "Mother of Tse-ne-gat Braves Terrors of Railroad Engines To Be at Son's Side," and "Indian Simplicity Baffles the Court."

The trial lasted nine days. The jury deliberated seven hours before returning a verdict of not guilty.

After the trial was over, Tse-ne-gat was lionized as a hero. A reporter gave him a ride on a motorcycle. "Chug horse go like hell," commented the passenger, "buck like hell, bump wind out of Tse-ne-gat." He posed for photos in the driver's seats of his admirers' autos. He allegedly received four offers of marriage from Denver women, and a fifth suitor, from Chicago, where she had been smitten by photos of the defendant, offered to pay his travel expenses if he would come to Illinois to accept her proposal.

Wearing "a string of cheap medals pinned on one side of his breast," Tse-ne-gat boarded the train to return to Utah. There he rejoined his father's people. Around Bluff, residents were convinced that the man had gotten away with murder, and they "tried to steer clear of him."

Tse-ne-gat did not have long to enjoy the freedom he had regained. While in Denver, he had been admitted to a hospital after complaining of chest pains. The doctors told him he had tuberculosis.

He died in January 1922, still only thirty-three years old.

◄◄ ►►

Tse-ne-gat's exoneration and his return to his old haunts changed nothing. For eight more years, the same tensions between the "renegade" Utes and Paiutes in Allen Canyon and along the San Juan River and the Anglos in Monticello, Blanding, and Bluff kept flaring into punitive action and sometimes into violence. Each episode might have provoked another battle like the one that played out on February 22, 1915, but cooler heads, acts of forgiveness, and sometimes simple fear kept a second "war" from breaking out. Yet underneath those years of tension pulsed a thread of inevitability, as if the ancient Greek gods of vengeance—the Eumenides, daughters of night; and Nemesis, "the Inescapable"—were in charge in San Juan County.

The deeds could be trivial: grazing a Ute horse in a field that belonged to a Mormon, cutting down fences the Indians had raised so that a rancher could move his cattle through, even so small an act as stealing food from a warehouse or storage shed. Some Anglo settlers hated all the Indians; others, like Henry McCabe, respected them greatly. (Knowing that his own cows ranged into Ute lands, he asked permission of those neighbors, and he trusted them not to pilfer from a cache of 1,500 pounds of sugar, flour, and honey he left unguarded—which the Utes didn't, though they were often plagued by hunger.) Yet over those eight years, familiarity bred the illusion of harmony. In Blanding, especially, the townsfolk got to know the friendlier Utes and Paiutes, and even the kids sometimes played together.

The anger and misunderstanding beneath the surface that would finally explode into "the last Indian war" had roots too deep for most of the principals fully to grasp at the time. By moving into the greater Bears Ears domain, building towns, planting fields, and running cattle and sheep, the Mormons had upended the ancient nomadism, based on a hunter-gatherer way of life, of the Numic people they displaced. The solution Anglos tendered—settling the Indians on reservations run by white officials—sprang from a myopia as to just how deeply interwoven were Ute/Pauite culture and that nomadism. Shortly after Poke and Posey returned from Salt Lake City in 1915, they were asked why they had not honored the pledge they had made to go to the Weeminuche reservation in Colorado. Both men denied they had ever promised to do so. The Ute translator, they insisted, had botched the courtroom exchange of words.

Posey was born near Navajo Mountain in the early 1860s. His father was Paiute; some say his mother was Mexican. His given name was Sagwageri (Green Hair), though he was never known to Anglos by that appellation. He gained the name Posey, at least as far as Mormons were concerned, because of his supposed admiration for a cowboy named Bill Posey. While young, he married Turah, the sister of Narraguinip or Polk, thus cementing his ties with Utes. After eight years of marriage, one day his gun misfired and he shot Turah by accident. A devastated Posey ran on foot to summon a midwife from Bluff, but Turah died three days later. According to one source, Posey "was heartbroken and mourned for her the remainder of his life." Later, after Posey became infamous for his hostility to the Mormons, he was accused by them of killing his wife in cold blood.

By the 1920s, Posey hung out in Allen Canyon in the warm months, along the San Juan west of Bluff through the winter. But he was also a familiar figure in the streets of Blanding. One longtime resident, William Riley Hurst, recalled half a century later the terror Posey struck in his heart when he was just "a little kid."

> Wesley Barton and I were riding up the road . . . about a mile south of [Blanding] and we met Old Posey. He was riding south and he had this famous black mare that he used to have. He was jogging down through the dust and he always wore that pearl-handled six shooter on his hip. Wesley was kind of a smart alec as a kid. . . . I had told him that I was scared of Posey and he said "Oh, I'm not scared of Posey. He's a good old Indian you know." When we got up there . . . , he made some kind of smart alec remark and Old Posey whipped that six shooter around and I looked in the end of that damned thing and I know it had a 4 inch hole in that barrel. Boy he wasn't fooling. I thought he was going to kill us. So he finally ripped off a lot of threatening talk in Ute which we couldn't understand and put his gun back in his holster and went on down the road.

The event that triggered "Posey's War" began as a depredation performed by two young Utes that might have had no more lasting repercussions than any of scores of insults and petty crimes that had taken place over the previous eight years. The perpetrators, though in their twenties, were known to the Mormons as Joe Bishop's Little Boy and Sanáp's Boy. (The patronizing tone of such namings may have been one more factor that contributed to the decades of antagonism between Indians and Anglos in Utah.) On January 10, 1923, those men killed a sheep that belonged to a Hispanic herder on a mesa just east of Blanding, and also robbed the man's camp. When the herder showed up, the Utes drove him away on foot. The herder happened to be Desidirio Chacón, a relative of Juan Chacón, killed near Navajo Springs in 1914.

Chacón complained to his boss in Blanding, who filed a complaint, but nothing came of it at first. Two months later, however, Blanding sheriff Bill Oliver, accompanied by Joe Bishop himself, drove up to the Ute camp and arrested the young men. Since Blanding lacked a jail, the sheriff turned the pair over to his deputy sheriff, who kept them for several days in the basement of a house he was building on the west edge of town, with a couple of volunteers wielding rifles to guard them. To ensure fairness, the young men's fathers showed up with their own rifles to guard the guards.

At this point, the story becomes complicated. One night, after eating scalloped potatoes served by the deputy sheriff's wife, Joe Bishop's Little Boy became very ill. The next day his older brother showed up, raging, "All night boy shook like poisoned coyote. Mebbe so die!" Blanding citizens would later conclude that the young Ute was faking his illness, but the deputy sheriff, relenting, released the two prisoners on the promise that they would show up for their trial in the Desidirio Chacón case.

And sure enough, the two did return for the trial. Joe Bishop's Little Boy and Sanáp's Boy were found guilty. The sentence would have been mild—perhaps ten days' confinement—but a quirky local law required a six-hour moratorium between verdict and sentencing. After the courtroom had emptied, Sheriff Oliver took the "boys" out for lunch. And at that moment, everything went wrong.

Two young Blandingites witnessed the fracas and recalled what they had seen decades later. Their oddly discrepant accounts reflect the ambiguity that would forever linger about the event that triggered Posey's War. Ervin Guymon, a seventh-grader, returned from his own lunch at home to the courtroom (which was in the basement of the school building) just in time to witness the outburst.

[Sheriff Oliver] mounted on his big brown horse and rode to where those two young fellows were and said, "Come on and I will take you to dinner." This one young fellow said, "You can go to hell." He could speak fairly good English. So the sheriff drew his six-shooter from his holster because he could see that this young fellow was trying to get away. He aimed the gun right to his head and pulled the trigger one, two or three times and his gun wouldn't go off. I was standing probably twenty feet from him, watching everything that was going on. Old Chief Posey was there. . . .

But Josephine Bayles, a fifteen-year-old who watched the confrontation from the school window, remembered:

I could see the Indians that were seated on the ground and on horses around in a circle. Of course, the Ute boys had quite a following of sympathizers who sat around in glum silence. The sheriff's horse stood in the circle with its reins dragging the ground. Joe Bishop's Boy sat twirling a round stick about two-feet long. As the sheriff stood up and walked toward his horse, the Ute boy strolled over to one of the Ute boys['] horses. . . . As the boy mounted the Ute horse, the sheriff took the horse's bridle. The Ute boy grabbed the sheriff's six-shooter from its holster as another boy attempted to cut the reins from the sheriff's hand. . . . The sheriff tried to snatch the gun, but the boy was too quick. He pointed the gun to the officer's face and pulled the trigger.

To say the least, we were all just breathless with fright. To our amazement the weapon didn't explode, it merely clicked. Twice more the trigger was pulled. Each time a click was the result.

Whatever sudden outburst set in motion the fatal chain of events, whoever pulled the trigger on the gun that three times failed to fire, the immediate aftermath is not in dispute. Joe Bishop's Little Boy took off on a horse, riding pell-mell through the Blanding streets, with Sheriff Oliver on his own horse in close pursuit. The sheriff appeared to be gaining on the escapee, when the Ute turned in the saddle and fired again. This time the six-shooter worked. The bullet struck the sheriff's horse in the chest. Whether the horse was "crippled" (Bayles) or only mildly stunned (Guymon), the skillful or lucky shot enabled Joe Bishop's Little Boy's getaway.

At this juncture, the strange incident might still have remained a localized disturbance. Whoever tried to shoot and kill, no one had yet been injured. But here the Furies intervened, casting their retributive spell on San Juan County.

In the confusion, Posey had likewise fled with Sanáp's Boy. Even while volunteers joined the sheriff in pursuit of Joe Bishop's Little Boy, others decided that "all the stray Utes around the country, men, women, and children, should be brought into town and held until the trouble was over." A kind of mass paranoia had seized Blanding, reinforcing the suspicion some residents held that Posey had planned some such uprising for weeks, even if it led to all-out war between Mormons and Indians.

In 1923 only the Utes and Paiutes closest to Posey could have known, and today, nearly a century on, the truth of it lies forever beyond retrieval— but a legend has come down to us that Posey had long envisioned a world freed for good of the Mormon invaders, even if it took an apocalyptic conflict to bring it about. Thus historians Steve Lacy and Pearl Baker assert, without either qualification or attribution, that as the fragile truce in southeast Utah began to fray,

> Posey was elated, but whether it was mere love of violence, or restlessness, or hatred is moot. He dreamed of taking his followers in a body, with their families, goats, and horses, into the canyons, and when the white men came, victory would be his. He only dreamed. He didn't make any plans to carry out a campaign, and before he knew it, the explosion came.

That legend may be merely the projection of Blanding paranoia. But it's also possible that Posey partook of the kind of messianic dream, often a visionary refuge for Native Americans under white oppression, that the Lakota shamans who revived the Ghost Dance in 1890 claimed to foresee.

The escape of Joe Bishop's Little Boy, along with the Blanding response to it, at once split the Indians into two camps. The roundup of "innocent" Utes and Paiutes was surprisingly effective, and after Blanding men built a stockade designed along World War I lines, complete with barbed wire and armed guards, more than eighty prisoners huddled in the center of town in fear and squalor (buckets in the corners serving for outhouses). Edward Dutchie, six years old when he was incarcerated, remembered his terror many years later: "What I heard . . . was that they were going to take us away from our parents and the older people's heads [would be] cut off. . . . One guy said, . . . 'Let it come. Let them cut your head off and forget about yourselves. Try to be brave.'"

Most of the Utes and Paiutes who escaped the roundup joined Posey in headlong flight first south, then west. The ad hoc posse followed, rifles and pistols drawn or ready.

This last of all Indian wars took place, of course, not in the 1890s but in 1923. Cartoonish though it may seem today, the Blanding pursuers called upon all the technology of the day to facilitate the chase. The Indians fled, as they would have in Geronimo's day, on horseback. But at first the posse went after them in Model T Fords. With six veterans of World War I among the pursuers, it's not surprising (though bizarre to contemplate) that there was talk of going after the renegades in airplanes mounted with machine guns. Newspaper reporters from as far off as Chicago descended on San Juan County, and their dispatches echoed the rhetoric of Verdun and the Somme. Blanding "has become more or less an armed camp," wrote the scribe for the *Salt Lake Tribune*. "It bears the aspect of a military headquarters. The arrival and departure of couriers from the front is a matter of public interest."

The general assumption among the lawmen was that Posey intended to lead a flight of his followers onto the Navajo Reservation, perhaps even to the immemorial sanctuary of Navajo Mountain, as the Utes and Paiutes had done in 1915. There was widespread fear that Posey's old ally Polk would join in the resistance. But when a contingent visited Polk in his encampment near Montezuma Creek, the aged Ute proclaimed indifference, even scorn for his old comrade-in-arms: "If you fellows shoot Posey," he was heard to say, "pretty good alright."

The fleeing Indians headed straight south from Blanding for five miles, along the line of today's highway 191, then veered west, crossing Cottonwood Wash to emerge on the low rim above Butler Wash. Among the pursuers, a murderous frenzy held sway, licensed by Sheriff Oliver's orders: "Every man here is deputized to shoot. I want you to shoot everything that looks like an Indian." But Posey was not only a better marksman than nearly all his pursuers, he was better armed, with a Krag .30-06 rifle, and he was mounted on his indomitable black mare. From the saddle he fired backward and sent a bullet through the Model T behind him that passed between two of its three occupants. With another shot he took down the horse ridden by the deputy sheriff.

The posse managed to score some strikes of its own, most notably when a man named Bill Young enticed Joe Bishop's Little Boy and Sanáp's Boy into turning to chase him. Young hid behind a stunted juniper as the two Utes rode by on either side, searching for their enemy. "I just waited until I could see that button on the boy's shirt," Young later said, "and pulled the trigger." Joe Bishop's Little Boy flew out of the saddle, killed with one shot. But Young let Sanáp's Boy escape, and later expressed remorse for his deed—a sentiment in short supply during Posey's War. "It was no fun to kill an injun," he told another member of the posse.

A very curious alternative story about the demise of Joe Bishop's Little Boy has come down to us. In this version, somewhere along the escape route, Posey encountered the young Ute whose breakaway from the Blanding courtroom had triggered the whole debacle. Posey "cursed him for starting the trouble. Weapons were drawn and Posey shot and killed Joe Bishop's Boy."

If this version were true, it would certainly contradict any theory that Posey welcomed or even planned the war that would be named after him in order to realize his apocalyptic dream of a canyon fastness free from Mormon invaders. More likely, it's one more by-product of the confusion that the sudden conflagration unleashed.

It was not Navajo Mountain or any part of the Navajo Reservation toward which Posey directed the fugitive flight. A stronghold far closer to Blanding—only thirteen miles as the crow flies—was his well-considered destination. The chase continued for four days, with the pursuers returning nightly to Blanding for food, ammunition, and reinforcements. The Indian escape took Posey's refugees across Butler Wash, up Comb Ridge to its spiky crest, down a tricky trail on the sheer west side, across Comb Wash, and into the mouth of Mule Canyon, on the eastern edge of Cedar Mesa.

The Anglo narrative of Posey's War is the one preserved in the written record. According to that account, the pivotal act was performed by a man named Dave Black, alleged to be a marksman equal to Posey, a veteran of the storied hunt for the Apache Kid in the 1890s, an antagonist of Pancho Villa, and a recruiter who had helped Mormons from the polygamous colonies in Mexico resettle in San Juan County.

Somewhere near the crest of Comb Ridge, Black caught sight of Posey, riding hard to catch up with members of his band. Black and other posse members started shooting. In one telling, "Posey was hanging down on the right side of his mare, running up the ridge as fast as he could make the little mare go, shooting under her neck as he used her for a shield. But his hind parts were high in the saddle. Dave Black drew down, and when he shot, they saw Posey wince and nearly fall off his horse."

Wounded or not, Posey still managed to escape Black and two other pursuers, as he disappeared into the corners of Mule Canyon. Incredibly, the denouement of Posey's War would not arrive for another month.

The stronghold where Posey settled in to wait out any Mormon attack was a small mesa off Mule Canyon, guarded on all sides by short cliffs, with a single slot between rock buttresses allowing passage to the top. For all their bravado, the posse members, even Sheriff Oliver and Dave Black, were unwilling to assault this refuge. Instead they focused on other Utes and Paiutes, some of them women and children, who in small groups approached their pursuers carrying white cloths to signal surrender. During the next few days, trucks arrived from Blanding to carry these prisoners back to the stockade or to a holding pen in Bluff.

But Posey never surrendered. All through April, men saw a small fire light up the sky each night from different positions on the well-defended mesa. The lawmen assumed these were signals Posey sent out in a desperate effort to rally his allies to his side. But for fear that there were already other warriors ensconced in Posey's hideout, none of the authorities dared launch an attack. When several young Indians, let out of the stockade to tend to Ute horses and goats, returned only days later, it was assumed that they had sneaked into the stronghold to bring Posey supplies. The newspaper headlines thrummed with hollow confidence: "Old Posey Will Be Captured If It Takes Year, U.S. Marshal J. Ray Ward Says."

At last, in late April, the signal fires stopped flaring in the sky above the mesa. At the end of the month, Marshal Ward arrived in a shiny Packard from Salt Lake City to resolve the mystery. Guided by several Utes who now believed Posey must be dead, Ward dared to climb up to the stronghold. He returned after several hours to report that he had found the body. "He is buried where no white man will ever find him," Ward announced. "I assure you that he is dead and everything is taken care of. Things are under control." With that declaration, he jumped into his Packard and headed back to Salt Lake City.

Ward had buried Posey to satisfy the feelings of the Utes who had guided him to the death site, but Blandingites resented the marshal's arrogance. On the very next day, some of them climbed the mesa, discovered the site, and dug up the body. They claimed to find the bullet wound that had transected Posey's hips, and concluded that he had died slowly, agonizingly, of blood poisoning. Dave Black was credited with the lethal shot.

During the following two weeks, three more parties climbed the mesa and again dug up the hastily reburied body. One group posed with Posey's nearly naked corpse laid out in front of them, like a wild animal killed in a trophy hunt. By 1928, the body had vanished.

◄◄ ►►

Thus the version of Posey's death that has come down in the written record. But many Utes and Paiutes refused to believe it. According to them, Posey died not from a gunshot wound but from poisoned flour. Harry Dutchie was one of the boys confined in the Blanding stockade during the 1923 outbreak. Interviewed in 1968, he explained how he thought things had transpired. "When this happened," Dutchie said, "several of the Ute boys come into Blanding and they would say, 'If you'd give me some flour and a blanket or two, I'll go out and find Posey,' you know? And they'd take off and go out there, and then they'd be back in a day or two and say, 'No, we couldn't find him.' And they'd say, 'Well, Where's your flour?' And they'd say, 'Oh, we ate it all,' or something you know?"

Asked by the interviewer, "The white man put poison in the flour?," Dutchie answered, "Uh huh."

Also in 1968, at the age of almost one hundred, Jim Mike, who had fled with Posey as the posse hunted the refugees down, was interviewed by an Anglo, using a Paiute interpreter as go-between. Jim Mike elaborated on the story: "It was Poke's little brother . . . that found him first. And he was laying down and he had a bread he was eating around him and he had a bread in his hand." The interviewer parried, "When they found him he also had a bullet in his side right here in his hip."

Jim Mike answered: "They didn't shoot him, he wasn't shot; he was poisoned with flour and he had flour on his hands. . . . Old Posey wasn't shot. He was buried and they dug him up and shot him. That's how the white man are, Mormon!" Jim Mike went on, quietly bitter: "So they can tell it the way they want to tell it. . . . So they can make a history of it."

With Posey's death in 1923, the spirit of violent resistance attenuated among his tribe, which really had never amounted to more than a loose band of loyal Paiutes and Utes. Never again would Native Americans in San Juan County mount anything like an armed battle against their white neighbors. And over the decades, the image of Posey among his former antagonists softened. While he lived, many whites regarded him as a villain, or at least as a dangerous man capable of atrocities and even murder.

By 1963, when he wrote *The Outlaw of Navaho Mountain*—a roman á clef for Posey and the last Indian war—Albert Lyman's views had changed. Lyman's initial contempt for the Paiutes had posited them as the most backward and evil of all tribes in the Southwest. Even in the early pages of that late novel, he reverts to snide aspersions about the "inbred indolence" of "the little snarl of Paiute invaders." But Lyman had known Posey since he was an eleven-year-old boy playing in the Paiute head-man's camp near Bluff. In an epilogue to *Outlaw*, forty years after Posey's death, Lyman insists, "I did not regard him as a bad man. He was not bad at heart. Deep in his undisciplined soul were the intrinsic elements of manhood—courage, loyalty, and love."

Likewise, after considerable research, local historian Bradley Jensen, too young to have known Posey, found him sympathetic, even noble. "My view of Chief Posey," Jensen wrote in 2009, "is now of a man who loved his family, his nation and his birthright. His core values are not unlike those of many of my heros [*sic*] like Washington, Lincoln and Churchill. He was willing to fight and die for what he believed in."

Yet neither has Posey been retrospectively elevated to the status of a hero martyred for his people, as such other Native American leaders as Geronimo, Chief Joseph, and Crazy Horse have been. He lingers, almost a century after his death, in a historical and moral limbo.

In the 1950s, Utes who owned land near Blanding started building houses on a prairie shelf along Highway 191 twelve miles south of that town. It soon became a community with its own gas station, convenience store, community center, and, yes, LDS church. Though only 15.5 square miles in size, with a population of roughly 380, White Mesa felt the need for more formal recognition. Yet it was not until the 1950s that the community became a reservation, though even then, technically, as an adjunct to the Ute Mountain Ute Reservation (founded in 1934) with headquarters at Towaoc, Colorado.

I'd like to learn how the folks at White Mesa feel today about Posey, but I know better than to just barge into town and start asking. In 2008, I got deeply involved in a mystery that sprang from a remembered tale of a Navajo elder, deceased by then, but alive in the heart of his granddaughter. One day in the 1930s, Aneth Nez was tending his sheep along the crest of Comb Ridge, a few miles south of the San Juan River. He heard cries and noises coming from a draw three hundred feet below. Peering from the rim, he watched several Utes chasing, then murdering, an Anglo youth who was traveling through with a pair of pack animals. After the Utes had gone, stealing the young man's belongings and animals, Nez had carried the body up to the crest of the Comb and buried it in a crevice.

The old tale uncannily jibed with the mysterious end of Everett Ruess, the vagabond poet-artist whose disappearance in Utah in 1934 had never been solved. I had written about Ruess before, and would soon write his biography. And for months several of us believed that we might well have found the crevice in which Everett had been interred.

During those months, the buzz about our possible discovery spread across Utah and beyond, for Everett Ruess had become a cult hero half a century after his disappearance.

One day I stopped at the gas station and the convenience store on White Mesa and started asking. Had anybody heard about the Utes who'd maybe killed a young Anglo wanderer not far south of here back in the 1930s? If so, what did they think about the story?

Nope, nobody had heard a word about this long-ago tragedy. Nobody knew about the fuss we were creating all over Utah as we sought out the young man's grave. Nobody even bothered to doubt whether the tale could be true.

That's what they told me in 2008. In 2020, I guessed, I wouldn't learn much more about Old Posey from the folks at White Mesa. What they thought, if anything, about that firebrand, that visionary, (that martyr?), ninety-seven years after his death, they'd keep to themselves. I couldn't argue. Posey was theirs, not mine.

EIGHT

COUNTDOWN TO SHOWDOWN

B y the beginning of 2020, more than two years had passed since President Trump had reduced the Bears Ears National Monument by 85 percent, leaving only 202,000 acres protected instead of Obama's 1.35 million. In the courts, the resolution of the dispute dragged on at its characteristic snail's pace. On September 30, 2019, a federal district judge ruled in favor of the Native American tribes and organizations such as Friends of Cedar Mesa and Patagonia, which had sued to reverse the evisceration of the monument. But Trump and two secretaries of the interior had vowed to take the case all the way to the Supreme Court, and supporters of full monument preservation tried to suppress their fears that the Trump-packed highest court, with new justices Kavanaugh and Gorsuch, might confirm the tattered patchwork that a presidential decree had flung in the faces of environmentalists on December 4, 2017. Meanwhile, months passed after the September 2019 ruling by the federal district judge without a new development.

Cautious optimists such as myself dared to wonder whether the best scenario might be a delay that crawled on through November 2020. Then, if Trump were defeated in his bid for reelection, might a new Democratic president simply put Obama's monument back on the map? But Josh Ewing, executive director of Friends of Cedar Mesa, threw a dishpan full of water on my hopes, outlining five different scenarios of what might unfold over the coming year, ranging from the best he could imagine to a defeat that would have him, he joked, "thinking about jumping off North Six Shooter" (a stunning pinnacle smack in the middle of the monument). Ewing concluded, "Anyway, it's clearly a lifetime project to see this area protected. . . . In no scenario is there not a boatload of work to be done in the next decade."

The bitter Utah conflict that pits residents and lawmakers who abhor federal control of the state's most stunning landscapes against wilderness advocates (many of them, like me, living far from Cedar Mesa) is no recent development. For many decades, Utah has been the state with the second-highest proportion of federal land to private and state-owned, at 64.9 percent of the total. (Nevada ranks first, at a whopping 84.9 percent, but for some reason the denizens of the Silver State have been slow to register their outrage.)

It's also worth reflecting that Utah, in the guise of the New Zion, was founded in 1847 with the Mormon exodus under Brigham Young in a messianic quest to escape forever from the leaden grip of the American fist. Total independence from Washington was what Young's Mormons dreamed of, and for decades they believed they were on the verge of realizing it. Accepting statehood in 1896 was a sour compromise, not the joyous embrace that was shouted through the streets of Denver in 1876 or San Jose in 1850 (Sacramento becoming the capital of California only in 1879.)

The opposition of Utah citizens to the creation of a national monument in 2016, then, was not some new thing. Back in 1964, Canyonlands was set aside as a national park against the strident opposition of folks not only from Moab and Monticello but all around the state. I was in the town of Escalante a few days after President Clinton announced the creation of Grand Staircase–Escalante National Monument in 1996. Many of the front yards brandished signs furiously denouncing the federal takeover. Half a dozen locals bent my ear to skewer Clinton as too gutless to make his proclamation from the land he was sequestering—he'd given his speech instead from the South Rim of the Grand Canyon. Had Clinton showed up in Escalante, a rancher and a motel owner both told me, he'd probably have been lynched.

The same warring camps that would train their artillery on each other around the Bears Ears after 2017 faced off on a much more minor scale, but with every bit as strong convictions, in a shallow canyon just east of Blanding three years earlier. It all had to do with a trail, or a track, or a road that meandered along the creek between cliffs no taller than two hundred feet. Whether that byway was a trail or a road, and when it was created, would turn out to fuel antagonisms that stopped just short of fisti-cuffs and even gunfire, as well as furnishing key points in the legal wran-gling that flowed from the confrontation for years afterward.

Unprepossessing though it seems, Recapture Canyon was a prime hang-out for the Anasazi. Blanding locals such as Winston Hurst had wandered unfettered up and down the canyon for decades, but it was federal land, administered by the BLM. And in 2007, that agency shut down the trail/track/road to motorized vehicles, citing severe damage already inflicted on ancient habitation sites and the threat of even worse if Jeeps and ATVs and motorbikes continued to barrel through the canyon.

In 2007 Durango journalist Andrew Gulliford had hiked through Recapture, and he was shocked by what he saw. As he later wrote in *High Country News*, a left-leaning publication strong on environmental issues,

> Somebody, or more likely several people, had created an illegal all-terrain vehicle trail on Bureau of Land Management land. Sections of the trail ran right through 1,000-year-old Ancestral Puebloan archaeological sites, bisecting one prehistoric village the size of a football field—all this in a place that archaeologists have described as a "mini-Mesa Verde." The scar through Recapture Canyon, just east of Blanding, Utah, is seven miles long and four feet wide.

Gulliford's smashing of the fire-alarm box was countered by locals who insisted that nobody was more respectful of ruins and rock art than Jeepers and ATVers, and that besides, the "trail" was no illegal recent concoction, but an "existing road" that showed up on regional maps dating back at least to 1968. As an "existing road"—San Juan County Road 5314, in fact—it lay, or so the locals argued, outside BLM jurisdiction. Nonetheless, the BLM shut it down in 2007, and so it remained for seven years.

In February 2014, San Juan County formally requested a right-of-way for the infamous road. Proponents argued that motorized access to the glories of Recapture might actually boost tourism: "We feel," they wrote, "this trail could generate national interest, and we may see many people making the ride." The BLM, with regional headquarters in Monticello, had long negotiated an uneasy truce with locals who deeply resented federal control of their favorite recreation areas. Now, instead of reasserting its 2007 closure of the road, the BLM opted for the lazy compromise of calling for public comment on the proposal.

A not-so-brief aside here. Like many outdoorsmen and outdoorswomen whose background, upbringing, and schooling are similar to mine, I've always despised all-terrain vehicles. My friend Vaughn Hadenfeldt assigns their drivers to the catch-all category "Bubbas." ATVs are of course illegal in the canyons on Cedar Mesa, but they're the favorite mode of transportation for pothunters, and far too often both Vaughn and I have come across their unmistakable tire tracks leading up to remote alcoves in which fresh gouges in the dirt betoken rampant looting. The cartoon image of a cigar-chomping, beer-swilling, overweight Bubba hotrodding his ATV across the cryptobiotic soil fits all too smugly in my private gallery of eco-villains. In 2019, on a visit to the Blanding cemetery in a search for pioneer gravestones, I was bemused to discover a handsome slab of white marble emblazoned with the names of seven members of a local family, the rubric "Our Children," and a single icon: that of a full-suited pilot (helmet, visor, leather gloves) at the controls of an ATV as he (she?) guns it toward the hereafter.

Yet when I stop and cross-examine that stereotype, I have to question my snobbish condescension to the Bubbas for whom the Bears Ears is the backyard playground in which they grew up. One January in the 1970s,

I led ten students from Hampshire College in western Massachusetts on a winter-mountaineering trip into the Crestone group of the Sangre de Cristo Range of Colorado. In ten days of hiking, camping, and climbing 14,000-foot peaks, we saw no one else. But on the hike out, tromping down South Colony Creek on snowshoes, we ran into four or five snowmobilers heading in. I stopped to talk to them. They were from Del Norte, the blue-collar town just across the San Luis Valley from the Crestones, out for a long weekend of fun in *their* backyard. My students refused even to say hello to these intruders on their noisy machines, and once we had parted ways with the Del Norte crew, a couple of Hampshire pundits held forth about how disgusting it was to have to share the wilderness with these gas-guzzling bozos.

By then I was starting to get fed up with my students' elitism, and beginning to question my own motives for teaching climbing (which was life itself for me) to dilettantes for whom it was just one more casual delight. So I stopped my charges in their tracks and delivered a tirade. How much gas did they think we had guzzled driving 2,000 miles in the Hampshire van from Massachusetts to Colorado? If you changed oil in an auto shop or waited tables in a café all week, why wouldn't you welcome a snowmobile ride into the outback you saw each morning looming on the eastern horizon? The students were unconvinced, and my sermon did nothing to disperse the black funk in which I clomped on down to the trailhead.

Still, in 2020, I'm not quite willing to open up Cedar Mesa to the ATV crowd, and in Recapture Canyon, I wouldn't have supported the county petition for a right-of-way along the "existing road." What turned the 2014 controversy from a tempest in a teapot into a gun-toting showdown was the arrival of activists from the Sagebrush Rebellion. In March and April 2014, Cliven Bundy's defiance of the BLM over unpaid grazing fees on federal land near Bunkerville, Nevada, had flamed into a nationwide controversy. So when San Juan County Commissioner Phil Lyman organized a protest ride down Recapture Canyon for May 10, it was not surprising that hotheads from the Nevada debacle, including Ryan Bundy, Cliven's son, would show up to lend muscle to the symbolic trespass.

BLM officials also showed up on May 10, determined at first to arrest anyone who rode. The day began in a Blanding park, as speakers detailed the outrages the BLM had perpetrated against locals over the years. The Blanding bust of 2009 was bitterly evoked, with recitations of the Gestapo-style arrests the federal agents had unleashed on the town's citizens, leading to the suicide of Dr. James Redd. Other speakers summoned up the memory of Calvin Black, the uranium magnate and county commissioner in the 1970s caricatured as the villainous Bishop Love in Edward Abbey's *The Monkey Wrench Gang*. Black, some said now, was the original Sagebrush Rebel. His invective against the feds still resonated in Blanding, as in his memorable boast at a meeting with BLM officials in 1979, when he spat out, "We've had enough of you guys telling us what to do. I'm not a violent man, but I'm getting to the point where I'll blow up bridges, ruins, and vehicles. We're going to start a revolution. We're going to get back our lands. We're going to sabotage your vehicles. You had better start going out in twos and threes because we're going to take care of you BLMers."

The speeches invigorated Ryan Bundy's troops, who revved up their motors for the ride, brandishing their guns to back up their civil disobedience. But now Phil Lyman realized he was caught in a bind. Though he had been one of the speakers decrying BLM overreach, now he urged the ATVers to back off the protest ride. According to reporter Jonathan Thompson, Lyman pleaded, "My fear is that this event is looking like conflict for the sake of conflict. I think we do more harm than good to actually cross that line today. It takes a lot of courage to go down that road, it takes a lot of courage to say you know it's going to do more damage than good for our cause today in the media."

Lyman's cautionary advice only further energized Bundy's rebels. "If we don't open it, then we might as well go home right now," Bundy himself shouted out. Another rebel yelled, "To hell with the media." In Thompson's account, "When an older local bemoaned the BLM 'police state,' someone said, 'You've got guns, too. By God, that's what they're for!'"

Swayed by the zeal of the Bundyites, and recognizing that by organizing the protest he had sparked the whole confrontation, Lyman decided to ride down Recapture. He would enter the closed area, but stop and turn around where the road dwindled to a mere trail. Most of the more sensitive ruins lay along that lower trail, which veered closer than necessary to Anasazi sites. In a last-minute decision, the BLM officials showed up not in uniform but in everyday clothes, defusing potential clashes. And they decided to arrest no riders on May 10.

Josh Ewing, who would later become executive director of Friends of Cedar Mesa, hiked into Recapture that day to observe the action. He stationed himself close to Lyman's turnaround point. During a couple of hours, he counted between fifty-five and sixty vehicles that passed by. Half the riders carried firearms, and a few toted assault rifles. Ewing guessed that about half the travelers were Blanding-Monticello folks, the other half Bundyites. Some of the former stopped to chat amicably with Ewing; several of the rebels taunted or provoked him.

Hiking on in the wake of the motorized assault, Ewing mused on the riders' impact. "Some of the places the ATVs passed through," he later wrote, "were so overgrown that it looked like a shredder had passed through. . . . Whenever the trail climbed out of the stream bed onto a bench, there seemed to be significant cultural sites. I saw three multi-room pueblo structures, all of which the old trail had passed through or very close to."

Thanks to the forbearance of the BLM officials and the deputies and officers who policed the event, none of the edgy confrontations between environmental watchdogs and ATV protestors burst into violence. None of the Sagebrush Rebels, in fact, ever got arrested. But a year and a half later, in December 2015, Phil Lyman was found guilty of organizing and participating in the protest ride. He was fined $1,000 and sentenced to ten days in jail, with three years' probation, and he and the sole other defendant, a local blogger who also rode down Recapture, were tagged with a $96,000 bill for restitution of the cultural sites alleged to have been damaged by the ATV caravan.

Lyman served his sentence in April 2016 in the ominously named Purgatory Correctional Facility near St. George in southwest Utah. He emerged defiant but broke. The terms of his probation required that he inform authorities whenever he came in contact with a person with a criminal record. "I said are you kidding?" he told a reporter. "I live in Blanding, Utah. Everyone has a criminal record thanks to you guys. I said my home teacher can't come without me checking in with you."

Three years later, Lyman got his revenge—of a sort. Newly elected to the Utah state House as a representative from San Juan County, he introduced as his first piece of legislation a bill that would make it a criminal misdemeanor for anyone to close or block a state or county road, punishable by ninety days in jail or a $750 fine. And in November 2019, Lyman sued the BLM for $10 million for unlawful collusion in the machinations that led to his arrest after Recapture. As of this writing, the bill has yet to pass the legislature, and the lawsuit is unresolved.

Though I have yet to meet up with the man, I began an e-mail correspondence with Phil Lyman in early 2019. I wasn't surprised that, five years after the protest ride, he was still worked up over the way the Recapture Canyon showdown and the punishment the feds had wreaked upon him had upended his life. "Recapture is not abstract to me," he wrote. "The road I traveled is not a pipeline maintenance road. It's a county road. . . . I was banking on the assumption that the enviro groups would respond exactly as they did—with lies and false accusations, and that the BLM would capitulate to the enviros as they always do."

Lyman had me pegged from the start as one of those "enviros," and so his e-mails were peppered with little digs, such as "If you have actually researched anything about my case. . . ." He even voiced his doubts about whether answering the questions I had sent him was worth the effort: "These are gotcha questions, so I will give them only the time they deserve. As Emerson said, One cannot spend the day in explanation." But as we kept volleying missives back and forth, he opened up in a way that I found moving.

In 2019, the wound inflicted by his critics in the "enviro" press still festered:

> I get people all the time saying things like, "I agree with you on
> a lot of things, but I don't agree with you running over the graves
> of Native Americans with your armed, fat, drunk, Mormon, racist
> group of Cliven Bundy ATV activist, anti American, domestic ter-
> rorist militia, blah blah blah". . . . At that point I know that I am
> speaking to an ideologue and they have set the die. No matter what
> I say, I am 90% sure it will be received on that same level of "sancti-
> monious" dismissiveness.

He took heart in the support he enjoyed locally: "One thing I do know is
that when I walk into a room of cowboys, they take off their hats. They
must believe something about me that the leftist enviros do not."

Indeed, the depth of that local support was impressive. Lyman forwarded to me an apologia for his stance on Recapture that he had posted
on Facebook in 2016. Among the comments from readers were many
that unabashedly portrayed the former county commissioner as a genuine martyr-hero. "Thanks for continuing to fight for our rights through
all the false accusations!" wrote one Amber Rose. "We know who you
are and what you stand for and so does God!" Offered Leslie Nielson,
"Thank you Phil. I totally agree with you, the BLM and the archaeologist
are the real looters." And Joy Howell declared, "I love you! You are a San
Juan County HERO!"

Lyman was aware of my struggles with cancer, and in one e-mail he
let his guard down to detail the personal tragedies he had borne during
his incarceration at the Purgatory Correctional Facility. They included
the death of his "baby sister" from stomach cancer, as well as a hideous
medical ordeal his own daughter endured from "necrotizing pancreatitis."
"The pain she went through and is still going through was unimagina-
ble," he told me. And I was touched by Lyman's almost shy expression of
concern for my own medical ordeal. "I just want you to know that I have
a very small understanding of the trial you are going through," he wrote,
"and my prayers go out to you and those who care about you."

But then, as if embarrassed at turning soft, he reverted to a jocular tone:

"You caught me at a weak moment. Please don't tell your wacko environmentalist friends that I am anything but an inbred Neanderthal."

Still, he closed that e-mail, by far the most personal in our exchange, by signing off, "Your friend, Phil."

◄◄ ►►

During the eleven months between Trump's taking office and his announcement of the vastly reduced Bears Ears monument, the president sent Interior Secretary Ryan Zinke on a tour of the area, as he ostensibly sought opinions about how much of Obama's 1.35 million acres should be preserved. At the same time the department asked for citizens all over the country to express their views online in a massive poll set up by the government. Of the 1.3 million responses available for tally, a remarkable 99 percent voted in favor of retention of the full Obama monument.

Zinke also swore that the needs of the oil and gas industry would have no bearing on the decision he and the president reached. But a leaked e-mail from Utah senator Orrin Hatch's office that offered a map preserving only lands that had no potential for oil and gas extraction ended up coinciding almost exactly with the "new" national monument Trump unveiled in December 2017.

Zinke made a splash on his tour by riding horseback, black cowboy hat on head, as he posed for photo-ops with the Bears Ears buttes in the background. It was no coincidence that the only two Anasazi sites he was guided to—the magisterial Moon House on Cedar Mesa and the winsome but insignificant Doll House up on Elk Ridge—were the two tiny islands of preservation thrown into the revamped monument as a sop to the "enviros."

Even before the Trumpian reduction, advocates for full Bears Ears protection were compiling testimonials to the beauty and cultural significance of those 1.35 million acres—2,109 square miles—of semi-wilderness. By 2020, the six books that had been published about the monument all pleaded for its protection, with titles such as *Voices from Bears Ears: Seek-*

ing Common Ground on Sacred Land and *Edge of Morning: Native Voices Speak for the Bears Ears*. Many of the most powerful testimonies came from Native Americans, whose voices had tended to be drowned out in the polemical uproar while Zinke made his show tour of the region. Regina Lopez-Whiteskunk, a former head councilwoman for the Ute Mountain Ute Tribe, said,

> If the land gets destroyed, we won't have a tool or a mechanism to teach the next generation. We all learn, we're all products of the land, we learn from it. We know how our ancestors adjusted to the adversities they faced, but if the land is plundered, we lose that knowledge because the land is our teacher.

Shonto Begay, a Navajo artist from Arizona, waxed poetic:

> From where I sit, I look into the sanctuary of my childhood. . . . My world was the circular line of the horizon. This was the place that harbored the ancient gods and animal beings that are so alive in our legends. The land is scarred with erosions of rain, yet the corn stands tall, offering yellow pollen for another year.

Yet as I read through these anthologies of impassioned testament, a pair of old qualms crept over me. The first: by stacking their decks so heavily in favor of wilderness advocates, were these books only preaching to the choir? The second had to do with a malaise that too often undercuts my appreciation of Native American rhetoric. There was no doubting the authenticity of the speakers' pleas, but the words that embodied them were so freighted with spiritual gravitas, so disconnected from pragmatic specifics, that it was hard to see how they might stand up against the legal sophistry that Zinke and Trump's technocrats would monger in the courts.

Far less palatable to my sensibility were the effusions of Anglos whose prose seemed to strive for mystical transport as an argument for preservation. It was almost as if these writers envied natives who really did see gods in rock formations rather than geology. An example, from writer Amy Irvine:

> I was born to this landscape, and still the only claim I can make honestly is this: to be a daughter of the desert is to have been born to Demeter, the goddess of fertile, fruitful sustenance as well as barrenness and famine. She rages and withholds, at our forgetting.
>
> Red granules fall like dry tears. Somewhere above the fallout, I can hear my mother's wails.

As I'd come to see, it was all too tempting to caricature locals who opposed the Bears Ears monument as soulless trolls who cared only about making money from oil, gas, uranium, or cattle, and who were indifferent to the ruins and rock art panels of the ancients. Alone among the six books, *Voices from the Bears Ears: Seeking Common Ground on Sacred Land* gives space to those monument naysayers, and their entries contain surprises for the more hidebound preservationists. Phil Lyman takes the editors on a drive into Devils Canyon near Blanding. They park, then Lyman points out a small Anasazi dwelling tucked under the opposite rim. It takes the editors a while to spot it. Says Lyman, "You could pull off anywhere and find ruins. This is one of the coolest." Still, the editors feel the need to add the gratuitous comment, "His appreciation for the Native American ancestral sites that dot San Juan's public lands seems genuine; there is a touch of wonder in his voice as he shares his thoughts."

Likewise Kay Shumway, of the generations of Blanding Shumways, including Utah's most flagrant and destructive pothunter, says almost peevishly, "I go to these places to pray, to take photographs, to look at stars, to look at the visual landscape. It's just as sacred to me as to a Navajo."

The careless use of the word "sacred" had long bothered me. In *Edge of Morning,* Wayland Gray contributes a short piece that he titles "Sacred is Sacred." Gray is a Muscogee (Creek) native from Oklahoma. He had gained a certain fame by "trespassing" on his people's ancestral grounds in

Alabama, on top of which a casino resort had been built. After his arrest, a jury found him not guilty of all charges, reaffirming the American Indian Religious Freedom Act. Gray has no direct linkage to the Bears Ears, but in his essay he argues passionately for civil disobedience in defense of all ancestral places: "To seek protection for our sacred lands we must fight Big Money and call on the Government to intervene." In an epigraph preceding his essay, Gray writes:

don't ask us what makes it sacred
believe our people believe the creator
our answer will always be Sacred is Sacred
remember the ancestors their spirits are strong

I concede that for a non–Native American such as myself, there's no arguing with assertions like Gray's. In March 2019, however, Friends of Cedar Mesa hosted a celebration of the Bears Ears in Bluff with a weekend crammed with meetings, speeches, scientific field reports, barbeques, and hikes (ultimately cancelled as rain turned every back road and trail into a quagmire of mud). I was invited to be the keynote speaker. As I listened to the other presentations, I couldn't help noticing how often "sacred" was bandied about, by Anglos and natives alike. So when I gave my own talk, I communicated my love of the canyons and mesas, particularly Cedar Mesa, which I confessed had become my favorite place on earth. I tried to evoke what each discovery of a new Anasazi granary (new to me) or frieze of petroglyphs meant. I extolled the fundamental beauty of the landscape. Then I added, "But I can't call these places sacred, because I don't believe in God."

That remark caused a mild disturbance in the crowd. As soon as I finished, Josh Ewing, who was emceeing the event, leapt to the podium and proclaimed that he had no problem with calling the Bears Ears a sacred place, despite his own agnostic tendencies. He did a good job of rationalizing his side of the argument, and it was clear that almost everyone in the spacious community center agreed with him.

One issue that *didn't* get touched on in the long day of speeches was whether national monument status was the best possible outcome for the Bears Ears. For years before Obama created the monument in 2016, a handful of folks most deeply involved in saving that outback from development argued that making the place a National Conservation Area would be a better solution. Vaughn Hadenfeldt was a leading voice for that view, and I was an early ally. The iconoclastic Winston Hurst saw monument status as a disaster, summing up the National Park System in a pithy epithet as a bureaucracy that ran tourist-thronged reserves where "everything not compulsory is forbidden."

In April 2015, as rumors swirled that President Obama might soon take action to save the Bears Ears from oil and gas and cattle and private leases, I wrote an op-ed piece for the *New York Times* arguing at first for the designation Vaughn and I championed. As I argued, "There's a showdown looming. Congress should designate Cedar Mesa a National Conservation Area, which would provide enhanced protections to the area's natural and cultural treasures, but without the fanfare and throngs of visitors that often accompany the creation of new monuments or parks."

The problem in 2015 was that only Congress, not the president, could create such an area. So, bowing to expediency, I closed by proffering my second choice:

> But it seems highly unlikely that the Republican-controlled House and Senate would take such a step. President Obama remains the best hope. He should use his authority to set aside Cedar Mesa as a national monument. Doing so would mean more visitors and new regulations, as happened at Grand Staircase-Escalante. But it would also protect the wonders of the ancients and the environment itself for future generations to explore.

In 2020, that compromise still bothers me.

The crux of the argument that defenders of the Bears Ears monument hope will persuade judges all the way up to the Supreme Court is the claim that presidents have no constitutional authority to reduce national parks and monuments, but rather only the right to decree new monuments. Yet even while the bitter wrangle lingered in judicial limbo, Trump went ahead with actions that chipped away at the fragile protection the impasse so tenuously guaranteed. In August 2019 the White House announced plans to permit drilling, mining, grazing, and motorized recreation—yes, ATVs on the loose almost wherever their drivers chose to ride—on the one million acres of the Bears Ears landscape that Trump had cut out of Obama's monument. The new head of the BLM, William Pendley, castigated by his critics as a man "who has devoted his professional life to selling off public land," proceeded to implement those plans with the hearty approval of his bosses all the way up to the president himself.

In December 2019 a coalition of ninety-one conservation groups sent a letter to Secretary of Interior David Bernhardt demanding that Pendley resign or face removal. During the previous six months, Pendley had served only as the acting director of the BLM, and his term was about to expire. Bernhardt's response was to extend Pendley's term indefinitely—still as acting director. As with so many of the members of his administration, Trump seemed more comfortable with an acting rather than an actual head of a department. In doing so in Pendley's case, Trump avoided the nasty Senate confirmation hearing that would likely unfold if Pendley were nominated to the post.

The greatest conservation battle in the United States in the twentieth century was waged over the construction of Glen Canyon Dam on the Colorado River, which created the gigantic reservoir of Lake Powell even as it drowned what many regarded as the most beautiful canyon in the country and obliterated thousands of prehistoric sites. The greatest battle of the twenty-first century so far is the struggle over the Bears Ears monument (as well as over Grand Staircase–Escalante National Monument, which Trump slashed by about 50 percent).

The turning-point decision about Glen Canyon dam came in April 1956. I was twelve years old at the time, too young (or too ignorant?) to be aware of what was going on. I'd seen the Grand Canyon from the South

Rim on a family vacation trip, but I had only the vaguest notion of what kind of wilderness lay upstream on the Colorado River. I have no hesitation, though, in folding myself into a collective "we" in 2020.

We lost that one. About this one, we've got our fingers crossed.

◄◄ ►►

"All politics is local," Speaker of the House Tip O'Neill famously said. In San Juan County, the undisputed locus of political power is the three-member county commission. Mark Maryboy, the godfather of the Bears Ears monument, or Diné Bikéyah, as many Navajos would have preferred to call it, managed to get elected county commissioner in 1986 at the age of thirty-one. He was not only the first Navajo on that board, but the first Native American in Utah to be elected commissioner in any of its twenty-nine counties.

During his four terms in office, Maryboy clashed dramatically with fellow commissioner Calvin Black, whose politics could not have been more antipathetic to the interests of the state's Native Americans. After retiring from the county commission in 2002, Maryboy threw himself into all kinds of public-service works, which culminated (as detailed in chapter 1) in the creation of the Inter-Tribal Coalition in 2015 that started the Bears Ears ball rolling.

San Juan County, at 7,933 square miles, is the largest county in Utah. It's also the poorest, with a median per capita income of $17,500. Take a look at the map of this odd-shaped entity. It looks vaguely like a heavy boot seen in profile, tapering upward from its long sole along the Arizona border to the narrower laces around La Sal Junction, only twenty miles south of Moab (which lies in Grand County). The Mormon heart of San Juan County, along the corridor that stretches from La Sal to Blanding, occupies only the northern half of the map. A surprisingly large chunk of the Navajo Reservation stretches across the southern third of the county, all the way from the Colorado border to the Colorado River, an airline distance of 140 miles. Blanding is by far the largest town in the county, with a 2017 population of 3,690. Monticello, the county seat, is second, at 1,995. But the smaller towns on the Rez, ignored by tourists, add their weight in population: Aneth at about 600, Montezuma Creek at 500, Halchita at 270, Navajo Mountain at 380. (Compare these numbers to Bluff's 250, Mexican Hat's mere 31 in the 2010 census.) The fact is that by 2010, 50.4 percent of San Juan County was Native American, compared to 45.8 percent white (with negligible percentages of African-American, Asian, and "other").

Yet the county commission continued, as it always had, to be dominated by Mormon Anglos—until 2016, when a US district judge ruled that the county had long been gerrymandered to ensure that Navajo residents were all crammed into one of the three districts, while Anglos controlled the other two. After the districts were redrawn, in 2018 two Navajo candidates— Kenneth Maryboy, Mark's brother; and Willie Grayeyes—were elected county commissioners. The sole holdover from white domination was Blanding's Bruce Adams, reelected from the single Mormon district.

The backlash was immediate and intense. Grayeyes lives at Navajo Mountain, the southwesternmost settlement in the county. To drive from his house to a council meeting in Monticello requires a journey of 217 miles and almost five hours, dipping first into Arizona, through Marsh Pass, Kayenta, and Halchita, before leaving the reservation on the San Juan bridge at Mexican Hat, then vectoring north through Bluff and Blanding.

Almost at once, Kelly Laws, the sore loser to Grayeyes in the election, filed suit in the Seventh District Court in Monticello, claiming that his victory should be nullified on the grounds that he didn't live in Utah. Born in 1946 on Piute Mesa, a few miles north of the Arizona border, Grayeyes lived in 2018 with his family at Navajo Mountain, although he also kept an office in Tuba City, Arizona, and visited his girlfriend there. Laws argued that his opponent's "primary residence" was in Tuba City, even though he had to acknowledge that Grayeyes had never registered to vote in Arizona, having voted in San Juan County since the age of eighteen. Seeming at times more amused than offended by Laws's attack, Grayeyes offered his umbilical cord as corroboration. In the Navajo tradition, it had been buried at birth in the place where he was born. It still lay, said Grayeyes, under the soil on Piute Mesa.

Yet as the trial over the councilman's legal residency proceeded, the controversy turned nasty, and it brought out the dormant racism among some of the San Juan County Anglos. On the Facebook page of the local newspaper, the *San Juan Record*, appeared such comments as "If you use your umbilical cord as proof of residency, you are full of $h1t," and "It's pretty fucked up that someone on a sovern [*sic*] nation have a decision over tax dollars first. . . . Then the bastard doesn't live in San Juan county as far as I'm concerned that fucker can rot in hell."

Other letters to the editor of the *Record* conjured up a conspiracy in which Maryboy and Grayeyes were mere puppets for ill-defined but nefarious "outside interests." A letter about Maryboy on May 8, 2019, written by one Larry Wells of Monticello, accused him of promoting socialism, which "always fails the mass of the people, as it has on the U.S. native reservations." Maryboy was "a tool, a bully," under the thrall of "unknown power mongers."

In the wake of the 2018 election, disgruntled Anglos tried to engineer legal changes that would boost the number of commissioners from three to five, or even divide San Juan County into two counties, separating Navajo Democrats from Mormon Republicans. None of these machinations came to fruition, and in January 2019, the court settling the question of Grayeyes's legal residency decided in favor of him and against Kelly Laws.

One of the first proposals the new county commission put forward was a resolution of full-scale support for restitution of the Bears Ears monument. But not the 1.35-million-acre monument decreed by Obama; rather the full 1.9-million-acre monument original proposed by Diné Bikéyah and the Inter-Tribal Coalition. The proposal passed by a two-to-one vote. For the first time ever, San Juan County was officially on board not only with the "wacko environmentalists," but with the Native Americans who had divined the threat to a region that embodied not so much favorite places to hike and camp as their ancestral lands. The greater Bears Ears, they thus declared, was (no other word will do)—sacred.

◄◄ ►►

On March 5, 2019, Sharon and I drove to Monticello to attend the county commission meeting. It was a bright, sunny, chilly day—35 degrees at 9:00 a.m.—and the snowbanks around town, after two weeks of storms, were the deepest I'd ever seen in southeast Utah. The meeting was held on the second floor of the stolid county courthouse. In a room that might hold sixty people, some thirty spectators took their seats. The three councilmen sat behind a makeshift dais, speaking into microphones that didn't work.

On the left sat Bruce Adams, tall, crewcut, clean-shaven, with a chiseled Mormon face. He wore a spiffy shirt with blue and white vertical stripes. Throughout the meeting, he cocked back in his chair, chewing gum non-stop. In the middle, as befit the chairman of the commission, Kenneth Maryboy wore blue jeans and a checkered shirt. He leaned forward, arms crossed on the table, and nodded a lot, though what he was thinking he kept closely guarded. On the right was Willie Grayeyes, far more flamboyant than his two colleagues in a red plaid shirt and a dark red letterman's jacket with the logo of the NaaTsis'Aan Community School Warriors. His long silver hair was slicked neatly back, and his expressive face was dominated by a bold gray mustache, halfway between chevron and horseshoe. Throughout the meeting, he kept taking his glasses on and off, while he scribbled notes left-handed.

The meeting dragged on for three hours, and most of it, frankly, was dull. It took an hour and a half for the first resolution to be brought to the table. Since the onset of my cancer in 2015, my hearing has gotten pretty bad, and even with hearing aids, I found it difficult to follow the debate over a proposal to install solar panels on a patch of state land just north of Bluff. I knew that my Bluff friends would be against such a development, even with eco-friendly solar panels. Vaughn Hadenfeldt, in fact, was at the meeting, and he rose from the audience to express the opposition of Friends of Cedar Mesa to any panels until the final verdict on the Bears Ears might come down. Bruce Adams voiced his concern that the panels, of which he was in favor, needed to be built tall enough to allow grazing beneath them. Whether the commission voted on this issue or not never became clear to me. Of the seven resolutions brought before the council that day, in fact, most were tabled.

Then, almost two hours into the meeting, an electrifying conflict burst onto the staid scene. A woman rose from the audience, addressed Kenneth Maryboy, and blurted out, "Who wrote these resolutions?" Maryboy paused a beat, looked at her without blinking, and uttered a response too soft for me to hear, which Sharon whispered in my ear: "In other words, you think we're too stupid to write them ourselves?"

The woman shrieked, "I didn't say that!," but she'd lost the fight. In that moment, all the racism lurking under the veneer of San Juan County had leaked to the surface.

The one item of business that really mattered was a resolution in support of the Bears Ears Expansion and Respect for Sovereignty Act, then on the floor of the US House of Representatives. That stab of activism, like the council's vote in its first meeting in January, would restore the full 1.9 million acres of the Bears Ears monument proposed by the Inter-Tribal Coalition. In the era of Trump, with a Republican Senate, even its passionate adherents knew it was more symbolic gesture than realistic piece of legislation. (As of this writing, the bill was stuck in committee, still far short of a vote even in the House.) But in Monticello that March day, the resolution passed by a predictable two-to-one vote. As the council adjourned just after noon, Bruce Adams had a look of weary exasperation on his face.

I invited Willie Grayeyes to lunch at the Peace Tree Juice Café, a hippieish oasis on the main street of staunchly traditional (Wagon Wheel Pizza, Doug's Steak & BBQ) Monticello. Over his fish tacos and sprout-rich salad, the seventy-three-year-old councilman grew expansive, even playful. He talked about hiking to the summit of Navajo Mountain when he was a kid, before "they" put up the radio towers. It took him only two or three hours, he claimed, to scale the four thousand feet of winding trail past War God Spring. I asked him about his letterman's jacket. "I'm the school board chairman," he said proudly. (I heard the echoes of the critics who had tried to disenfranchise him as an Arizona resident.)

I asked him what clan he belonged to. "Red Kilt clan," he deadpanned. When I looked confused, he broke out a grin and pealed, "I'm Scottish! Can't you tell?"

But when we discussed the council meetings since he had been installed in January, he grew more somber. "It's been nothing but insult and onslaught," he said. Sometimes he and Maryboy had exchanged a few words in Diné during the meetings, only to have audience members erupt with the demand that they speak English. "All we were saying was 'yes' and 'no.'"

We came back to the acrimony over his legal residence, and the mischievous side of Willie Grayeyes resurfaced. "I told 'em, 'Go ahead and dig my umbilical cord out of the sheep corral,'" he said. "'Test the DNA, find the match—if you really want to go that far.'"

Now he gave me the straight answer about his clan membership. "I'm Reed Clan, born for Salt Clan," he explained. But then things got complicated, as he brought in the affiliations of his grandparents. Folding Arm Clan and Big Water Clan were part of Grayeyes's makeup. He grew animated, as he delved into migration stories. Suddenly he seized a couple of Coke cans on our table, some silverware, and what was left of his fish tacos, and moved them here and there through the centuries. The tacos represented "a body of water," he said. "My people built a lot of hogans. They called themselves Many Hogans. We kept our people in control."

I popped the question I can't resist asking Navajos, once I feel comfortable in their company. Did he believe the Diné, as Athapaskans, had migrated from subarctic Canada? "No!" he answered fiercely. "We were here! The mountains were on fire!"

I was lost. Pointing to the remnants of the fish tacos, I asked, "What body of water is that?"

Willie Grayeyes paused, then pointed to his forehead. "Up here," he muttered.

I paid the bill. As we rose to leave, I asked a last question: "Why is it that there are some Navajos who actually oppose the Bears Ears monument?"

The look on his face was unmistakably dark. "Those are the Navajos," he said, measuring his words, "who are affiliated with the Mormon church."

THE BEARS EARS I'LL
NEVER KNOW

The year was 1980. Vaughn Hadenfeldt ran a climbing store in Glenwood Springs, Colorado, with his wife, Marcia. His passion was mountaineering. Along with repeating classic routes and putting up new ones in the Rockies, he'd guided clients on an expedition to Denali. At Colorado State University in Fort Collins, he'd started a major in anthropology before dropping out. Although the two professors who tried to mentor him were distinguished Southwest archaeologists, the Anasazi bug failed to infect him. As a kid, Vaughn had dabbled with prehistoric sites near his home, but a more serious engagement with archaeology on the ground came during a couple of marathon backpack trips into the Wind River Range in Wyoming, where he and a friend headed out for as long as a month at a time without resupply. Above timberline, Vaughn was beguiled to come upon the fugitive leavings of the Sheepeater Indians, also known as the Tukudeka: chert and obsidian projectile points, awls, scrapers, and the like. The Tukudeka are now considered either extinct or completely assimilated into other Shoshonean peoples, but a single trip report Vaughn wrote for a CSU class in 1972 would win him kudos decades later as a pioneer of alpine archaeology in Wyoming.

Now, however, a friend named Jimmy Archambeault was badgering him to take a trip over to Utah and up onto a place called Cedar Mesa, where Archambeault had briefly worked as a BLM ranger in the 1970s. "Jimmy had never been in Slickhorn," Vaughn told me in 2019. "But he'd heard a rumor that there was an intact kiva somewhere in that canyon, somewhere up near the head. He wanted me to go with him on a backpack trip and explore the whole darn canyon, with all its branches.

"So just to get him to quit buggin' me, I agreed to go. Left Marcia to run the store while I was gone. We hopped into Jimmy's little VW and headed off. Got to Cedar Mesa and loaded up our packs for a week of exploring. It was early spring, but pretty perfect weather. We headed into a side canyon of Slickhorn, determined to check out the whole system. In those days, there were no beaten paths anywhere. We didn't even bring a tent—just slept under overhangs. It was still legal to build fires in the canyons then, so we didn't even carry a cook stove. And we didn't have a water purifier. That was back in the day when none of us were too scared of the outdoors. The water purification companies hadn't intimidated us yet about being wary of every patch of water in the backcountry.

"We felt like we were pioneering our own routes. Didn't see another person in a whole week. That was way cool. It didn't take me long to get sucked into the red-rock landscape. And then we started finding things— habitation sites with dwellings and granaries, cordage, corn cobs, everything so exquisitely preserved. And the rock art. All I'd seen before were stone tools, up in the Wind Rivers and other ranges.

"Our goal was to find the intact kiva Jimmy had heard about. We systematically worked our way up the canyon, exploring every ledge and side-branch, finding stuff everywhere. But three days out we were starting to get discouraged, almost ready to give up. Then we climbed one more hill, a steep one, up onto a ledge in an alcove, and there it was.

"The funny thing is, we didn't see the kiva at first. We saw the granaries and the mealing bins. But then we realized that what looked like the level floor of the alcove was actually the roof of the kiva, covered with sand. And the poles of the intact ladder were sticking out of the square entryway in the roof. We were pretty excited. The Perfect Kiva, as it's called now, made the whole trip worth it."

Vaughn was hooked. On the way back to Glenwood, Jimmy introduced him to Fred Blackburn, who had been Jimmy's boss with the BLM, initiating a friendship that would soon come to glorious fruition with the Wetherill–Grand Gulch Project—which in turn would lure me to Cedar Mesa in 1992. After 1980, Vaughn started taking trips out to the Utah desert every spring and fall, even though it was a drive of 300 miles from Glenwood to Bluff. He and Marcia brought their friends to Cedar Mesa, along with assorted kids, who would play in the mud building tiny replicas of the ruins they'd discovered in the canyons. Vaughn started leading trips for the Colorado Mountain Club, and in 1995 launched his own guiding service, calling it Far Out Expeditions.

But it was hard to make the break, to sell the lucrative climbing store, to give up climbing itself for the canyon exploring that had seduced him away from the mountains. It was especially hard for Marcia to contemplate moving from a town of 6,000, where she served as a city councilwoman, to a hamlet of 250, where jobs were scarcer than lunar eclipses. There was no checking the obsession, however, that had taken hold of the erstwhile anthro-major dropout. In 1994 Vaughn bought property in Bluff, restored a hundred-year-old house that sat derelict on it, then built a beautiful new house to soften Marcia's apprehensions. And that year, after eighteen happy years in Glenwood, Vaughn and Marcia moved to Bluff for good. Vaughn set up his Far Out shingle in front of the house and started booking clients. It was there, only months later, that I met both Vaughn and Marcia for the first time, launching a friendship based on the Anasazi mania that has lasted now for twenty-six years.

After I'd showed up on my *Smithsonian* assignment to check out the Wetherill–Grand Gulch Project, I'd been led by Fred Blackburn and his cronies to some of the sites that the Mancos cowboy's teams had dug in the 1890s. Those short outings were mere teasers hinting at the glories of the Bears Ears landscape, but I was hooked, just as Vaughn had been a dozen years earlier. So in April 1992, Sharon and I decided to do our own eight-day backpack trip down upper Grand Gulch, thirty-eight miles from the head of Kane Gulch to Collins Spring. Except we wouldn't hump our sixty-five-pound packs ourselves; instead we'd stash our gear and food (and extra goodies like bottles of wine) in the saddlebags of a pair of llamas we'd lease from Jim Hook at Recapture Lodge. Two years before, I'd rented llamas with Jon Krakauer for a sybaritic jaunt into the Wind Rivers and written a piece for *Outside* about it, and while that mode of travel had left the ascetic Krakauer unpersuaded, I was an enthusiastic convert to llamaturgical exploration. With a backpack strapped to your groaning torso, tilted forward in counterbalance, you tend to trudge along staring at the ground just ahead of your feet. With ten pounds in your daypack (water bottle, camera, a couple of candy bars, maybe an extra sweater), you can hold the llama lead in one hand while you scan the cliffs on either side for prehistoric clues, raising the binocs when a new ruin swims into your ken. Or you can link two llamas together and leave your partner unencumbered to wander at will. Or tie the leads off to willows and hike up a side canyon.

Needing to cover only five miles a day, Sharon and I poked along and reveled in the discoveries each new canyon bend revealed. Penstemon, globe mallow, and Indian paintbrush were coming into bloom, and the stream ran clear. Campfires were still allowed in Grand Gulch, and we stayed up late each night, our tent usually pitched on a south-facing shelf fifty or a hundred feet above the canyon floor, shifting our gazes from the flames below to the constellations above. Day after day we passed by amazing ruins: Junction, Split Level, Turkey Pen, Lion Tracks, Bannister, and others that didn't seem to have even unofficial names. And dazzling panoplies of rock art such as the Quail and Big Man Panels.

During those eight days, we saw only a small party of kindred devotees camped at Junction Ruin, then, a couple of days later, a hippie pair near the mouth of Green House Canyon who seemed lost before we straightened them out. We hummed back at our llamas when they hummed, and untangled their long leashes from snarling bushes each morning. That April Sharon and I were both forty-eight years old. We'd hiked and climbed in Alaska, Canada, Colorado, and New England for years, but this was one of the best trips we'd ever shared, with most of its pleasures utterly new to us. And we saw more Anasazi wonders than we thought a single canyon could contain.

It was only years later that we learned how much we had missed. Fourteen miles in, for instance, we paused at the narrow chute, covered with tall cattails, where Sheiks Canyon comes in from the left. Our National Geographic map of Grand Gulch Plateau indicated Green Mask Spring only two-tenths of a mile up Sheiks. I also studied the USGS quadrangle. We didn't need a spring; we had plenty of good water; so we skipped the side canyon. A couple of years later, when I hiked down Sheiks, I realized that Sharon and I had missed one of the two most stunning and extensive collections of rock art on all of Cedar Mesa, which a fifteen-minute llama-less detour would have brought us to. (Why didn't the name "Green Mask" tip us off? But there was no guidebook in 1992, and precious little advice anywhere in print about the glories of Grand Gulch. Nowadays, in the era of GPS and online "trip reports," I look back on that geographic innocence with keen nostalgia.)

On one of our day trips, Fred Blackburn had told me that he had a rule of thumb for seeking out the full measure of the Anasazi achievement. To do anything like a thorough job, checking each band of cliffs and ledges on walls that might rise eight hundred feet on either side, in a hard day's work you could canvass only one mile of one side of a canyon per day. I thought he was exaggerating. Soon I recognized how true Fred's dictum was.

Three years after Sharon's and my llama trip through upper Grand Gulch, I repeated most of it in the reverse direction, entering via the Government Trail and exiting at Kane Gulch. My three companions included Fred Blackburn. Once again, we leased llamas at Recapture Lodge, this time from veteran wrangler Larry Sanford. Fred, a dyed-in-the-wool mule- and horsepacker, disdained the instructions Sanford offered us and loaded up our beasts of burden the way he wanted to, with a liberal dose of his favorite squaw hitches ("basket hitches," in p.c. parlance). When the llamas hummed their disapproval, Fred cursed them and pulled the ropes even tighter.

During our seven days in Grand Gulch, with my climbing skills I was able to get Fred into a couple of vertiginous alcoves he'd long coveted. But he repaid my assistance in spades, thanks to his intimate knowledge of the canyon from the years he'd toiled there as a BLM ranger. That connoisseurship was epitomized in a single moment on the third or fourth day. "Tie 'em off," Fred abruptly ordered. "I want to show you guys something." We cinched the llamas tight to cottonwood limbs, then followed Fred through a dense thicket of willows until we ran smack into the north wall of the Gulch. For a few minutes Fred scouted right and left, bashing willow tangles impatiently aside, searching for something. . . . "Here it is," he said quietly.

At chest level on the smooth brown sandstone, three tiny petroglyphs interrupted the monotone geology. They were bighorn sheep, carved by some ancient in characteristic profile, the largest no bigger than seven inches long. There are tens of thousands of bighorn sheep etched all over Cedar Mesa; for reasons no archaeologist has been able to explain, they're the animal by far the most often rendered by the Anasazi. Three more petro-sheep in the middle of nowhere would hardly have been worth the detour, but as I stared, I realized that these were the most exquisite portrayals of that once ubiquitous bovid I had ever seen. "Wow," I whispered.

"I call it the Miniature Panel," said Fred.

"How'd you find it?"

"Pete Steele showed it to me years ago."

Pete Steele. The name rang a very distant bell in my head. I knew that as early as the late 1940s, a handful of local Utah men had led guided trips through Grand Gulch, for clients who craved more esoteric wilderness jaunts than such neatly packaged outings as mule trips down the Bright Angel Trail to Phantom Ranch in the Grand Canyon or ranger-led tours of Spruce Tree House and Cliff Palace at Mesa Verde. A few names besides Pete Steele's had crept into a corner of my brain: Carl Mahon, Kent Frost, Ken Sleight. But that moment with Fred in front of the Miniature Panel conjured up the fragile threads by which the oral lore of one generation got passed to the next, and then, with luck, to the next. . . . I'm older than Fred Blackburn, but that day in Grand Gulch I was in the second generation to receive the blessing of the Miniature Panel. Actually, I should place myself in the third generation, for it was Carl Mahon who taught Pete Steele, who taught Fred, who taught me. That handing down by word of mouth, on journeys into outbacks that few explorers could ever know well, seemed in a small way to mirror the great age of the Mountain Men (1806 to 1842?), when John Colter might have told James Beckwourth where a hidden hot spring on the Yellowstone River lay, and Beckwourth might have told Kit Carson. All of that lore kept in heads, in part because most of the trappers were illiterate, but also because broadcasting their expertise would cut right into their profits in beaver pelts.

Back in the early 1990s, Fred and Vaughn told me they were planning to collect the stories of those early Cedar Mesa guides, maybe with the help of Winston Hurst, before it was too late, and publish them in a book. I thought it was a terrific idea. (I craved those old guides' stories, not directions to the Miniature Panel.) Fred and Vaughn had already interviewed a few of those pioneers. I nudged them as hard as I could for years to keep after the Pete Steeles, but one thing or another got in the way, and now it's too late.

I know that today I could never find the Miniature Panel again. I wonder if Fred still could. Doesn't matter: it's out there, waiting to be rediscovered by some patient, tireless canyon sleuth. Thank God we had no GPS devices in 1995. I don't want to find those perfect petroglyphs again by homing in on them with an electronic gizmo. I may have jotted notes that day with Fred, but by now the notebook itself is lost.

In her lyrical 1978 paean to Cedar Mesa, *Wind in the Rock,* Ann Zwinger recounts a horseback trip through upper Grand Gulch led by Pete Steele at the end of his tenure as a Cedar Mesa guide. Right off she characterizes him as "among other things a uranium miner, a wrangler and rancher, and, that most demanding of professions, a rodeo clown. He now lives in Monticello, Utah. . . ."

Alas, Zwinger misses all the chances she had to bring Pete Steele to life, to repeat any of the tales he must have told around the campfire, as she devotes her long chapter on upper Grand Gulch to an (excellent) exegesis of the archaeology of the place. Richard Wetherill, dead some sixty-five years, is a more vivid character in Zwinger's book than the veteran guide who helps her mount her horse and coaches her down a steep incline.

In 1992, when Sharon and I llama-packed upper Grand Gulch, Ken Sleight was still running horseback trips through the canyon. The crony on whom Edward Abbey based the anarchist maverick Seldom Seen Smith in *The Monkey Wrench Gang* is still alive at age ninety, living at his beloved Pack Creek Ranch outside Moab. I interviewed Sleight in 1998 because I'd heard a rumor that he had found a "NEMO" inscription—the cryptic alter ego Everett Ruess had adopted in the last months before he disappeared in 1934—carved into a granary wall in Grand Gulch, a very long way from where Everett's last camp was found in Davis Gulch, a tributary of the Escalante. Sleight's discovery had come on a pack trip some thirty years before I talked to him, and though his memory was already getting fuzzy, Fred, Vaughn, and I were able to find the granary, and with subtle tricks with a headlamp and binoculars Fred thought he could pick out a faded but unmistakable "NEMO" etched in the mud. That inscription remains a tantalizing clue in the unsolved mystery of Everett Ruess's demise.

As far as I know, though, nobody has mined Ken Sleight for his lode of tales about guiding Grand Gulch long before it became a destination on every Southwest dabbler's to-do list. And if Ken himself ever thought of writing a memoir, he hasn't done so yet, and now, as he recently told a reporter, with a laugh, "I can't hear, I can't see, and I can't speak."

The only one of those pioneer guides who has left behind a written record of his adventures is Kent Frost. *My Canyonlands*, published in 1971, is a quirky, folksy, charmingly unvarnished ramble through decades of poking around, often solo, all over southeast Utah. Unfortunately, only three pages of the book narrate Frost's adventures in Grand Gulch, focusing on his first trip there, solo, in winter, without a sleeping bag! ("After midnight I forced myself to stop and make camp at a driftwood pile.") One paragraph, however, resonated deeply with me, for after many trips into Grand Gulch, I've worked out "secret" shortcuts just like the ones Frost discovered over the years.

On subsequent visits I surprised myself by finding obscure passage-
ways from the rim that took me all the way to the bottom—although
when hiking down there one would think he was locked in by those
smooth and often overhanging walls. They were blind exits from
within the canyon. I named one my "secret Indian trail," as broken
pieces of pottery and chert chips along the way told me the ancient
Indians had also preferred this way of entering.

Kent Frost was born in 1917, a year before my mother, so I guess a solid
gap of one generation separated him from me. (He lived to be ninety-six,
expiring only in 2013. I kick myself now that in none of my many trips
through Monticello did it occur to me to stop and try to arrange a chat
with the old-timer who so loved every inch of the Bears Ears landscape.)
That generation gap, however, spans a radical difference in our ethics of
exploring. Near the end of *My Canyonlands*, Frost recounts one of his finest adventures. Off solo as usual, this time in the Maze district of Canyonlands National Park, he's discovered a short, narrow canyon that he can
find no way to enter. He returns year after year, stymied every time, until
he comes upon an obscure side slot that may give access.

One lip of rock overhung a twenty-foot wall that I could negotiate,
if I could get to it.
  "I could return with climber's gear, or . . . ," I speculated. In a
few weeks I came back alone with the "or"—six sticks of dynamite.
I dug a small channel above the lip, placed the six sticks of dynamite end to end in it, and covered them deeply with dirt. My fuse
was short, about a foot long. So, after lighting it, I scrambled to the
cover of a protective rock, 200 feet away. A few seconds later the canyon suddenly filled with the thunder of blasting dynamite. Rocks
rolled and tumbled to the ledges below. . . . I cleaned out the debris
and climbed down, cutting several Moqui steps with my hammer.
In twenty minutes I was at the bottom of the canyon that was so
important to me. As I walked along in wonder and triumph I found

several Indian spearheads and skinning knives out in the open. Had anyone else been here, they would have removed them. So perhaps I was the first. . . . The thrill was very great.

No backcountry aficionado of my generation would dream of using dynamite to blast a passage into some inaccessible canyon, or even of pounding out a hand-and-toe trail with his hammer. But Frost's tone is utterly unashamed: nothing wrong with a little dynamite if you can't climb it free. It doesn't even seem to occur to Frost to wonder how the Anasazi or the Fremont people who left the spearheads and skinning knives had found their way to that inviolate refuge in the first place.

Appalling though that passage in *My Canyonlands* seems to me, I'll cut Kent Frost a lot of slack. (After all, cavers of his generation used dynamite to "improve" tight crawls.) The sheer exuberance of the man's discovery, the innocence of his "triumph," win me over. And as I've often reflected, no doubt a future generation of hyper-p.c. canyon explorers will condemn the kinds of practices in which Vaughn or Fred or I routinely indulge, like picking up potsherds to admire them before dropping them back in the dirt.

In the Doris Duke Oral History Collection at the University of Utah, I found another trove of Frostiana. One amusing exchange from the mid-1970s covered his Monticello neighbors' reactions after *My Canyonlands* was published. "Right after that," Frost recalled, "a lot of my friends came around to me and said, 'Kent, we want to borrow some money to pay off our house with. We want to borrow some money to buy a new car with.' They thought that I was a rich man as soon as my book came out. Then the people started calling me Mr. Frost. . . . Now that has been over two years ago, and so now they are getting back in the old habit of just calling me old Kent."

On one of his trips into lower Grand Gulch, Frost came across a magnificent arch—the biggest, it turns out, in the whole fifty-five-mile-long canyon—whose north wall was adorned with a dazzling array of pictographs and petroglyphs, including a swirl of flung paint that might have

emanated from the brush of an Anasazi Jackson Pollock. He thought he
had made the Anglo discovery of the sandstone span, and so he felt enti-
tled to name it. The uninspired title Grand Arch is what came to him.
(Almost surely, earlier explorers, including Richard Wetherill's teams or
McLoyd and Graham in the 1890s, or Nels Nelson in 1920, had visited the
arch before Frost found it. In fact, Jim Knipmeyer claims to have found an
1891 inscription from McLoyd near the arch, though I managed to miss it
on my first trip down lower Grand Gulch in 1994.)

In 1958 Frost jotted down an account of his discovery "by memory."
After parking his Jeep at Collins Spring, hiking solo as was his wont, he
made fast time down the canyon. Even in late winter, he didn't bother carrying a sleeping bag or pad. Instead he'd find a "driftwood pile," use it to
build a campfire, let the flames thaw the frozen ground, then settle in to
sleep in his clothes on warmed-up dirt. On that undated jog down lower
Grand Gulch, Frost covered thirty-four miles down-and-back in two and
a half days. (In 1994, again with llamas, Sharon and I stretched the same
trip into eight leisurely days.)

Proud though he was of his "discovery" of Grand Arch, Frost devotes a
bare two sentences to the find, and he makes no mention of the spectacular pictograph panel on its northern face. Yet having regained his Jeep, he's
still unsatisfied, so he drives six miles south from Collins Spring along the
west rim of the Gulch, along a "road" that no longer exists (one I'm sure
Phil Lyman would be eager to reclaim). After the road peters out in huge
rounded boulders, Frost rim-walks on. He's delighted to see his Grand
Arch from above, but he keeps going. A few miles farther south, he spots
the tell-tale ladder poles of an intact kiva "in a great cave below." Somehow he'd missed this ancient wonder on his dash down the canyon bottom
a few days earlier. Frost is frantic to explore the kiva, even though it's 800
feet below the rim.

The day's running short, so he heads back to his Jeep and camps another
night, this time "nice and warm" in a double sleeping bag he hadn't wanted
to lug into the canyon. The next morning, back to the overlook. And now
Frost's pluck at route-finding comes into play. Poking around, he discov-

ers "a very narrow crack, which was a tight squeeze in getting through." And soon he's finding "broken pieces of pottery along this trail and chips of jasper [chert]." This is Frost's "secret Indian trail."

At the kiva, he spends a couple of blissful hours climbing down the ancient ladder and surveying the interior, which "appeared to be in practically its natural state of repair except the rodents and pack rats had dug into the sandy walls." Before he leaves, a very strange thing happens.

> I had heard about these Night-hawk Birds which migrate through the country in the summertime and I understood these birds would hibernate to spend the long winter months. Near this kiva I was looking around on the ground and here was a Nighthawk setting by the stone and I thought it extremely unusual so I picked up this bird in my hand and looked at it closely. While I was looking at this bird, he blinked his eye and opened his mouth as if yawning so I . . . set him back down in his original place and this is the only time I have ever seen one of these birds in the hibernation state.

Then all the way back to his Jeep, in a single short day in February or March. In his four-page account of that outing, Frost sums up his happiness in his usual homely fashion: "I was over-joyed with my discovery of this secret Indian trail. . . . [I] drove back to Monticello satisfied that I had a sufficient exploration and a very enjoyable time being out in the country for a few days."

Man, they don't make 'em like that any more! I know of no one else who has ever climbed down Frost's secret trail, but reading his account makes me hungry to head out to Collins Spring and give it a rim-walking whack. Even in my prime, though, I think it would have taken me three days to do what Kent Frost did in one.

I've got a pretty good idea which intact kiva Frost found, though it's one Sharon and I missed in 1994. I didn't find my way to it until more than fifteen years later, and then only thanks to directions from Fred Blackburn, who had found it during his ranger days. As Fred told me, "I knew Kent

Frost had been there, but he was pretty secretive about it. It made my hair stand on end, it was so pristine." The kiva's still there, still intact, though when Greg Child and I explored it in early spring, no night hawks were hibernating nearby.

A gloomy footnote about nomenclature. On the USGS topo map, Grand Arch is titled "Shaw Arch." That may well be its official designation, according to the US Board on Geographic Names. That appellation was bestowed in memory of an incompetent Boy Scout leader who in 1963 managed to kill twelve of his charges and himself, and injure twenty-six others, when he lost control of his cattle truck on a hairpin curve on the Hole-in-the-Rock road, far out on the Escalante Desert. Shaw had never been anywhere near Grand Gulch. Even before the accident, thanks to the predilection of cows to fall off the embankment to their deaths, the hairpin bend had been graced with the appropriate (if macabre) name Carcass Wash.

◄◄ ►►

My favorite piece of Frostiana among the rich archives of the Doris Duke Oral History Collection is the tale he wove for an interviewer in 1973 about a great adventure he'd undertaken thirty-four years earlier, at the age of twenty-two. One day in 1939, Frost and his seventeen-year-old cousin, worn out after a summer of work on the Monticello farm, joined a picnic outing somewhere high in the Abajos. "We decided we wanted to go on a short vacation," Frost recalled, so the two young men took off on foot, telling friends and family they'd be gone for a few days on a "hiking trip."

That spontaneous lark evolved into a month-long ramble across huge stretches of Southwest wilderness. The two young men were formidable hikers, regularly covering forty miles in a day. After descending White Canyon to the Colorado River, they decided to build a boat and head on downstream. Three days out, they ran out of food. Here's a sample from the rambling oral account of the journey:

"I had a thirty-eight Colt pistol that I could shoot good with," Frost said. Soon a beaver floated within range. Frost's second shot nailed the animal, which promptly sank to the river bottom. "I jumped in with my clothes on and it just happened that I could find the beaver with my feet. I pulled him up to the surface. We put him in the boat and skinned out the hind legs and back."

Famished, the boys camped early and roasted their catch. It was not a success: "There was no way we could eat that beaver. It was the toughest, worst tasting stuff we had ever tried."

No problem. The boatmen got out their "fish lines" and baited their hooks with pieces of beaver. "We were pulling catfish out one right after another . . . , and we were eating them just as soon as they got roasted in the coals of the fire. Oh, they was good. They were the best catfish we had ever."

The boys make it all the way to Lees Ferry, 185 river miles downstream from White Canyon. Then they hitchhike erratically all over Utah until a "preacher" gives them a ride back to Monticello. "Our folks were glad to see us," Frost closes his story.

I like to think that I set off in my youth on hiking jaunts as challenging as Frost's with his cousin in 1939—a forty-mile backpack in to Mount Deborah in Alaska's Hayes Range, for instance, when Don Jensen and I were both twenty-one. But I've never accomplished a pilgrimage one whit so blithe, so improvisatory, so seat-of-the-pants as the one those two young ramblers accomplished more than eighty years ago. Is such a voyage even possible in our day and age? Or have we forgotten how to hear the siren song of wanderlust?

The eighteen-day traverse of Comb Ridge from one end to the other that Vaughn Hadenfeldt, Greg Child, and I accomplished in 2004 felt like a serious outing. But we planned it like generals, laying caches of bottled H_2O along the first fifty-one waterless miles and arranging for three resupplies along the route. There was nothing spontaneous about that backpack.

In March 2019 I met Zak Podmore, an avid young river runner ambitious to become a writer. Four years earlier his wife, Amanda, had been offered a job at Friends of Cedar Mesa. As he recounted, "She asked me, 'Do you want to move to Bluff?' I jumped right on it."

Zak had already spent many days exploring Cedar Mesa. Now he resuscitated the defunct local monthly newspaper, *Canyon Echo*, as a hip online periodical acutely tuned in to the ongoing controversy over the Bears Ears. "Before we moved to Bluff," Zak told me, "I was really drawn to the landscape. Remote canyons where you could go out for days and not see anyone else. The archaeology was cool, but it was something I just sort of stumbled upon. But since we moved to Bluff and I've spent time with archaeologists, I'm starting to be really drawn to the prehistory."

Almost off-handedly, Zak mentioned a solo trip he'd taken in 2017 that filled me with admiration and envy. "I wanted to do a big circle loop right out of Bluff," he said. "So I just walked down to the San Juan from our house and put in with a ten-pound pack raft. Three days of paddling past Mexican Hat, through the Goosenecks, down to the mouth of Slickhorn Canyon. Then I hiked up Slickhorn, carrying maybe sixty or seventy pounds. At the head of Slickhorn, I stashed the raft, paddle, dry suit, and life jacket to pick up later.

"Hiked down Road Canyon to Comb Wash. Then I climbed the old Moqui steps that lead up to Procession Panel on the Comb." Comb Ridge is relentlessly steep on its west face, averaging seventy or eighty degrees along the twenty-mile stretch between Routes 163 and 95, but the Anasazi, always impatient with circuitous detours, had crafted a series of hand-and-toe trails from Comb Wash up to the crest of Comb Ridge. I'd down-climbed the steps by the Procession Panel myself.

"From there," Zak went on, "I hiked down the Comb, then climbed a prehistoric route to the top of Tank Mesa, and then down the canyon that comes out by the transfer station. From there, it was only a short walk back to my house."

"Wow," I said. "Impressive. How many days?"

"A good seven."

"How many miles?"

It seemed as though Zak had never pondered the matter before. "Let's see," he said, "maybe sixty or seventy down the San Juan to Slickhorn. Then forty or fifty hiking back to Bluff."

"Call it one ten?"

"Something like that."

Granted, Zak's marathon loop had required a lot of pre-planning and a careful study of the maps. It lacked the aleatory splendor of Kent Frost's month-long truancy from the Monticello farm. But what it had in common with the 1939 ramble was a certain organic integrity: a far-ranging odyssey, mixing river descent with cross-country hike, starting and ending at the front door of the place one called home. In all my years of hiking on Cedar Mesa, such a journey had never occurred to me; nor, I thought, had it tickled Vaughn's fancy. When we set out to explore, we automatically hopped into our vehicles and drove to the trailhead.

◄◄ ►►

For me, in the canyons of the greater Bears Ears, the archaeology was always foremost. And that took me by surprise, for before the age of forty, I'd been relatively uninterested in prehistory. I'd taken a couple of anthro courses in college, but Raymond Firth's *We the Tikopia* failed to enthrall me the way Heinrich Harrer's *The White Spider* did. As a mountaineer obsessed with unclimbed peaks in Alaska, I craved a wilderness where no humans had ever been, where every glacial cirque I traversed was truly unexplored.

My first encounter with Cedar Mesa came not in 1992, when Fred Blackburn took me to ruins he and his pals were trying to match to Richard Wetherill's field notes, but in 1987, on a kind of one-off outing, when a friend and I spent three days in Bullet Canyon, a tributary of Grand Gulch. Expecting only good hiking and camping between graceful sandstone walls, I was stunned by the perfection of Perfect Kiva ruin (the other Perfect Kiva, besides the one in Slickhorn) and Jailhouse ruin. And there I found the same small but eloquent artifacts that had so mesmerized Vaughn on his Slickhorn quest: potsherds and chert flakes and twists of yucca fiber lying in the dirt, where their makers had left them more than seven centuries before.

It took a few years, though, before the charm of total wildness faded for me, to be replaced by what I called in a youthful poem the appeal of "the finding of the found." Once it did, every hike I took on Cedar Mesa became a search for ruins and rock art. I recognized that merely collecting Anasazi sites could become a sterile fetish, akin to what climbers sneer at as "peak-bagging." Instead, I felt driven by the need to learn everything I could about the archaeology of the Southwest. As my passion started to cohere in a plan for a book—which became *In Search of the Old Ones*, still my favorite among the ones I've written—I knew I had to crisscross the country from Phoenix to Durango, from Paquimé in Chihuahua to Salt Lake City, to beg the experts to share their insights into not only the Anasazi, but the Fremont, the Mogollon, and the Hohokam as well.

That passion led me to one of the greatest of all American archaeologists, Bill Lipe, a charming, shy, profoundly erudite fellow who more than anyone else has figured out what was going on on Cedar Mesa before AD 1300.

As mentioned briefly in chapter 4, during four summers from 1972 to 1975 Lipe and his colleague, R. G. Matson, ran field camps based in tents near the head of Todie Canyon. In an era when major excavations of big pueblos were still being carried out elsewhere in the Southwest, Lipe and Matson laid a light hand on the landscape. Instead of digging, they opted for survey. Dividing the spacious mesa into sections, they chose five to focus on; within those five, they marked off seventy-six "quadrats"—like-sized rectangles of ground to ensure statistical randomness. Then the teams went out and identified and mapped every single Anasazi *thing* they found, from two-story dwellings to one-hand manos (grinding stones), from chains of white-paint humanoids holding hands on a sandstone wall to six-inch strings of woven yucca. In all, the researchers documented 340 sites. The only practice that the teams engaged in that would later go out of fashion was to collect nearly all those artifacts for study back in museum labs. (When I discovered Moon House by accident in 1993, before its exis-

tence was known to more than a small clutch of cognoscenti, my only disappointment was that the site was bereft of potsherds and lithics.)

Lipe and Matson's teams made some remarkable discoveries that applied
to all of Cedar Mesa. The place seemed to have been thoroughly inhabited,
if only by small bands whose average size was the single household, during
three periods: from AD 200 to AD 400, then from 650 to 725, and finally
from 1060 to 1270. But, enigmatically, the mesa was just as thoroughly
abandoned during the two long intervals between those occupations, first
from 400 to 650, then even longer, from 725 to 1060. Population size is
always a tricky business to gauge, but Lipe and Matson estimated a pretty
continuous habitation of 440 to 880 folks during the first phase, of 600 to
1200 during the second, and of 750 to 1,500 during the final, just before the
mass abandonment of nearly all of the Colorado Plateau.

What could have caused those major disruptions, those mini-
abandonments? If Cedar Mesa was a happenin' place for the Anasazi
through most of the seventh century, why was it shunned completely
through the Pueblo I period (750 to 900), when places like Chaco Canyon and the Dolores River Valley saw huge and vital Anasazi incursions?
What made Cedar Mesa bad juju for 300 years?

Lipe and Matson pondered explanations: climate variability, the deple-
tion of resources from slash-and-burn agriculture, population pressure
from areas peripheral to the mesa. Yet even those savvy archaeologists
seemed less than satisfied with their speculations. We can imagine that
the Anasazi might have cut down most of the piñons and junipers on
Cedar Mesa, in a frenzy of building and firewood gathering. But it doesn't
take 300 years for trees to grow back. Today's Puebloans—especially the
Hopi—often argue that migrations and abandonments are dictated not by
environmental crises but by spiritual mandates given to them by their gods.
That's not the kind of explanation that archaeology can prove or disprove.

Bill Lipe was not done with Cedar Mesa after 1975. For decades, he
kept returning to investigate remarkable sites such as Moon House and
Turkey Pen ruin, and a string of grad-student theses and dissertations
wrung new insights from the dirt. Over the years, Lipe has kept his sense

of humor, as the titles of some of his publications reflect ("How Many Turkeys Did It Take to Make a Blanket?"). One of the correctives that archaeology inflicts on our sentimental dreams is a stout dose of icono-clasm. For example: at Moon House, where one of Lipe's teams got the latest tree-ring date of all on Cedar Mesa (AD 1268), an in-depth study came up with a surprising truth. Everyone who visits that unique ruin in McLoyd Canyon, with its delicate inner rooms hidden by its windowless façade, its painted bands with drooping triangles, the apparent representa-tions of full and crescent moon that give it its name, comes away stunned by its beauty. Moon House must have been a palace, we muse, or a sacred shrine where shamans sought their visions. Nope: as a Lipe-run research probe discovered, the place was a regional storage center, a glorified Ana-sazi silo where several years' supply of corn was stored up against the next drought or famine.

If there was one thing about Cedar Mesa that I thought Lipe and Mat-son overlooked, or at least understated, it was the extreme defensiveness of its thirteenth-century cliff dwellings and granaries, which drove the build-ers to wild feats of acrobatic prowess. Over my years of prowling across the mesa, I've been proudest of using my climbing skills to get to redoubts that I'm quite sure no one had reached since the last Anasazi packed up and headed south. How *they* not only got to those scary ledges, but built and eked out survival there, is an enduring mystery. Yet all that Lipe and Matson grant is the tepid remark: "Defensive structures and arrangements are also common in the cliff sites, and many are associated with storage complexes. . . . It may be, then, that groups in the general Cedar Mesa area raided one another after harvest had been completed and food stored." (Blink and you missed it.)

For years, I argued with my go-to Southwest guru, Steve Lekson, that because archaeologists are seldom rock climbers, they've completely failed to recognize the astounding virtuosity that prehistoric daredevils unleashed to get to ledges and alcoves that even modern climbers find daunting and frightening to reach. In 2005 in Range Creek, in east-central Utah, Greg Child and I were able to rappel to a crazy double granary sixty-five feet up an overhanging wall that Fremont people had built a thousand years ago. (Ropes are allowed to access ruins on the Tavaputs Plateau, as they're not on Cedar Mesa.) It was only after I showed Lekson photos of our *outré* maneuvers that he finally stroked his chin and said, "I think I'm beginning to see what you mean."

Lekson and Lipe are longtime friends, with great respect for each other. In 2019, Lekson went on record with this comprehensive appraisal of his colleague:

> Bill Lipe is the Grand Old Man of Four Corners archaeology, in part because he's been doing it for . . . ever. Along the way, he's cranked out fundamental research for understanding its past. Bill has a first-class analytical mind. He can read what your write or hear what you say and, in very short order, tell you—with a smile—exactly how far your head is up your logical hole. He's also very smart, very funny, and a genuinely decent fellow.

Yet about Cedar Mesa, the two men have a fundamental disagreement. Lekson sees the Anasazi who eked out a living there during their three epochs of habitation as marginal, even unimportant, compared to what was going on in the much larger pueblos in the southwest corner of Colorado—not up at Mesa Verde (itself peripheral, he would insist), but in aggregated communities on the open plains such as Lowry, Yellow Jacket, and Yucca House. Not very sexy to look at, those sites: instead of pristine rooms and kivas sheltered by graceful alcoves, those pueblos unfold as row-upon-row of rubble, pounded into submission by the centuries of rain and wind. But no one denies their importance as Anasazi villages.

Lekson's dismissal of Cedar Mesa pains Lipe, since so much of his career has been dedicated to elucidating the lifeways of its aboriginal inhabitants. Yet even Lipe admits that there was something weird going on in this prehistoric hinterland. When I talked to him way back in 1995, he cited a strange ruin in Slickhorn Canyon that he had named Wooden Kiva. In the forty years he'd already toiled in the Southwest, he'd seen nothing like it. "On Cedar Mesa," he told me, "the Anasazi were really going their own way. These people were escaping the confines of normative thought."

Lipe and others estimate that there are at least 100,000 prehistoric sites in the 1.35 million acres that Obama decreed for the Bears Ears monument, ranging from ten- or fifteen-room ruins to small lithic scatters. No other region of comparable size in the United States is as archaeologically rich. One problem with evaluating the significance of all that prehistory is that only Cedar Mesa has been thoroughly studied. Beef Basin, for instance, which is rich in Anasazi structures of a very different kind from the ones Lipe and Matson analyzed—many of them eerie, free-standing towers and complexes, sometimes built of dry-laid stone—has spurred only a single, relatively cursory study based on fieldwork performed back in the early 1950s.

As the momentum built through 2016 toward the designation Obama would make in the last month of his term, then-Interior Secretary Sally Jewell arrived in Bluff to hold a public meeting about the proposed monument. Vaughn Hadenfeldt guided Jewell to such sites as Procession Panel on Comb Ridge, and it was obvious to Vaughn that she "got it" at once. Alas, the next year, when Ryan Zinke made his show tour of the same region, Vaughn and Josh Ewing sensed only the most token reception to their ardent advocacy for Bears Ears protection. I'm sure Vaughn would have been glad to jerk Zinke off his horse—or out of his Black Hawk helicopter—long enough to hike to the Citadel or the Green Mask panel, but the secretary never asked.

One thing I really admire about Bill Lipe is that as the Bears Ears controversy heated up, he threw himself into championing the full monument. Even at age eighty-five, he's staunch and tireless in his engagement with archaeology in the service of saving the irreplaceable past. In 2017, he was instrumental in organizing a two-day meeting of experts in Bluff to lay down strategies to bring archaeology to bear on preserving the landscape Trump (and the Utah legislature) want to turn over to developers. Some of his recent publications bespeak that passionate partisanship, with titles such as "Bears Ears Controversy: Some Monumental Issues."

In March 2019 I got back in touch with Bill, and I mentioned my sadness that cancer now prevented my revisiting some of my favorite places on Cedar Mesa. His response, full of his usual whimsy and self-deprecation, moved me:

> Sorry that your ailment has curtailed your hiking. I have heard vague stories that you've been slowed down by some ailment. My knees started to go bad 20 years ago, and my only good one is the one I had replaced in 2015, and my last fieldwork on Cedar Mesa was in 2012. I guess an advantage of being a biped is that you only have two knees to worry about. I feel sorry for all those older spiders whose joints have started to go. Also now and then I am getting twinges of angina—it comes and goes. Thinking of getting together a show called "The Angina Monologues," where some of us geezers can voice our stories of about how we don't get no respect.

◄◄ ►►

By the spring of 2020, I'd been heading out to Cedar Mesa from Boston every year for twenty-eight years straight. Not just Cedar Mesa, for I'd spent some of my happiest days searching for relics of the ancients in Range Creek, along the Escalante River and its tributary canyons, in the Navajo heartland of the Dinétah in northwest New Mexico, at Chaco Canyon, among the cavates carved out of soft tuff in and around Bandelier National Monument, on the Navajo Reservation (including two five-day backpacks into the magnificent Tsegi Canyon system), at lordly Paquimé in the Mexican state of Chihuahua, as well as other Mogollon refuges deep in the Sierra Madre—in these outbacks, as well as half a dozen others in the greater Southwest.

Yet I keep coming back to Cedar Mesa. Among the hundreds of days I've spent there rim-walking or scrambling into arcane chasms, I can count on the fingers of one hand the outings that have "skunked" me, when six or eight hours of wandering have led to the finding of not a single gray potsherd or flaked sliver of chert. As Vaughn often says, affecting the Swedish-farmer drawl of the neighbors he grew up with near the Colorado-Nebraska border, "Cedar Mesa sure do spoil ya."

In my first years, I checked out the "standard" itineraries—if any trip on Cedar Mesa can be called "standard": the two llama-packing runs through Grand Gulch with Sharon; the classic Fish-and-Owl loop, to which I devoted a pokey four days. Yet even then, I sought out the unpredictable, and it was sheer serendipity that nudged me to the accidental discovery of two of the mesa's most wonderful ruins, Moon House and the Citadel. In 1993 and 1994 I was lucky enough to find the two most extraordinary artifacts I would ever stumble across on Cedar Mesa: a big, intact corrugated pot tucked away on a dead-end ledge in a then little-traveled canyon; and a fantastically well-preserved yucca or willow basket, with a colored triangular decoration woven in, in an even more obscure canyon. The pot and the basket served as the framework for *In Search of the Old Ones*, though I never anticipated (and would eternally regret) the impact my semi-disclosure of those finds would have on too many readers, which was to encourage them to treat my book as if it were a treasure map. I also tasted the sting of backlash, from fellow Cedar Mesa devotees who thought that writing about the place at all was sacrilege. That scorn was distilled in the pithy formula the Kane Gulch ranger, Scott Edwards, delivered after a few beers to Vaughn one evening: "Tell Roberts to shut the fuck up."

On thirteen expeditions to the mountains of Alaska in my twenties and early thirties, not once did I repeat a route that other climbers had put up before me. It was always the quest for new routes and unclimbed peaks that motivated me. Not surprisingly, then, my keenest passion on Cedar Mesa (and elsewhere in the Bears Ears landscape) was to search for ruins or rock art panels that few wanderers before me, or even none, had found. As a kid, on a family outing, I had dutifully followed a park ranger through a tour of a couple of the finest ruins in Mesa Verde National Park, only to come away with the dead feeling of having sat through a lecture in art history. As part of my research for *Old Ones*, I joined a group of forty-five on a tour of Cliff Palace, partly to see if my boredom decades earlier could be dismissed as twelve-year-old attention deficit. The earnest but clueless canned spiel the ranger fed us in 1993, as he herded us through the site in the prescribed sixty minutes flat, rang even deader in my ears than its counterpart had in the 1950s. Perhaps cruelly, I devoted several pages in my first chapter to a sardonic rehash of that error-riddled performance.

What has kept me coming back to Cedar Mesa every year for almost three decades is the freedom I've had to go wherever I pleased, to camp in spots I chose on my own, to figure out routes from rim to canyon floor the way Kent Frost did in the 1940s. Now, even though I've raised my voice in solid support of Obama's national monument, I dread the loss of freedom that designation will inevitably dictate. If in the future five or ten or even fifty times as many people come to the Bears Ears as bothered to before 2016, then there's no way the rangers will allow them to visit Moon House or the Citadel on their own. I've tried to imagine what Moon House would mean to me if I'd hiked down the zigzag trail, equipped in the Park Service future with handrails, then sat on the shelf in front of the guardian façade with thirty other tourists while a uniformed ranger described the wonders that lay behind the portal on the right—for of course the inner, painted rooms would be too fragile to tolerate trespass. And then I remember the enchanted late November afternoon in 1993, when as far as I knew my friend and I were the only people at that moment in all of McLoyd Canyon, as we crawled through the portal and discovered the Moon House that had measured out the silence of the centuries. It's not a happy comparison.

Even gloomier, to my way of thinking, is the very real possibility that after the Bears Ears becomes a national monument, the volume of visitation will dictate the closing of Moon House, the Citadel, and a few other prime sites for good. Not so far-fetched: many of the finest ruins at Mesa Verde have been off-limits to visitors for decades.

One blazing-hot August day in the late 1990s, I set off alone to rim-walk part of Cedar Mesa between two short unnamed side canyons. Two hours in, with binoculars, I spotted what looked like some kind of Anasazi structure half a mile away on the opposite cliff, mostly obscured by a big piñon that grew in front of it. A tricky downclimb of a layback crack and a scratchy bushwhack later, I hiked into the alcove. The proverbial shiver seized the appropriate parts of my body. There in front of me stood a nearly intact kiva, and from the stone-squared entryway in the pristine roof protruded the twin poles of the ladder the Anasazi had used to climb in and out. As far as I knew—and later queries supported the surmise—I might actually have been the first person in modern times to visit this obscure site.

I resisted the urge to clamber inside the kiva, for the ladder poles really were too fragile. Instead I peered and shined my headlamp, noting every detail its weak beam lit up. Late that afternoon, back in Bluff, I sought out Vaughn and breathlessly described my discovery. "No way!" I think he said (or so memory would have it). The next day I led Vaughn and his Far Out Expeditions sidekick Jay Willian to the site. Their own delight was interlaced with unmistakable envy, and by the end of our outing they were teasing me about how this would be the perfect place to bring a group of clients (were they Girl Scouts from Provo?) they had lined up next week.

There's no getting around the fact that for many of us who cherish such discoveries in the prehistoric wilderness, the quest is a competitive sport. Vaughn Hadenfeldt and Greg Child, the two friends with whom I've done the most sleuthing on Cedar Mesa, are fiercely competitive fellows, no matter how well they camouflage that penchant, and I'm certainly their match in that respect. Well do I remember the moment early on the third day of our Comb Ridge traverse when Greg suddenly blurted out, "There's one!," only to have Vaughn exclaim, "I saw it too!" Keeping my mouth shut, I threw off my sixty-pound pack, even while an internal dialogue volleyed between *Nice find, Greg!* and *Shit, if he hadn't been two paces in front.* . . . But the happiness we shared was genuine, as we fondled the perfect Basketmaker dart point, chiseled out of creamy white chalcedony with streaks of red, before tucking it back in the sand exactly where we'd found it.

The spasm of wonder that arrives with such a discovery in the Anasazi outback is deepened, for me at least, by the realization that very few others have ever beheld the object of my rapture. Those moments are indelible in memory. I think of a single petroglyph tucked around a corner on a short band of cliffs high on a plateau north of Cedar Mesa that Sharon and I came upon one day. Atlatl Man, I call him: with a single plume arcing from the top of his head, wearing what look like mountain boots or galoshes, he holds a fending stick in his lowered right hand, a half-moon-painted shield raised in his left, all to no avail, for his enemy has struck home with an atlatl dart planted solidly in his chest. Or the Frankenstein panel, as Greg and I call it, fifty feet up on a ledge in Grand Gulch that Greg brilliantly figured out a way to get to: a row of ghostly gray, narrow-cheeked, silently screaming heads painted who-knows-when by the Edvard Munch of the Cedar Mesa Anasazi.

Or the dazzling swaths of shining lithics scattered across the summit of Pollys Island. Or a granary I soloed to way up near the rim of Grand Gulch that could be seen from below only from a single vantage point in a side canyon a mile away. Or the two-story ruin tucked under a massive sloping caprock that Vaughn and I figured out how to hike to after he glassed it from far down-canyon on the opposite side, the account of which I splashed across the opening pages of this book. . . .

In recent years, some clever revisionists have turned what was long regarded as the glorious cavalcade of exploration and discovery on its head by arguing that the quest for the unknown is inseparable from the dismal Western tradition of imperialism and conquest. In this rereading, even such blithe adventurers as Eric Shipton and Bill Tilman, who always forswore any taint of jingoism or nationalist goals, stand indicted along with the grand poo-bahs who subjugated India under the Raj or wept at the thought of the sun setting on the British Empire. Lewis and Clark, the revisionists claim, were as guilty of colonizing Native Americans as Andrew Jackson.

My initial reaction to these critiques was a hearty British "Balderdash!," followed by the discomforting thought, *Maybe there's something to it after all*. No game was more ruthlessly competitive than the Great Game, the struggle between British and Russian explorers in the nineteenth century to seize control of central Asia. The quests for the North and South Poles at the beginning of the twentieth century were fiercely nationalistic, pitting Brits against Norwegians against Americans. Likewise the campaign to claim the first ascents of the fourteen highest mountains in the world from 1950 to 1964, which matched British, French, Swiss, German, American, Italian, Austrian, and even Japanese and Chinese climber-heroes against one another.

But could these strictures tell me anything about my passion for Cedar Mesa? When I found a rock art panel almost nobody had seen before, was I fetishizing it in my pride, even appropriating it as belonging to me (if only intellectually), and thereby marginalizing the ancients who had created it? Could a new national monument, with designated campgrounds, hiking fees and permits, ranger-led tours, and sites accessed by paved trails and cordoned off behind guardrails perversely steal the numinous past from Native Americans by turning their legacy into a thing for white folks to "do" on their vacations?

Climbing has always been an unabashedly competitive pursuit. If you put up a new route, it gets named after you—the Steck-Salathé on Sentinel Rock, the Bonatti Pillar on the Petit Dru. Not so the search for the vestiges left behind by the Old Ones. The kiva with the intact ladder I found in the nameless side-canyon that hot August day will never be known, thank God, as "Roberts's kiva." Yes, I'll grant, when I find something strange and unique in the backcountry I feel the faint temptation of ownership; the babbling id brags, *I found it, it's mine.* But sentience and curiosity take over. *It's mine* dissolves into the far more potent *What's it all about?*

There are profound unsolved questions raised by what the Anasazi made and did that archaeology so far has been powerless to answer. I'll mention one. All across the Southwest, Anasazi rock art panels rigorously observe a set of stylistic conventions. The atlatl or spear-thrower is always engraved as a straight line bisecting a circle, iconic shorthand for the shaft and the double finger loop the hunter uses to propel his weapon. Mountain lions are always portrayed with the same bold ellipse of jagged teeth and spiraling dangle of toes. Flute players are always limned in profile, sometimes with massive erections, sometimes supine with their legs kicking air. Basketmaker humanoids invariably have triangular or trapezoidal torsos that taper from massive shoulders to slender waists. Duck-headed humans proliferate (what are they about?) Even the representations of abstract things—spirals, concentric rings, "rakes" that may or may not signal rain, "tabbed lobes" (and what are *they* about?)—hew to rigid conventions.

So here's the puzzle. How could a people who never organized in bands much larger than the extended family, who had no chiefs or governments or schools, produce a rock art that for centuries, across hundreds of miles, repeated again and again the exact same ways of engraving a bighorn sheep or painting a headpiece? Why didn't every extended family produce its own art, Grandma Moses miniatures in Slickhorn Canyon, Edward Hopper tableaux in Fish? How did aesthetic orthodoxy seep into the yucca brushes and stone knives of artists so far apart that they'd never met those distant strangers, or even heard a word spoken in the strange dialect they mouthed?

It's a question that archaeology hasn't tackled, so far as I know. The same conundrum animates Anasazi pottery. Mesa Verde Black-on-White looks very different from Tusayan Polychrome, as befits the 125-mile–odd gap between the centers of their contemporary workshops. But with Mesa Verde Black-on-White, the same lines of dots, the same zigzag bands, the same diamond squares chasing squared-off spirals into stair-step interiors grace pot after pot. And over in the Tusayan, the same swatches of bold orange and black polygons prevail.

Each time I stare at an Anasazi rock art panel, I ponder this mystery again. And in those moments, as I try to see the world as the ancients might have, my own ego shrinks, or so it seems. It's what *they* did that matters, and why—not whether I'm the first or the one-thousandth modern to find the cliff on which the Old Ones let their visions and their stories all hang out.

With a mountain, one shot was enough, unless we failed and had to give it another shot. After climbing the west face of Mount Huntington or Shot Tower in the Brooks Range, I never needed to come back. If decades later, I could hire a bush pilot to fly near so I could take photos, that was gratification enough. But on Cedar Mesa, or elsewhere in the prehistoric Southwest, I never tire of returning to a familiar site. By now I must have hiked to Moon House or the Citadel twenty or thirty times each, but those eloquent ruins never grow old.

During my first years of Cedar Mesa pilgrimage, I was keen to find something new on every trip. But after a while I started taking friends to my favorite sites. The vicarious enjoyment I absorbed from their own "aha!" moments furnished a whole new reason for returning to the canyons. A few of my friends—it always surprised me which ones—were unmoved by the Anasazi phenomenon. Then the disappointment was as sharp as the pleasure of winning over a new devotee had been. It was like playing a CD of a favorite piece of music, or reciting a favorite poem, only to have that listener hear only noise. Even worse—because the exercise stretched across the better part of a day, and my anticipation built through the hours of hiking on approach: "Just around the next bend. Wait'll you see it."

During the last fifteen years, I thought I'd found my perfect recipe for Cedar Mesa visits. If I could mix forays into new canyon stretches looking for things I'd never found before with jaunts to favorite sites that almost always won the jaw-drop approval of one friend after another, I could pack a week or three of hiking and camping on Cedar Mesa and beyond so full of delight that the journey always supplied one of the high points of my year. I imagined an indefinite future of more of the same. I saw myself tottering over my ski poles, like Gene Foushee in his mid-eighties heading into Davis Gulch, as I explored my favorite place on earth until I could no longer walk.

◄◄ ►►

Then in July 2015, I was diagnosed with stage 4 throat cancer. Sharon and I had planned our usual trip to Cedar Mesa for the coming autumn, but after seven weeks of intensive radiation (thirty-four zappings under a green mesh mask that bolted my head immobile to a rigid plank) and chemotherapy (the loss of all my hair, extreme nausea and fatigue, vomiting, insomnia, colitis, daily migraines, fainting), I knew it would be impossible to get to Utah. In September, alarmed by my inability to swallow normally, the doctors decreed that I needed to have a feeding tube inserted in my stomach. After that, lunch and dinner became bottles of Osmolite and Ensure flushed down the tube direct to my stomach. Just as well—hunger itself had become a distant memory.

I spent good parts of September and October 2015 not camped at Muley Point, but in Brigham and Women's Hospital, where I had to call a nurse for help, or at least surveillance, each time I staggered out of my bed and over to the adjoining bathroom to deliver a weak stream of piss. Sharon came every day, and often spent the night curled uncomfortably in a chair. The deep frown of worry on her face scared me more than my own nightmares.

There was more pain, dulled but not eliminated by Oxycodone, than I'd experienced in the first seventy-two years of my life put together. At my nadir, hospitalized this time for aspiration pneumonia, the pain was bad enough that I realized I didn't care much whether I'd live or die.

In November, back home in Watertown, I took my first halting hikes. To navigate one block west from the corner on which we lived and back, I needed to rest three times on neighbors' front-yard walls. Jon Krakauer flew out from Colorado for a week to help Sharon care for me and to try to boost my spirits. On one walk—appropriately enough in the Mount Auburn cemetery—I got twelve feet from the car before I crumpled to my knees and had to be helped back to the passenger seat. Jon said later that he seriously thought he might be watching me die.

I wasn't sure how soon I would expire, but I clung to the life raft of the conviction that at least my mind was intact. A lifelong compulsive reader, now I devoured books maniacally, and even though I was too weak to go to the library to do research, I started writing the book that would become *Limits of the Known*.

During the first eight months after my diagnosis, Sharon and I traveled no farther than twenty-five miles from our house in Watertown, always with her at the wheel. Through many sleepless hours in bed, I ruminated on the losses cancer had already inflicted, and on the ones that the madly reproducing cells had waiting for me in the future. Seven months of Osmolite and Ensure instead of lamb chops or tuna sandwiches or beer was a big loss. My hearing, excellent most of my life, had turned patchy in my late sixties, and I'd started wearing hearing aids in 2014. But chemo dealt a further blow, and for a year I had a kind of tinnitus that never let up in my left ear, and if I slept on my left side, my heartbeat was broadcast direct from ear to brain. Listening to music, I had trouble separating chemical screech from woodwind harmony, and that was a loss, especially of my beloved Schubert. So was the difficulty I now had catching conversations around a table, or even hearing Sharon clearly at home. "What?!" had always seemed to me a rude injunction, but now I fired it her way twenty times a day, always with mixed sorrow and irritation.

But I was alive. In February 2016 I accomplished my first hike of six full blocks, which felt like a real triumph. In April Sharon and I played eighteen holes of golf with a cart, and while I couldn't pretend that was serious exercise, it was fun and it was in the outdoors. The doctors at Dana-Farber held out the cautious hope that the radiation and chemo had gotten all the cancer. So I was ready to be bold.

I invited my two oldest climbing buddies, Matt Hale and Ed Ward, to join Sharon and me on Cedar Mesa. Matt had hiked there often with us; Ed never. In May we flew to Denver, then drove more than four hundred miles to Bluff. I had no idea what hikes I could manage, but since Ed knew nothing of Anasazi wonders, we could start easy (Target House, the Mule Canyon towers) and work up. We even managed to get to the Citadel—by far the strongest effort I had yet undertaken, at five miles round-trip and some four hundred feet of altitude gained and lost. In years and years of climbing, backpacking, and sports, Ed had wrecked his knees, reducing them to cartilage-less bone grinding on bone. He was able to hobble at about my pace, in worse pain, so our four-person team struck a steady pace of one mile per hour. (A year later Ed had surgery to replace both knees with artificial joints.)

No sooner had we come back home than the joy of hiking on Cedar Mesa again, however circumscribed, was dashed by bad news. Somehow my cancer had provoked an irreversible ailment called SIADH—the acronym for the abstruse condition called syndrome of inappropriate anti-diuretic hormone secretion. What it meant was that for the rest of my life I would have to take massive doses of sodium (salt pills), and that I should never drink "free water" (what a strange term for the wonderful stuff I'd guzzled from mountain streams since I was a teenager). All my water from now on would have to be adulterated with electrolytes.

But there was worse. The throat cancer had metastasized to my lungs.

Thus in the summer of 2016, I once more reconciled myself to hospitals, and to the likelihood that I would die relatively soon, and not in any pleasant way.

◄◄ ►►

Four years later, I'm still alive. This despite two more metastases, the first to my adrenal glands, the most recent, in December 2019, to my abdomen. I owe my survival not to any pluck or toughness or willpower of my own, as cancer victims who stay alive are routinely hailed for marshaling. (The metaphor that truly sets my teeth on edge is "the battle against cancer," which while it aims to celebrate survivors, ends up shaming those who die as losers.) No—the credit goes to my brilliant oncologists at the Dana-Farber Cancer Institute, and to a radical new treatment, immunotherapy, that rightly earns the chemicals that enact it the old cliché, "miracle drugs." All through my years of treatment, friends and strangers have sent me messages that insist, "You climbed all those mountains, you wrote all those books, you can beat this." Sorry: it's not the discipline I applied to Mount Huntington or the Comb Ridge traverse or *Limits of the Known* when I was feeling lousy that's kept me out of the grave, but pembrolizumab, nivolumab, and ipilimumab.

So far. For once cancer metastasizes, it's incurable. For the last five years, I've lingered in that limbo the medical profession likes to call "palliative care."

Since that May 2016 trip with Matt Hale and Ed Ward, Sharon and I have returned to Cedar Mesa—and to other parts of the greater Bears Ears domain—no fewer than seven times. On every one of those trips, we've taken friends along to show them places that still send my heart soaring and my brain cogitating. Along the way, I've learned my physical limits, limits I think I'll not surpass in the few years I have left. The most miles I've managed to cover on slickrock or in canyon bottom is about six, round-trip. The greatest gain and loss of altitude, about 800 feet. Only seven years ago, before cancer, I was still capable of hiking fifteen miles and cruising up and down some 2,500 feet on a long, hard day, but not one that truly wiped me out. Never again.

On none of those eight post-cancer trips have I been able to go off the way I used to and explore corners of the Bears Ears where I hadn't been before. The joy I've felt, though, at sharing the genius of the Anasazi with my friends has been deeper than ever before. Yet every time on Cedar Mesa, it hurts to come to the edge of places I used to count among my favorite day-trip destinations, and realize that I can no longer get to them. (Sharon could get to some of them, but she'd rather stay with me.) The hurt is visceral: I taste it on my radiated tongue.

Beyond me now forever are Sheiks Canyon down to Green Mask panel, around the head of Water Canyon to the Great Gallery, the full McLoyd loop, Step and Pine Canyons down to the Quail Panel, the Hardscrabble entry to Grand Gulch . . . and many others. On several of our recent trips, Sharon and I have gone halfway, then sent our younger or stronger friends onward, armed with sketch maps and promises to take photos. There's a reward in that, but of course it's not the same.

Bears Ears: the places where I planned to go, and now never will. Bodie

Canyon. The full west fork of Salt Creek. The summit of Bridger Jack Mesa. Youngs Canyon, and lower Dark. Mancos Mesa. Gravel, Hideout, and K and L Canyons. Harts Draw. Lockhart Basin. . . . Together those places make up, in Tennyson's words, "that untraveled world whose margin fades/ Forever and forever when I move."

I've always been aware, of course, that my way of learning and loving the Bears Ears is only one of many. Al Scorup and Kent Frost had their own agendas out there, different from mine. So did Posey and Jim Mike. For the Native Americans who first launched the crusade to save that irreplaceable landscape from oil rigs and private inholdings and ATV trails—the Navajos, Utes, Paiutes, and Puebloans who put their muscle behind the Inter-Tribal Coalition—the Bears Ears has a spiritual power deeper than any transport I can summon up there. What matters is that their need to keep the place inviolate dovetails with mine, and Vaughn's, and Greg's, and Fred's. The ones for whom the Bears Ears had the deepest meaning, of course, were the ancients who made it their home, century after century. But we'll never know what they thought or felt or knew.

In September 2019, Sharon and I hiked a good ways out along the rim of one of Cedar Mesa's canyons with Bill Briggs and Larry Graham. Bill grew up with me in Boulder, and we attended the same schools, a few years apart. We lost touch, then reunited several years ago. He's a legendary pioneer of Colorado climbing, but it was Sharon and I who got him hooked on Cedar Mesa and the Anasazi. Larry is Bill's climbing partner, as well as a world-class pianist, and now he's hooked too.

More than ten years ago, on a solo jaunt, I discovered a remarkable ruin on a ledge about 150 feet below that rim. It's a major site, with possibly two kivas and a couple of pristine rooms with intact roofs. I couldn't figure out any way to get to it. In 2013 I went back, determined to try. After two false stabs, I inched along the ruin ledge from around the corner to the left. Though I got to a place that I knew was only about a hundred feet from the site, which remained out of view, I was stopped cold by a seamless vertical buttress that blocked the way. Unclimbable, even for the Anasazi.

In September 2019, Bill and Larry stared at the ruin from where I had first spotted it more than a decade before. There wasn't time to try to get to it, and the hike back to the car exhausted me. But we've been scheming up a return ever since. Bill and Larry have a couple of plans. As keenly as I'd love to share the discovery with them, if they can pull it off, I know it's more than I can handle. And more than Sharon can.

So when we go back, Sharon and I will wait and watch, maybe from that same rim overlook. This time it won't hurt. Whatever discovery Bill and Larry can make, somehow we'll be part of it. For me, it will be enough to recline on the slickrock, close to the person I've loved more than anyone else in my long life—next to the woman who, even more than the doctors at Dana-Farber, has kept me alive through five years of cancer— as we linger for another few charmed hours in that corner of my favorite place on earth.

ACKNOWLEDGMENTS

During the last three decades, I've been blessed with the company of many of my best friends as we explored the matchless domain of the Bears Ears. All of them shared my astonishment at the vestiges of the ancients we discovered there, undimmed since my first foray into Bullet Canyon in 1987, as well as reveling in the pristine beauty of the canyons, mesa tops, and piñon-juniper forests. In my dedication, I salute the three—Fred, Vaughn, and Greg—who most profoundly influenced the ways I discovered and understood this semi-wilderness.

Those friends are too numerous to name here, but among those who have come back several times, or expressed a limitless curiosity about how the Old Ones did it, I must mention above all my longtime buddy and climbing partner Matt Hale, who has partnered with me in more than a dozen Bears Ears outings. Also (in no particular order) Mary Tobin, Nils Bonde-Henriksen, Bill Briggs, Larry Graham, Irene Owsley, Charley Lecompte, Karen Roos, Judi and Rick Wineland-Thomson and their daughter Erica Landerson, Shannon O'Donoghue, Ariann Child, Connie Massingale, Deanna Clay, Kara Faciszewski, Ed Ward, Emmett Lyman, Sarah Keyes, Alissa Doherty, John Gassel, the late Marie-France Moisi, Stephanie Scott, Kelly Adair, and Caty Enders.

In Bluff, Jim and Luanne Hook, my hosts for thirty years at Recapture

Lodge, as well as at their adjunct lodgings in Adams House and West House, have become great friends, logistical saviors (Jim organized the resupplies for our Comb Ridge traverse), and limitless sources of Bears Ears lore. Gene Foushee, who as much as anyone put a revived and invigorated Bluff on the map, served as a sage for the region until his death in 2017. Bluff is where I've periodically reunited with Gus and Sandra Scott, pioneer explorers of the whole Southwest, whose knowledge supplemented that of Gene and Jim and Luanne. Larry Sanford, ace llama wrangler, organized my jaunts with friends into the Dark Canyon wilderness, lower Fish Creek, and upper Grand Gulch, where his uncomplaining, sure-footed camelids turned our journeys downright cushy. Marcia Hadenfeldt, a pillar of the Bluff community, has served for decades as my friend, informant, and critical advisor. And Josh Ewing, in his role as director of Friends of Cedar Mesa, steered me skillfully through the shoals of Bears Ears politics.

I benefited handsomely from in-person interviews, both on and off the record, with folks who knew all kinds of things I barely grasped: Vaughn and Marcia Hadenfeldt, Jim Hook, Fred Blackburn, Josh Ewing, Willie Grayeyes, Jonathan Till, Kay Shumway, Robert McPherson, Winston Hurst, Andy Nettell, Ariann Child, and Zak Podmore. Adam Vitale, a Harvard grad student in archaeology whom I hired as a research assistant, smoothly turned those tape recordings into transcripts. By e-mail, I gained many insights from Gavin Noyes, Phil Lyman, Bill Lipe, Winston Hurst, and my touchstone Southwestern archaeologist, Steve Lekson. Winston's mordant iconoclasm, sharp wit, and profound understanding of Bears Ears prehistory have kept me hanging on his every word for thirty years.

At the Marriott Library of the University of Utah in Salt Lake City, I dredged up reams of invaluable oral testimony from the Doris Duke Oral History Collection and the Doris Duke American Indian History Project. I found useful bits of info at the Grand County Public Library in Moab and the Utah State Historical Society in Salt Lake City, and relied on many crucial sources in Widener and Tozzer libraries at Harvard.

Numerous sagacious scholars plowed the Bears Ears ground from which I plucked a rich harvest. Citations of their work can be found in my bibliography.

As they have so often with my books, Matt Hale and Ed Ward read several chapters in draft and offered their valuable comments. Thanks to them for that.

Charley Lecompte took on for me what is always the most fiendish of bookmaking tasks: researching historic photos and securing permissions for them. He did a masterly job, organizing everything with an efficiency I never expected. In addition, he crafted the pair of excellent maps that appear at the beginning of this book. Bravo, Charley! (Alpha Bravo Charley . . . ?)

This is my sixth book for Star Lawrence, the legendary editor at W. W. Norton and Company. I've come to rely on his eagle eye for my errant flights of self-indulgence or soft writing. In this case, at the beginning of a long section about one of the eccentric oddballs in Bears Ears history—a narrative I had great fun writing—Star penciled in the margin, "What in God's name is this story doing in this book?," then proceeded to cut the next thirteen pages. He was right.

At Norton, Nneoma Amadi-obi performed all the crucial and fussy tasks of turning draft pages into a book and catching the glitches that could lead to embarrassment (or worse, legal action) with grace and patience, especially when I grew a bit churlish about toeing the line. Erin Lovett managed the vital business of publicity, making sure our book wedged its elbows into the fiercely competitive publishing market, with her usual aplomb. My copy editor, William Avery Hudson, did a fine and scrupulous job of catching my mistakes, especially those misspellings that slide past the eye of many a diligent proofreader.

I've had the great good fortune to be represented for the last twenty-one years by one of the best literary agents in existence, Stuart Krichevsky. This is our seventeenth book together, and during the course of our long association we've become friends in a way that I think is rare between author and agent. We trade jibes about the Red Sox and Mets, about steak and Schubert (strange as that sounds), but more and more I find myself confiding some of my deepest fears and hopes to Stuart about matters that I'm not ready to share with my readers. At Banff in November 2019, Stuart once again hosted the raucous and genial private dinner for "his" writers, and once again it was the high point of the book-and-film festival for me. In recent years, I've been able to steer several younger writers his way, whose books have flourished and won acclaim under his nurturing touch: a small favor compared to all those he's done for me. What I admire most about Stuart is his deeply moral center. There are books he knows would make money that he won't take on because of whom they might hurt, or because he senses the psychic toll they would inflict on their creators. In the cutthroat business of publishing, this is a very rare virtue.

At the Stuart Krichevsky Literary Agency, once again Laura Usselman and Aemilia Phillips flawlessly handled all kinds of tedious tasks that end up making a career as a writer viable, from negotiating contracts for audiobooks to asking luminaries for blurbs to funneling royalties to the author's bank. Without them, the loneliness of the long-distance scribbler would be lonelier (and poorer) indeed.

In my last three books (including this one), I've sung the praises of my wife, Sharon Roberts. Most authors do so, at least at the end of their acknowledgments. But during the five years since I was afflicted with cancer, Sharon has literally kept me alive. I know how much the effort has cost her—the decision abruptly to end her flourishing career as a psychoanalyst so she could take care of me marked a great loss. For this book, she typed half the chapters from dictation and critically read the chapters I was able to peck out with my single right index finger. More importantly, she's been my companion through every day of our last nine trips to the Bears Ears region, all the journeys we've made there since I "got" cancer.

We've been married now for more than fifty-two years. Whether oddly or predictably, the last five have been our happiest together. I don't like to think how easily it could have been otherwise, without her magnanimity and love. I simply cling to it as the greatest blessing I've received toward the end of my life.

NOTES

Two: In Search of a Lost Race

12   **"It signifies the relationship of all people"**: Gavin Noyes to author, May 2019.

13   **"You know how muddy that road gets"**: Jim Hook to author, March 2019.

15   **The only surviving account of this journey**: Camp, ed., *George C. Yount*, pp. x, 85.

16   **"the longest, crookedest, and most arduous"**: Hafen, quoted in Camp, *George C. Yount*, p. x.

16   **In charge of a team, grandly titled**: Madsen, *Exploring Desert Stone*, pp. xvi–xix, 64–78.

18   **"I cannot conceive of a more worthless"**: Macomb, quoted in Madsen, *Exploring Desert Stone*, p. 75.

18   **"the wildest and most fantastic scenery"**: Newberry journal, quoted in Madsen, *Exploring Desert Stone*, pp. 75, 77.

18   **"[L]ooking around there met our eyes"**: Dimmock diary, quoted in Madsen, *Exploring Desert Stone*, p. 75.

20   **The Navajo name for the panel**: Allen, *Utah's Canyon Country*, vol. 2, p. 538.

23   **"There is no key to the meaning"**: Morris, "An Unexplored Area of the Southwest," p. 502.

27   **This grand enterprise was entrusted**: McPherson and Neel, *Mapping the Four Corners*, pp. 8–9, 29–30, 32.

28   **"Not only did they stay all night"**: Holmes, "Field Notes," quoted in McPherson and Neel, *Mapping the Country*, p. 102.

28   "Nearly the whole of this canyon region": Cuthbert Mills, *New York Times,* September 9, 1875, quoted in McPherson and Neel, p. 126.

29   "The ruins were so numerous now": Jackson and Driggs, *The Pioneer Photographer,* p. 266.

29   "In a long shallow cave ... we discovered": Jackson, *Time Exposure,* p. 238.

30   In 1923, Samuel Guernsey, a Harvard professor: Guernsey, *Explorations in Northeastern Arizona,* pp. 45–53.

31   Seizing this opportunity was a coterie: Knipmeyer, *In Search of a Lost Race,* pp. 9, 15.

31   "no articles of scientific value have been contributed": ibid., p. 13.

32   "The ... Expedition will begin its labors": ibid., pp. 14–15.

32   Five miles into their float trip: ibid., pp. 48–52.

33   From their camp at Noland's, the team: ibid., pp. 77–84.

33   On May 5 the team packed up their camp: ibid., pp. 89–90.

34   "There is no interest whatsoever in camp life": ibid., pp. 101–102.

35   "As a conclusion, we would say": ibid., p. 123.

35   Out of all their hard work, the IAEE: ibid., p. 150.

Three: Manuelito's Dirge

36   Manuelito, one of the greatest Navajo leaders: Correll, "Manuelito," p. 11B.

36   Among the epithets his people bestowed: ibid., p. 11B.

36   While still a youth, Manuelito married a daughter: McNitt, *Navajo Wars,* p. 120.

36   (Navajo: "scratch for water"): *WPA Guide to 1930s New Mexico,* p. 338.

37   Instead, the Navajos utterly routed: Correll, "Manuelito," p. 11B.

37   Two years later, Manuelito played: ibid., p. 11B.

38   "If the muskets and cannons of the Americans": McNitt, *Navajo Wars,* p. 120.

38   "[I]n the future if the Navajos stole": ibid., pp. 118–119.

38   "We have waged war against the New Mexicans": Zarcillos Largos, as translated by Captain Horatio Hughes, quoted in ibid., p. 118.

39   In July 1849, several Navajos murdered: ibid., pp. 135–146.

40   In Diné lore, he had always been wary: Bighorse, *Bighorse the Warrior,* pp. 13, 100.

40   "It is a tragic irony that the American Indian": Ryan Winn, "Robert Kennedy's Indian Commitment," *Tribal College: Journal of American Indian Higher Education,* June 1, 2018 (web exclusive), https://tribalcollegejournal.org/robert-kennedys-indian-commitment/.

41   In 2018 Maryboy recalled Kennedy's visit: Robinson and Strom, *Voices from the Bears Ears,* pp. 51–52.

41   "lead a quiet life, free of controversy": ibid., p. 53.

42 **"The ethnographic mapping interviews at Bears Ears":** Gavin Noyes to author, April 2019.

42 **"My name is Desbaa', 'Warrior Woman'":** "Item #0703: John Sampson Yazhi, Desbaa' 'Warrior Woman', Kit'siili 'Old Ruins' (Navajo) (1/18/61)," *UAIDA Oral Histories Transcripts*, J. Willard Marriott Digital Library, University of Utah, https://collections.lib.utah.edu/details?id=347276.

43 **Also in January 1961, the Doris Duke program:** "Item #0704: John Sampson Yazhi, Desbaa' 'Warrior Woman', Kit'siili 'Old Ruins' (Navajo) (1/18/61)," *UAIDA Oral Histories Transcripts*, J. Willard Marriott Digital Library, University of Utah, https://collections.lib.utah.edu/details?id=347283.

44 **Mark Maryboy insists that he is Manuelito's:** Carson Bear, "'The Spirits Are Still There': A Personal Reflection on Bears Ears National Monument," National Trust for Historic Preservation, May 24, 2017, https://savingplaces.org/stories/mark-maryboy-personal-reflection-bears-ears-national-monument#.XKN-aqR7lc8.

44 **One of his sons, Bob Manuelito, was interviewed:** "Interview with Manuelito, Bob," Center for Southwest Research, University Libraries, University of New Mexico, American Indian Oral History Navajo Transcripts, Tape #345, February 1969, https://nmdigital.unm.edu/digital/collection/navtrans/id/147/.

44 **"Maryboy's people have always been leaders":** Rob Schultheis, "Deep in Bears Ears Country," *Alta*, January 8, 2019, https://altaonline.com/bears-ears-last-stand/.

45 **"Manuelito, born five miles south":** McPherson, *As If the Land Owned Us,* p. 97.

46 **"There are always surprises, but I can":** Robert McPherson to author, February 2019.

46 **"Manuelito was born near 1818":** Van Valkenburgh, *Diné Bikéyah*, p. 91.

46 **"Following their release from Fort Sumner":** McPherson, *A History of San Juan County*, p. 121.

47 **"only the Utes could justify a strong":** ibid., pp. 121, 135.

47 **McPherson repeats and endorses the oft-cited:** ibid., p. 297.

48 **"on anyone who 'knowingly places'":** Brian Maffly, "New Utah Legislator," *Salt Lake Tribune*, January 30, 2019.

48 **"a great friend and a truly great historian":** Phil Lyman to author, January 2019.

48 **"Here's the problem, as I see it":** Phil Lyman to author, January 2019.

49 **The nadir of the Mormon perspective:** Christopher Smart, "Navajo Elder Says," *Salt Lake Tribune*, June 9, 2017; Vaughn Hadenfeldt to author, July 2019; Zac Podmore, "Native Voices Aren't Being Heard," *High Country News*, December 21, 2017.

49 **"His brother, Cayetanito, rescued him":** Correll, "Manuelito," p. 11B.

50   **"He sure fought like a cat":** "Interview with Manuelito, Bob."

50   **In maturity Manuelito was very tall:** ibid., p. 120.

51   **Brigadier General James H. Carleton, appointed:** Trafzer, *The Kit Carson Campaign,* p. 58.

51   **The epic tragedy that unfurled:** e.g., Bailey, *The Long Walk*; Bailey, *Bosque Redondo*; Trafzer, *The Kit Carson Campaign*; Kelly, *Navajo Roundup*; Thompson, *The Army and the Navajo*; among others.

52   **"All Indian men of that tribe":** Carleton to Carson, October 12, 1862, quoted in Kelly, *Navajo Roundup*, p. 11.

53   **Thus one officer arriving at the Bosque:** Roberts, "The Long Walk to Bosque Redondo," p. 50.

53   **"People were shot down on the spot":** Curly Tso, in *Navajo Stories of the Long Walk Period*, pp. 103–104.

53   **"The U.S. Army fed corn to its horses":** Mose Denejolie, in *Navajo Stories of the Long Walk Period*, p. 242.

53   **For almost four years from the inception:** Kelly, *Navajo Roundup,* pp. 151–167.

53   **According to Lee Correll, the Utes stole:** Correll, "Manuelito," p. 14B.

54   **Manuelito rallied the remnants of his band:** Trafzer, *The Kit Carson Campaign*, p. 221.

54   **A best estimate gives the following numbers:** Roberts, "The Long Walk to Bosque Redondo," pp. 48–49, 54.

55   **In 1863, at about age thirty-five, Hashkéneinii fled:** Roberts, *The Lost World of the Old Ones*, p. 173.

55   **Robert McPherson claims that during the next few years:** McPherson, *Comb Ridge and Its People*, p. 86.

55   **an interview with Hashkéneinii's son, Hoskinini-Begay:** Kelly, "Chief Hoskaninni," pp. 219–226.

55   **In 2013 Greg Child and I spent five:** Roberts, *The Lost World*, pp. 173–186.

56   **As Hoskinini-begay later told:** Kelly, "Chief Hoskaninni," p. 222.

56   **"[H]e told them that he was right":** "Interview with Manuelito, Bob."

56   **The Navajo Way hangs on a belief:** Roberts, "The Long Walk to Bosque Redondo," p. 54.

57   **"It was the Diné's own fault to be rounded up":** Charley Sandoval testimony, in *Navajo Stories of the Long Walk Period*, p. 142.

57   **At Fort Sumner, in recognition of his sway:** Correll, "Manuelito," p. 14B.

57   **Carleton himself had requested reassignment:** Kelly, *Navajo Roundup*, pp. 168–169.

57   **In May 1868 they won a significant concession:** Thompson, *The Army and the Navajo*, pp. 151–152.

58 **Finally, in May 1868, Sherman met:** "Treaty between the United States of America," pp. 1–25.

58 **"The day came of their return":** "Interview with Manuelito, Bob."

59 **"When we saw the top of the mountain":** quoted in Thompson, *The Army and the Navajo*, p. 140.

60 **"Death and everything connected with it":** Kluckhohn and Leighton, *The Navaho*, p. 184.

62 **In Canyon de Chelly in 2008:** see Roberts, *The Lost World of the Old Ones*, pp. 155–172.

63 **Two years later, Fred Blackburn and I:** see Roberts, *Escape Routes*, pp. 239–252.

66 **In the middle of our eighteen-day traverse:** see Roberts, *Sandstone Spine*, pp. 97–99.

68 **Three months later, I read in the newspaper:** Dennis Romboy, "Utah Man Faces Federal Murder Charge," *Deseret News*, December 14, 2018.

75 **In 2003, as I joined a group of visitors:** Roberts, *The Pueblo Revolt*, p. 94.

76 **A corroborating source fell into my hands:** Ingstad, *The Apache Indians*, pp. 2–3.

77 **"Brugge was the preeminent non-Navajo expert":** Steve Lekson to author, August 2019.

77 **Then in 2012, seemingly out of the blue:** Brugge, "Emergence of the Navajo People," pp. 124–149.

80 **"I think Brugge's probably right":** Steve Lekson to author, August 2019.

80 **As Barboncito, the eloquent speaker:** Correll, "Manuelito," p. 15B.

80 **"From a list they made of men suspected":** ibid., p. 15B.

80 **In 1880, Manuelito agreed to try to curb:** ibid., p. 15B.

81 **The school's motto, a purportedly humanitarian:** Yurth, "Manuelito's Legacy," [n. p.].

81 **But already by 1882, reservation inspector:** Correll, "Manuelito," p. 15B.

81 **According to a contemporary quoted:** ibid., p. 15B.

81 **Shortly before he died, Manuelito:** Correll, "Manuelito," p. 16B.

82 **I had read an article in the *Navajo Times*:** Yurth, "Manuelito's Legacy," [n. p.].

Four: Shumway's Shovel

84 **It was early morning, June 10:** Mozingo, "A Sting in the Desert."

84 **He was known for ministering extensively:** "Legacy of Kindness: James Redd, The Man Bullied to Death by the BLM," *Free Range Report*, February 11, 2017, http://www.freerangereport.com/legacy-of-kindness-james-redd-the-man-bullied-to-death-by-the-blm/.

85   **The raid, planned in secret for months:** Mozingo, "A Sting in the Desert."

85   **The Redds were driven twenty-five miles north:** ibid.

85   **The next morning, before dawn, after a sleepless:** ibid.

86   **"In 1973, I was helping out one of the cattlemen":** Fred Blackburn, interview with author, March 2019.

87   **"He couldn't stand my sermonizing":** Helen O'Neill, "A Utah Town's Love of Indian Artifacts Backfires," *Aspen Times*, October 4, 2009.

87   **After Redd committed suicide, according to reporter:** Mozingo, "A Sting in the Desert."

87   **"It's just incomprehensibly tragic":** "Conversation: The Looters Next Door," [n. p.]

88   **"As for memoirs. . . . A life of foolish":** Winston Hurst to author, January 2019.

88   In 2011, in the quirky but invaluable local journal: Hurst, "Collecting This, Collecting That," pp. 46–48.

92   **The sting that so dramatically hit Blanding:** Mozingo, "A Sting in the Desert."

92   **According to reporter Joe Mozingo, who has dug:** ibid.

93   **As a BLM ranger on Cedar Mesa in the 1970s:** Fred Blackburn to author, March 2019.

94   **"he was back in business, representing wealthy":** Mozingo, "A Sting in the Desert."

95   **"I know a few of the folks who participated":** Burrillo, "The Pillagers."

96   **"[T]hey . . . came in this time and arrested":** "Conversation: The Looters Next Door," (Q & A with Winston Hurst), [n. p.].

96   **More than nine hundred people attended his funeral:** Mozingo, "A Sting in the Desert."

96   **Longtime Blanding resident Kay Shumway outlined:** Kay Shumway interview with author, March 2019.

97   **Dr. Redd had been arrested in 1996:** Mozingo, "A Sting in the Desert."

97   **Another defendant charged in the sting:** ibid.

98   **"he would tie Gardiner to a tree":** ibid.

98   **"On Feb. 27, 2010, [Gardiner] called Tina Early":** ibid.

99   **"Jeannie Redd ended up with three years":** Burrillo, "The Pillagers."

99   **"About a month after Dr. Redd's death":** Haun, "BLM Agent Dan Love."

99   **But in 2017, he was fired for a host:** Brian Maffly, "Utah BLM Agent Used Position to Get Burning Man Perks," *Salt Lake Tribune*, February 1, 2017.

100 **"Thanks to the Burning Man escapades":** Phil Lyman to author, March 2019.

100 **In 2015, a team from *Smithsonian* magazine:** Sharp, "An Exclusive Look at the Greatest Haul."

103 **The canyon was named in 1879 by scouts:** Allen, *Utah's Canyon Country Place Names*, vol. 1, p. 297.

103 **"What the Anasazi called this many-headed":** Lipe, "Three Days on the Road from Bluff," revised edition, pdf sent to author, March 2019.

103 **Yet according to inscription expert:** Knipmeyer, *Butch Cassidy was Here*, p. 99.

104 **"one of the least frequented and probably also":** Nelson, unpublished report, quoted in McNitt, *Richard Wetherill: Anasazi*, p. 61.

104 **"Few places in the world are so cut off":** ibid., p. 61.

104 **Thanks to the indefatigable sleuthing of Fred Blackburn:** Blackburn and Williamson, *Cowboys & Cave Dwellers*, pp. 27–28, n. 172.

105 **Fred's team was able to reconstruct:** ibid., pp. 28, n. 172.

107 **Nordenskiöld has been widely credited with turning:** ibid., pp. 22–25.

107 **"the first major record of archaeological work":** McNitt, *Richard Wetherill: Anasazi*, p. 43.

107 **Before he set sail for Europe, however:** ibid., pp. 42–43.

108 **That he did, and as soon as he got back:** Blackburn and Williamson, *Cowboys & Cave Dwellers*, p. 24.

108 **Before his untimely death in 1895:** "Finland to Repatriate American Indian Artefacts to the United States from Its National Collections," Kansallismuseo—The National Museum of Finland, March 10, 2019, https://www.kansallismuseo.fi/en/articles/suomi-luovuttaa-yhdysvalloille -intiaanikansojen-jaanteita-kansalliskokoelmista.

108 **In the days that followed, a consortium:** Simpson, "More Than a Century Ago."

109 **McLoyd and Graham were friends of the five Wetherill:** Blackburn and Williamson, *Cowboys & Cave Dwellers*, pp. 30–31, 47.

110 **Whether or not it was Nordenskiöld who had:** Richard Wetherill to Talbot Hyde, fall 1893, quoted in ibid., p. 49.

112 **Besides performing an invaluable service to Southwestern:** Fletcher, ed., *The Wetherills of Mesa Verde*, p. 25.

113 **In 1900, the then president of New Mexico Normal:** McNitt, *Richard Wetherill: Anasazi*, pp. 188–190.

114 **In charge of two young grad students from Harvard:** Givens, *Alfred Vincent Kidder*, pp. 14–20.

115 **"Grand Gulch . . . is the most tortuous cañon":** Wetherill field notes, quoted in McNitt, *Richard Wetherill: Anasazi*, p. 53.

116 "One animal fell off of a bridge and broke its neck": ibid., p. 155.

116 "Tent camps are also part of the 'romance'": Lipe, "Three Days on the Road from Bluff."

117 At Patokwa, a site in northern New Mexico: Liebmann, *Revolt,* pp. 88–89.

117 Researching *In Search of the Old Ones*: Roberts, *In Search of the Old Ones,* pp. 42–44.

119 The controversy fanned into flames over Kennewick Man: "Kennewick Man," Wikipedia, https://en.wikipedia.org/wiki/Kennewick_Man.

120 "I was asked, over and over, first by *ricos*": Lekson, *A Study of Southwestern Archaeology,* pp. 220–221.

120 "his enthusiasm for artifact collection was not matched": Hurst, "The Professor's Legacy," p. 2.

120 the blatantly fraudulent Frank Hibben: Preston, "The Mystery of Sandia Cave," passim.

121 "We were camping down at the mouth of Grand Gulch": Fred Blackburn, interview with author, March 2019.

122 "It was the most effective deterrent we ever had": Blackburn to author, October 21, 2019.

123 "'Stiles,' he said, 'How would you like it'": Stiles, "When 'Bears Ears' Had TOO MUCH Protection?"

123 "Blackburn sustained a crushed vertebrae": ibid.

124 "It was our Vietnam," he told me: Fred Blackburn, interview with author, March 2019.

124 In the late 1980s, poking through the archives: Hurst, "The Professor's Legacy," pp. 1–19.

124 "In a field where documentation and publication": ibid., p. 5.

124 "Kerr's field work had little to do with archaeology *per se*": ibid., p. 5.

125 "We want the biggest collection of Utah": cited in ibid., p. 5.

125 "Kerr used his annual field budget from the university": ibid., p. 6.

125 "Professor Kerr . . . came down here quite often": "Moki Digging in Southeastern Utah," Southeastern Utah Oral History Project, July 19, 1973, quoted in ibid., p. 7.

126 "The only difference between archaeology and pothunting": ibid., p. 12.

126 "Around here it's not a crime": Egan, "In the Indian Southwest, Heritage Takes a Hit."

126 By his mid-twenties he was bragging openly: ibid.

126 He taunted federal agents by letting them know: Fisher, "Earl K. Shumway: The John Dillinger of Archaeological Looting."

126 Along with his pothunting, Earl dabbled in burglary: "Shumway Releaded from Prison after Four Months," *Moab Times-Independent,* July 24, 1986.

126 **Despite his cockiness, Shumway was busted:** Fisher, "Earl K. Shumway."

127 **That attitude was voiced, for instance:** "Blanding Mayor Says Sleeping Giant Awake after 'Gestapo' Raids," *Moab Times-Independent*, May 15, 1986.

127 **Six years later (in the narrative reconstructed by prosecutors):** "United States of America, Plaintiff-appellee," *Justia US Law*, May 6, 1997.

128 **All this business finally came to trial:** Fisher, "Earl K. Shumway."

129 **In March 2019 I sat down in the museum:** Jonathan Till, interview with author, March 2019.

130 **In 2019 I interviewed Kay Shumway in his Blanding home:** Kay Shumway, interview with author, March 2019.

Five: O Pioneers!

132 **As for American citizens first planting:** Embry, *La Sal Reflections*, pp. 4–5.

133 **"the answer to every cowman's prayer":** Kelly, *The Outlaw Trail*, p. 17.

133 **By 1882 they even had a post office:** Embry, *La Sal Reflections*, pp. 7–8.

133 **"Only two men had previously penetrated":** Kelly, *The Outlaw Trail*, p. 17.

133 **The Negro was William Granstaff or Grandstaff, known locally:** Knipmeyer, *Butch Cassidy Was Here*, pp. 82–83.

133 **According to the 1941 Works Progress Administration:** *Utah: A Guide to the State*, p. 427.

133 **Other sources claim that William Grandstaff:** Burr, "Utah's Negro Bill Canyon Renamed."

134 **"The men are gathering up guns to hunt Indians":** *Utah: A Guide to the State*, p. 425.

134 **"fine herds of cattle and horses, located on the best range":** Kelly, *The Outlaw Trail*, p. 17.

134 **In the 1930s, Kelly managed to track down:** ibid., pp. 17–18.

134 **"I was born and raised by as good parents":** "History of Tom McCarty," quoted in ibid., p. 18.

134 **During the next decade, Tom McCarty parted ways:** ibid., pp. 18–32.

135 **"stockily built and bubbled over with uncontrolled energy":** ibid., p. 20.

136 **"It is a wild country—regular painted-rock desert":** Warner, *The Last of the Bandit Raiders*, pp. 68–69, 77.

137 **In the mid- to late-1870s, cattlemen from Kansas:** Sheire, *Cattle Raising in the Canyons*, pp. 6–7.

139 **"the highest type of pioneer endeavor that broke the wilderness":** Miller, *Hole-in-the-Rock*: [dedication], pp. ix–x.

140 **In brief: from the southern Utah towns, a reconnaissance:** ibid., pp. 17–38.

142 **"It is certainly the worst country I ever saw":** Platte D. Lyman, diary, December 1, 1879, quoted in ibid., p. 62.

142 **"We have just sent our last five dollars":** Elizabeth M. Decker, diary, January 19, 1880, quoted in ibid., p. 76.

144 **There were no fewer than twenty-five Deckers:** ibid., p. 144.

144 **While the emigrants piled up at Forty-Mile Spring:** ibid., pp. 106–107, 119–122.

145 **"[O]ur meat and everything else had give out":** E. I. Decker, "Sketch of My Life," quoted in ibid., p. 195.

146 **"Last night was the coldest night I ever experienced":** Platte Lyman, "Journal," quoted in ibid., p. 168.

146 **Accounts of this incident indicate that near bloodshed:** ibid., p. 127.

147 **"It's the roughest country you or anybody else":** "Letter Written at Grey Mesa, February 22, 1880," quoted in ibid., p. 197.

148 **"The water is very bad and feed pretty good":** Platte Lyman, "Journal," March 31, 1880, quoted in ibid., p. 169.

148 **In 1977, Fred Blackburn joined Lynn Lyman:** Fred Blackburn to author, November 2019.

149 **As he retraced the emigrants' route in 1954:** Miller, *Hole-in-the-Rock*, p. 123.

149 **On the face of the northern wall, at least:** Knipmeyer, *Butch Cassidy Was Here*, pp. 78–79.

149 **"We cannot follow up the river, so we":** Platte Lyman, "Journal," April 1, 1880, quoted in Miller, *Hole-in-the-Rock*, p. 169.

149 **"Here again seven span of horses were used":** Charles Redd, "Shortcut to San Juan," quoted in ibid., p. 138.

150 **"Today we held meeting and by unanimous":** Platte Lyman, "Journal," April 25, 1880, quoted in *ibid.*, p. 171.

151 **"Most of us secretly feel," she said:** Roberts, *Devil's Gate*, p. 261.

152 **"wacko environmentalists":** Phil Lyman to author, March 2019.

152 **A Danish farmer converted to the faith:** Carpenter, *Jens Nielson*, pp. 9–16.

152 **Within two years of his arrival in Salt Lake City:** ibid., pp. 18–39.

153 **"go on whether we can or not":** Miller, *Hole-in-the-Rock*, p. 56.

153 **"stickie-ta-tudy":** ibid., p. 67.

153 **With Jens on the long peregrination came:** Carpenter, *Jens Nielson*, pp. 67–68, 142.

153 **It's a measure of Mormon perspicacity:** ibid., p. 67.

154 **Somehow the scale of the riverside terrace:** ibid., pp. 40–41.

154 **"Self-interest had almost destroyed in days":** ibid., p. 41.

154 **The first town hall was not erected until the autumn:** ibid., pp. 54, 66.

154 **One barometer of the schism that divided:** ibid., p. 43.

155 **"Many of the homes had doorways without doors":** ibid., p. 65.

155 **To defend against that menace, they built a fort:** ibid., p. 65.

155 **In January 1880, as Platte Lyman was directing:** Hardy, "Mormon Missionary Diaries: Albert Robison Lyman."

156 **"The Navajo or Piute not skilled in the essential art":** Lyman, *Fort on the Firing Line*, pp. 66, 68.

158 **"a white and delightsome people":** [Joseph Smith], Book of Mormon, 2 Nephi 30: 6–7.

160 **The 1941 WPA guide to Utah recorded:** *Utah: A Guide to the State*, p. 435.

160 **"An occasional automobile kicks up a plume":** Lavender, *One Man's West*, p. 185.

Six: Cowboys and Characters

162 **By 1880, much bigger outfits based in Kansas:** Sheire, *Cattle Raising in the Canyons*, pp. 5–6.

163 **"Texas cowboys from the big outfits became":** ibid., p. 10.

163 **"When he was just a kid . . . , he came to San Juan":** Grant Bayles interview by Mary Risher, July 7, 1971, Doris Duke Oral History Collection (DDOHC).

163 **On his first visit to Bluff, Al spent a night:** Lambert, "Al Scorup, Cattleman of the Canyons," p. 304.

163 **"He was very attractive," Emma later told:** Stena Scorup, *J. A. Scorup: A Utah Cattleman*, p. 25.

163 **"He saw lots of grass," Grant Bayles remembered:** Bayles interview, DDOHC.

164 **"could find the cattle in the maze of cracks, washes, and cliffs":** Lambert, "Al Scorup," p. 303.

164 **"The way they would catch those wild cattle":** Bayles, interview, DDOHC.

164 **"there was no room for him around White":** Lambert, "Al Scorup," p. 304.

165 **"Jim was a hard-twisted youngster":** Lavender, *One Man's West*, p. 192.

165 **"I really wanted to go back":** Stena Scorup, *J. A. Scorup*, pp. 27–28.

165 **"The cows mill around on the edge":** Lambert, "Al Scorup," p. 305.

166 **"One can only guess at his reaction":** ibid., p. 306.

166 **"[A] cow just a few hundred yards away":** ibid., p. 308.

167 **Longtime Blanding rancher Dereese Nielson remembered Adams:** Dereese Nielson, interview by Mary Risher, July 17, 1971, DDOHC.

168 **"We saw a mountain ahead of us that looked like":** Stena Scorup, *J. A. Scorup: A Utah Cattleman*, [n. p.].

169 **Harve Williams, a protégé of Al Scorup:** Lambert, "Al Scorup," p. 307.

169 **According to Grant Bayles, the legendary wolf:** Grant Bayles, interview by Mary Risher, July 7, 1971, DDOHC.

169 **"By living in caves and shanties; eating sourdough":** Lambert, "Al Scorup," p. 308.

170 **Meanwhile the big cattle companies, after nearly:** Sheire, *Cattle Raising in the Canyons*, pp. 12–13.

170 **"At the end of the 1897 roundup":** ibid., p. 13.

170 **"Unmolested now for years, generations":** Lambert, "Al Scorup," p. 311.

171 **"You couldn't lay that rope on in any fancy way":** Young, "Wild Cows of the San Juan," p. 258.

171 **By 1928, his domain stretched across:** Sheire, *Cattle Raising*, p. 16.

172 **"Al would have no 'nonsense' from his cowboys":** Lambert, "Al Scorup," p. 317.

173 **It was the first and only mineral rush triggered:** Ringholz, *Uranium Frenzy*, p. 11.

173 **"It was a vivid and sometimes crazy time":** ibid., p. 12.

173 **Ringholz builds her narrative around Charlie Steen:** ibid., passim.

174 **"Charlie reached into the Jeep and pulled":** ibid., p. 58.

175 **"Poverty and I have been friends for a long time":** ibid., p. 79.

175 **Between 1949 and 1959, in fact, no fewer than:** Topping, *Glen Canyon and the San Juan Country*, p. 137.

175 **Way back in 1899, several prospectors whose names:** James Knipmeyer, Place Names Note Cards, quoted in Allen, *Utah's Canyon Country*, vol. I, p. 325.

176 **In 1946, a road contractor from Monticello:** Ringholz, *Uranium Frenzy*, p. 77.

176 **The only road was a dirt track barely negotiable:** Buckley Jensen, "The Bronsons, Joe Cooper, and the Fabled Happy Jack," *San Juan Record*, October 14, 2009.

177 **After several stabs at interesting other companies:** Ringholz, *Uranium Frenzy*, p. 77.

177 **"a primitive backwater, inhabited mostly by Native Americans":** Jensen, "The Bronsons."

178 **"With that kind of money, Fletch, Grant and Joe":** ibid.

178 **"Finding radioactive rock along the outcroppings":** ibid.

178 **"I recall one January the first, when I was expecting":** Cleone Bronson Cooper Hansen, interview by Dorothy Erick, August 12, 1970, "Uranium Oral Histories," University of Utah Marriott Library Digital Library.

179 **"Water was hauled from Fry Canyon":** Dorothy R. Rossignol, interview by Rusty Salmon, December 23, 2005, Eastern Utah Human History Library.

180 **Even as early as 1950, there were reasons:** Ringholz, *Uranium Fever*, pp. 41, 95–96.

180 **A government-authorized study to assess:** ibid., pp. 84–85, 87.

181 **"Well first I'll take my needle-nosed pliers and remove":** Edward Abbey, *The Monkey Wrench Gang*, p. 296.

181 **"Dr. Saccomono in Grand Junction makes":** Calvin Black, interview by Milan Pavlovich and Jeffrey Jones, July 24, 1970, DDOHC.

182 **"I hear rumors that you've come down":** Buckley Jensen, "Cal Black."

185 **In 2017, for the *New York Times*:** Max Read, "Navigating Uphill," *New York Times*, April 19, 2017.

185 **"Make no mistake, serious acrophobes should not take":** Judith Anderson, "A Wild Corner of Utah," *New York Times*, December 11, 1994.

Seven: Posey's Trail

187 **Back in favor in 1891, Lyman:** Carpenter, *Jens Nielson*, pp. 290–291.

188 **By early 1905, Bishop Nielson, now eighty-four:** ibid., p. 301.

188 **With the passing of its spiritual leader:** ibid., p. 303.

189 **Zane Grey's most popular novel:** Zane Grey, *Riders of the Purple Sage*, pp. 3, 5, 244, passim.

189 **"fairly drips with anti-Mormon rhetoric":** Gary Topping, "Zane Grey in Zion," p. 484.

190 **In fact, it was named by Zane Grey:** Allen, *Utah's Canyon Country Place Names*, vol. 2, p. 735.

191 **Interviewed in 1972, Johnson recalled:** John A. Johnson, interview by Pat Whitaker, July 7, 1972, DDOHC.

192 **In 1959, a geologist named Gene Foushee:** Gene Foushee, interview by Pat Whitaker, July 11, 1972, DDOHC.

192 **The town had gotten electricity only two:** Andrew Gulliford, "The Soul of Bluff."

192 **"It seemed to me that Bluff was a beautiful place":** Foushee, interview by Pat Whitaker.

193 **"He always pointed a stubby pencil":** Gulliford, "The Soul of Bluff."

196 **"a reminder that these two deities":** Robert S. McPherson, *Thru Navajo Eyes*, pp. 11–12.

197 **Over the years, the towers have been called:** Allen, *Utah's Canyon Country Place Names*, vol. 2, p. 532.

197 **Born near Agathla, the volcanic plug on the south:** Robert S. McPherson, *As If the Land Owned Us*, p. 303.

197 **It is possible that when still a child:** Stanley Warren Bronson, *The Ute Spiritual Cross*, p. 8.

197 **"I saw Jesus, and he called me by my Secret":** ibid., p. 15.

198 "Just before they came to Cottonwood Wash": ibid., pp. 15–16.

199 "This writer believes that Christ's appearance": ibid., p. 16.

200 "Who actually discovered Nonnezoshe": Neil Judd, "The Discovery of Rainbow Bridge," in *Rainbow Trails*, p. 3.

200 The Utes and Paiutes are Numic peoples: McPherson, *As If the Land Owned Us*, pp. 13–17.

201 According to one version of the story: ibid., pp. 212–213.

202 "Me no Paiute. Paiutes scared": Forbes Parkhill, *The Last of the Indian Wars*, p. 19.

202 "we were afraid of this Indian and his father": deposition of Ca-vis-itz's son, May 18, 1914, quoted in Lacy and Baker, *Posey*, p. 63.

202 "The Narraguinip band is composed": *Ute Mountain Country*, June 28, 1884, quoted in ibid., p. 32.

203 In September 1914, Deputy Marshal: McPherson, *As If the Land Owned Us*, p. 213.

203 The band of loyalists his father commanded: ibid., p. 214.

203 The winter of 1914–15 was a harsh one: ibid., pp, 214–215.

204 "Bluff at Mercy of Hostile Redskins": *Salt Lake Tribune*, February 22, 2015, cited in Lacy and Baker, *Posey*, p. 77.

204 "Nebeker made the mistake": R. E. Pool, *Outlook*, [date not specified], quoted in ibid., p. 73.

204 "booze fighters, gamblers, and bootleggers": ibid., p. 67.

204 Nebeker had hoped to surprise the Indians: McPherson, *As If the Land Owned Us*, p. 215.

205 Posey, on the west side of the encampment: ibid., pp. 215–216.

205 "Indians Surround Marshal's Posse": *Salt Lake Herald-Republican*, February 22, 1915, cited in Lacy and Baker, *Posey*, p. 76.

206 By the beginning of March, the Polk-Posey: ibid., pp. 92, 96–97.

207 "Pony die," he complained: ibid., p. 97 [source not indicated].

207 Scott earnestly insisted that he wanted: ibid., p. 97.

207 "We are going to do just what": McPherson, *As If the Land Owned Us*, p. 220.

207 "These Indians are poor ignorant grown-up": Lacy and Baker, *Posey*, p. 98.

207 At Thompson Springs, north of Moab: ibid., pp. 104, 112.

207 In the courtroom, Scott himself took on the role: ibid., p. 115.

208 "put his hand on his heart and declared": McPherson, *As If the Land Owned Us*, p. 221.

208 Before they left Salt Lake, the acquitted Indians: Lacy and Baker, *Posey*, pp. 112–113.

208 **"He recognized that the murder victim":** McPherson, *As If the Land Owned Us*, pp. 221–223.

209 **A reporter gave him a ride on a motorcycle:** Lacey and Baker, *Posey*, p. 123.

209 **"a string of cheap medals pinned on one side":** McPherson, *As If the Land Owned Us*, p. 223.

209 **Around Bluff, residents were convinced:** Lacey and Baker, *Posey*, p. 129.

210 **Knowing that his own cows ranged:** McPherson, *As If the Land owned Us*, p. 229.

210 **Shortly after Poke and Posey returned:** ibid., p. 228.

210 **Posey was born near Navajo Mountain:** Buckley Jensen, "Fascinating Life of Chief Posey."

210 **He gained the name Posey:** McPherson, *As If the Land Owned Us*, p. 178.

210 **After eight years of marriage, one day:** Jensen, "Fascinating Life."

211 **"Wesley Barton and I were riding up the road":** William Riley Hurst, interview by James DeMar Redd, September 14, 1971, DDOHC.

211 **On January 10, 1923, those men killed:** Lacy and Baker, *Posey*, p. 134.

212 **One night, after eating scalloped potatoes:** McPherson, *As If the Land Owned Us*, pp. 236–237.

212 **"[Sheriff Oliver] mounted on his big brown horse":** Ervin Richard Guymon, interview by Suzanne Shelton, June 1, 1978, DDOHC.

213 **"I could see the Indians that were seated":** Grant L. and Josephine Harris Bayles, interview by Mary Risher, July 7, 1971, DDHOC.

213 **Joe Bishop's Little Boy took off on a horse:** Guymon, Bayles interviews.

214 **In the confusion, Posey had likewise fled:** McPherson, *As If the Land Owned Us*, p. 237.

214 **"all the stray Utes around the country":** Bayles interview.

214 **"Posey was elated, but whether it was":** Lacy and Baker, *Posey*, p. 133.

215 **"What I heard . . . was that they were going":** Edward Dutchie, interview by author, May 21, 1996, quoted in McPherson, *As If the Land Owned Us,* p. 238.

215 **With six veterans of World War I among:** ibid., pp. 239, 242–243.

215 **"has become more or less an armed camp":** "Piute Indians Are Reinforced," *Salt Lake Tribune*, March 24, 1923, quoted in ibid., p. 243.

215 **But when a contingent visited Polk:** ibid., p. 238.

216 **"Every man here is deputized to shoot":** ibid., p. 239.

216 **But Posey was not only a better marksman:** Lacy and Baker, *Posey*, p. 137; McPherson, *As If the Land Owned Us*, p. 239.

216 **"I just waited until I could see that button":** Lacy and Baker, *Posey*, p. 143.

216 **"It was no fun to kill an injun":** McPherson, *As If the Land Owned Us*, p. 240.

216 "cursed him for starting the trouble": Jensen, "Fascinating Life of Chief Posey."

217 alleged to be a marksman equal to Posey: Lacy and Baker, *Posey*, p. 141.

217 "Posey was hanging down on the right side": ibid., p. 143.

217 Instead they focused on other Utes: McPherson, *As If the Land Owned Us*, pp. 241–242.

218 "Old Posey Will Be Captured If It Takes": [unspecified newspaper], April 5, 1923, cited in Lacey and Baker, *Posey*, p, 166.

218 At the end of the month, Marshal Ward: ibid., pp. 167, 170.

218 On the very next day, some of them climbed: McPherson, *As If the Land Owned Us*, p. 242.

219 "When this happened," Dutchie said: Harry Dutchie, interview by Gary Shumway, July 15, 1968, Doris Duke American Indian History Project, Item # 0517.

219 "It was Poke's little brother . . . that found him first": Jim Mike, interview by Gary Shumway, with interpreter Anna Marie Ketchum Nat, June 20, 1968, Doris Duke American Indian History Project, Item # 550.

220 "I did not regard him as a bad man": Lyman, *The Outlaw of Navaho Mountain*, p. 231.

220 "My view of Chief Posey," Jensen wrote: Jensen, "Fascinating Life of Chief Posey."

Eight: Countdown to Showdown

222 But Josh Ewing, executive director of Friends: Josh Ewing to author, January 2020.

224 "Somebody, or more likely several people": Andrew Gulliford, "Recapture Canyon and an Illegal ATV Trail," *High Country News*, February 12, 2014.

224 Gulliford's smashing of the fire-alarm box: "The Federal Government Lied about Who Owns Recapture Canyon Road," "the Petroglyph Editor," *Petroglyph*, March 6, 2019.

225 Proponents argued that motorized access: Gulliford, "Recapture Canyon."

226 What turned the 2014 controversy from a tempest: Jonathan Thompson, "A Reluctant Rebellion in the Utah Desert," *High Country News*, May 13, 2014.

227 The day began in a Blanding park, as speakers: ibid.

228 Josh Ewing, who would later become: Josh Ewing, "Recapping the Recapture Canyon ATV Protest," May 13, 2014, https://www.friendsofcedarmesa .org.

228 But a year and a half later, in December: Thompson, "A Reluctant Rebellion."

228 **Lyman served his sentence in April 2016:** Dennis Romboy, "Commissioner Phil Lyman Tells of Jail, 'Hamilton,' and His Right to Public Land," *Deseret News*, August 13, 2016.

229 **"Recapture is not abstract to me":** Phil Lyman to author, March 19, 2019.

230 **"I get people all the time saying things like":** Lyman to author, March 30, 2019.

230 **Lyman forwarded to me an apologia:** Phil Lyman, "Setting the Record Straight on Badgers," Facebook, July 18, 2016.

230 **Lyman was aware of my struggles with cancer:** Lyman to author, March 30, 2019.

231 **During the eleven months between Trump's:** Yessenia Funes, "Documents Show Ryan Zinke Ignored Public Support for Bears Ears in Favor of Oil and Gas," March 2, 2018, https://earther.gizmodo.com/documents-show-ryan -zinke-ignored-public-support-for-be-182461754.

232 **"If the land gets destroyed":** Regina Lopez-Whiteskunk, "Fighting for the Land and Building Healing from Within," in *Edge of Morning: Native Voices Speak for the Bears Ears*, p. 31.

232 **"From where I sit, I look into the sanctuary":** Shonto Begay, "The View from the Mesa," in *Red Rock Stories: Three Generations of Writers Speak on Behalf of Utah's Public Lands*, p. 83.

233 **"I was born to this landscape":** Amy Irvine, "Seeing Red," in ibid., p. 97.

233 **"You could pull off anywhere and find ruins":** *Voices from the Bears Ears: Seeking Common Ground on Sacred Land*, p. 62.

233 **"I go to these places to pray":** ibid., p. 41.

233 **In *Edge of Morning,* Wayland Gray:** Wayland Gray, "Sacred is Sacred," in *Edge of Morning*, pp. 153–154, 169.

235 **"There's a showdown looming":** David Roberts, "Saving What's Left of Utah's Lost World," *New York Times*, April 11, 2015.

236 **In August 2019 the White House announced:** Jeff Moag, "Land Stripped from Bears Ears and Grand Staircase Open for Drilling," *Adventure Journal*, September 4, 2019.

236 **In December 2019 a coalition of ninety-one conservation:** Steven Mufson, "Interior Secretary Extends the Tenure of Federal Lands Chief," *Washington Post*, January 2, 2020.

238 **The fact is that by 2010, 50.4 percent:** "San Juan County, Utah," Wikipedia, https://en.wikipedia.org/wiki/San_Juan_County,_Utah.

238 **The backlash was immediate and intense:** Zak Podmore, "Editorial: Commissioner Willie Grayeyes' Residency Claim Rests on Far More than Cultural Beliefs," *Canyon Echo*, January 25, 2019.

239 **"If you use your umbilical cord as proof":** ibid.

239 **A letter to Maryboy on May 8:** Larry Wells, "A Line That Concerns Me," *San Juan Record*, May 8, 2019.

Epilogue: The Bears Ears I'll Never Know

244 **"Jimmy had never been in Slickhorn":** Vaughn and Marcia Hadenfeldt, interview by author, March 2019.

249 **"among other things a uranium miner, a wrangler":** Ann Zwinger, *Wind in the Rock*, p. 55.

250 **"I can't hear, I can't see":** Maggie McGuire, "Don't Touch Beauty: Ken Sleight Still Speaks Out," *Moab Sun-News,* October 3, 2019.

250 **Unfortunately, only three pages of the book:** Kent Frost, *My Canyonlands*, pp. 92–94.

251 **"One lip of rock overhung a twenty-foot wall":** ibid., pp. 157, 159.

253 **"Right after that," recalled Frost:** Kent Frost, interview by Albert Page, July 20, 1973, DDOHC.

253 **In fact, Jim Knipmeyer claims to have found:** Allen, *Utah's Canyon Country Place Names*, vol. 2, p. 685.

253 **In 1958 Frost jotted down an account:** Kent Frost, "Discovery of Grand Arch, from the Top," [undated typescript], DDOHC.

254 **"I knew Kent Frost had been there":** Fred Blackburn to author, ca. 2014.

255 **On the USGS topo map, Grand Arch:** Allen, *Utah's Canyon Country Place Names*, vol. 1, p. 113; vol. 2, p. 685.

255 **One day in 1939, Frost and his seventeen-year-old:** Kent Frost, interview by Albert Page, July 20, 1973, DDOHC.

257 **"Before we moved to Bluff":** Zak Podmore, interview by author, March 2019.

259 **In an era when major excavations:** R. G. Matson, William D. Lipe, and William R. Haase IV, "Adaptational Continuities and Occupational Discontinuities: The Cedar Mesa Anasazi," in *Journal of Field Archaeology*, vol. 15, no. 3, 1988, pp. 245, 250, 251, 253.

261 **"Defensive structures and arrangements are also":** ibid., p. 255.

262 **"Bill Lipe is the Grand Old Man":** Steve Lekson to author, April 2019.

262 **When I talked to him way back in 1995:** David Roberts, *In Search of the Old Ones*, p. 133.

264 **"Sorry that your ailment has curtailed":** Bill Lipe to author, March 2019.

268 **In recent years, some clever revisionists:** e.g., Aidan Hamilton, "How Did the Age of Exploration Lead to European Imperialism," https://prezi .com/u421xgqioy7y/how-did-the-age-of-exploration-lead-to-european -imperialism/.

BIBLIOGRAPHY

Abbey, Edward. *The Monkey Wrench Gang*. New York City: HarperCollins Publishers, 2006 [originally 1975].

Allen, Steve. *Utah's Canyon Country Place Names*, two vols. Durango, Colorado: Canyon Country Press, 2012.

Aton, James M., and Robert S. McPherson, *River Flowing from the Sunrise: An Environmental History of the Lower San Juan*. Logan, Utah: Utah State University Press, 2000.

Babbitt, James E., ed. *Rainbow Trails: Early-Day Adventures in Rainbow Bridge Country*. Page, Arizona: Glen Canyon Natural History Association, 1990.

Bailey, Lynn R. *Bosque Redondo: The Navajo Internment at Fort Sumner, New Mexico, 1863–1868*. Tucson: Westernlore Press, 1998.

———. *The Long Walk: A History of the Navajo Wars, 1846–68*. Tucson: Westernlore Press, 1988.

Bighorse, Tiana. *Bighorse the Warrior*. Tucson: University of Arizona Press, 1990.

Bronson, Stanley Warren. *The Ute Spiritual Cross of the San Juan Mission*. [privately printed], 1999.

Brugge, David M. "Emergence of the Navajo People," in Deni J. Seymour, ed., *From the Land of Ever Winter to the American Southwest*.

Burr, Thomas. "Utah's Negro Bill Canyon Renamed Grandstaff Canyon by Federal Board," *Salt Lake Tribune*, October 12, 2017.

Burrillo, R. E. "The Pillagers." Draft essay, April 2019.

Camp, Charles C., ed. *George C. Yount and his Chronicles of the West.* Denver: Old West Publishing Company, 1966.

Carpenter, David S. *Jens Nielson, Bishop of Bluff.* Provo, Utah: BYU Studies, 2011.

"Conversation: The Looters Next Door." *Archaeology*, September-October 2009, vol. 62, no. 5.

Correll, J. Lee. "Manuelito, Navajo Naat'aani," *Navajo Times*, September 9, 1965.

Doris Duke American Indian Oral History Program, Marriott Library, University of Utah: https://collections.lib.utah.edu/search?q=Doris +Duke.

Egan, Timothy. "In the Indian Southwest, Heritage Takes a Hit," *New York Times*, November 2, 1995.

Embry, Jessie L., ed. *La Sal Reflections: A Redd Family Journal.* [Provo, Utah]: Charles Redd Foundation, 1984.

Ewing, Josh. "Recapping the Recapture Canyon ATV Protest," May 13, 2014, https://www.friendsofcedarmesa.org.

Fisher, Jim. "Earl K. Shumway: The John Dillinger of Archaeological Looting," Jim Fisher True Crime (blog), December 7, 2017.

Fletcher, Maurine S., ed. *The Wetherills of Mesa Verde: Autobiography of Benjamin Alfred Wetherill.* Lincoln, Nebraska: University of Nebraska Press, 1977.

Frost, Kent. *My Canyonlands.* London: Abelard-Schuman, 1971.

Givens, Douglas R. *Alfred Vincent Kidder and the Development of Americanist Archaeology.* Albuquerque: University of New Mexico Press, 1992.

Grey, Zane. *Riders of the Purple Sage.* Roslyn, New York: Walter J. Black, Inc., 1940 [originally 1912].

Guernsey, Samuel James. *Explorations in Northeastern Arizona: Report on the Archaeological Fieldwork of 1920–1923.* Cambridge, Massachusetts: Papers of the Peabody Museum, vol. 12, no. 1, 1931.

Gulliford, Andrew. "Recapture Canyon and an Illegal ATV Trail," *High Country News*, May 13, 2014.

———. "The Soul of Bluff: Visionary Gene Foushee Built, Restored Desert Town," *Durango Herald*, October 13, 2017.

Hansen, Cleone Bronson Cooper. Interview by Dorothy Erick, August 12, 1970, "Uranium Oral Histories," University of Utah Marriott Library Digital Library.

Hardy, Jeffery S. "Mormon Missionary Diaries: Albert Robison Lyman," https://lib.byu.edu/collections/mormon-missionary-diaries/about/diarists/albert-robison-lyman/.

Haun, Marjorie. "BLM Agent Dan Love: A Cruel and Unusual History," https://redoubtnews.com/2017/02/blm-agent-dan-love-cruel-history/.

Hurst, Winston. "Collecting This, Collecting That: Confessions of a Former, Small-Time Pothunter." *Blue Mountain Shadows*, Fall 2011, vol. 44.

———. "The Professor's Legacy: Some Historical Insights into Southeastern Utah's 'Pothunting' Tradition." Draft MS, June 2009.

Hurst, Winston, and Christy G. Turner II. "Rediscovering the 'Great Discovery': Wetherill's First Cave 7 and Its Record of Basketmaker Violence," in *Anasazi Basketmaker: Papers from the 1990 Wetherill-Grand Gulch Symposium*. Salt Lake City: United States Department of Interior, Bureau of Land Management, 1993.

Ingstad, Helge. *The Apache Indians: In Search of the Missing Tribe*. Lincoln, Nebraska: University of Nebraska Press, 2004.

"Interview with Manuelito, Bob." New Mexico Digital Collections: https://nmdigital.unm.edu/digital/collection/navtrans/id/147/

Jackson, William Henry. *Time Exposure: The Autobiography of William Henry Jackson*. New York: Cooper Square Publishers, Inc., 1970.

Jackson, William H., and Howard R. Driggs. *The Pioneer Photographer: Rocky Mountain Adventures with a Camera*. Yonkers-on-Hudson, New York: World Book Company, 1929.

Jensen, Buckley. "Cal Black," *San Juan Record*, October 1, 2008.

———. "Fascinating Life of Chief Posey," *San Juan Record*, September 23, 2009.

————. "The Bronsons, Joe Cooper and the Fabled Happy Jack," *San Juan Record*, October 14, 2009.

Johnson, Broderick H., ed. *Navajo Stories of the Long Walk Period*. Tsaile, Arizona: Navajo Community College Press, 1973.

Keeler, Jacqueline, ed. *Edge of Morning: Native Voices Speak for the Bears Ears*. Salt Lake City and Torrey, Utah: Torrey House Press, 2017.

Kelly, Charles. "Chief Hoskaninni." *Utah State Historical Quarterly*, July 1953, vol. 21.

————. *The Outlaw Trail: A History of Butch Cassidy and His Wild Bunch* (revised edition). Lincoln, Nebraska: University of Nebraska Press, 1996.

Kelly, Lawrence. *Navajo Roundup: Selected Correspondence of Kit Carson's Campaign against the Navajo, 1863–1865*. Boulder, Colorado: Pruett Publishing Company, 1970.

Kluckhohn, Clyde, and Dorothea Leighton. *The Navaho*. Cambridge, Massachusetts: Harvard University Press, 1946.

Knipmeyer, James H. *Butch Cassidy Was Here: Historic Inscriptions of the Colorado Plateau*. Salt Lake City: University of Utah Press, 2002.

————. *In Search of a Lost Race: The Illustrated American Exploring Expedition of 1892*. [n.p.]: Xlibris Corporation, 2006.

Lacy, Steve, and Pearl Baker. *Posey: The Last Indian War*. Layton, Utah: Gibbs Smith Publishers, 2007.

Lambert, Neal. "Al Scorup, Cattleman of the Canyons," *Utah Historical Quarterly,* Summer 1964, vol. 32, no. 3.

Lavender, David. *One Man's West*. Lincoln, Nebraska: University of Nebraska Press, 1977 [originally 1943].

Lekson, Stephen H. *A Study of Southwestern Archaeology*. Salt Lake City: University of Utah Press, 2018.

Lipe, Bill. "Three Days on the Road from Bluff," revised edition, 1975 (pdf courtesy of author).

Liebmann, Matthew. *Revolt: An Archaeological History of Pueblo Resistance in 17th Century New Mexico*. Tucson: University of Arizona Press, 2012.

Lyman, Albert R. *Fort on the Firing Line*. Provo, Utah: BYU Print Services, 2012 [originally 1948].

———. *Indians and Outlaws: Settling of the San Juan Frontier.* Salt Lake City: Bookcraft, 1962.

———. *The Outlaw of Navaho Mountain.* Salt Lake City: Deseret Book Company, 1963.

Madsen, Steven K. *Exploring Desert Stone: John N. Macomb's 1859 Expedition to the Canyonlands of the Colorado.* Logan: Utah State University Press, 2010.

Matson, R. G., William D. Lipe, and William R. Haase IV. "Adaptational Continuities and Occupational Discontinuities: The Cedar Mesa Anasazi," in *Journal of Field Archaeology*, vol. 15, no. 3, 1988.

McNitt, Frank. *Navajo Wars: Military Campaigns, Slave Raids, and Reprisals.* Albuquerque: University of New Mexico Press, 1972.

———. *Richard Wetherill: Anasazi: Pioneer Explorer of Southwestern Ruins.* Albuquerque: University of New Mexico Press, 1957.

McPherson, Robert S. *A History of San Juan County: In the Palm of Time.* Salt Lake City: Utah State Historical Society, 1995.

———. *As If the Land Owned Us: An Ethnohistory of the White Mesa Utes.* Salt Lake City: University of Utah Press, 2011.

———. *Comb Ridge and Its People: The Ethnohistory of a Rock.* Logan: Utah State University Press, 2009.

———. *Life in a Corner: Cultural Episodes in Southeastern Utah, 1880–1950.* Norman: University of Oklahoma Press, 2015.

———. *Thru Navajo Eyes: Bluff to Monument Valley.* [n.p.]: Four Corners Digital Design, 2014.

McPherson, Robert S., and Susan Rhoades Neel. *Mapping the Four Corners: Narrating the Hayden Survey of 1875.* Norman: University of Oklahoma Press, 2016.

Morris, Earl. "An Unexplored Area of the Southwest." *Natural History* 22: 498–515 (1922).

Mozingo, Joe. "A Sting in the Desert," *Los Angeles Times*, September 21, 2014, http://graphics.latimes.com/utah-sting/.

Nordenskiöld, G. *The Cliff Dwellers of the Mesa Verde.* Mesa Verde

National Park, Colorado: Mesa Verde Museum Association, 1990 (facsimile reprint).

Oral History Stories of the Long Walk: Hwéeldi Baa Hané. Crownpoint, New Mexico: Office of Indian Education Programs, 1990.

Parkhill, Forbes. *The Last of the Indian Wars.* New York: Collier Books, 1961.

"The Petroglyph Editor," "The Federal Government Lied about Who Owns Recapture Canyon Road in San Juan County, Utah," *Petroglyph,* March 6, 2019.

Podmore, Zak. "Editorial: Commissioner Willie Grayeyes' Residency Claim Rests on Far More than Cultural Beliefs," *Canyon Echo,* January 25, 2019.

Preston, Douglas. "The Mystery of Sandia Cave." *New Yorker,* June 12, 1995.

Ringholz, Raye C. *Uranium Frenzy: Boom and Bust on the Colorado Plateau.* Albuquerque: University of New Mexico Press, 1991.

Roberts, David. *Devil's Gate: Brigham Young and the Great Mormon Handcart Tragedy.* New York: Simon & Schuster, 2008.

———. *Escape Routes: Further Adventure Writings of David Roberts.* Seattle: The Mountaineers, 1997.

———. *Sandstone Spine: Seeking the Anasazi on the First Traverse of the Comb Ridge.* Seattle: The Mountaineers, 2006.

———. "Saving What's Left of Utah's Lost World," *New York Times,* April 11, 2015.

———. "The Long Walk to Bosque Redondo." *Smithsonian,* December 1997, vol. 28, no. 9, pp. 46–57.

———. *The Lost World of the Old Ones.* New York: W. W. Norton and Company, 2015.

———. *The Pueblo Revolt: The Secret Rebellion That Drove the Spaniards Out of the Southwest.* New York: Simon & Schuster, 2004.

Robinson, Rebecca M., and Stephen E. Strom. *Voices from the Bears Ears: Seeking Common Ground on Sacred Land.* Tucson: University of Arizona Press, 2018.

Rossignol, Dorothy R. Interview by Rusty Salmon, December 23, 2005, Eastern Utah Human History Library.

Schultheis, Rob. "Deep in Bears Ears Country," *Alta*, January 8, 2019, https://altaonline.com/bears-ears-last-stand.

Scorup, Stena. *J. A. Scorup: A Utah Cattleman.* Privately published, 1945.

Seymour, Deni J., ed. *From the Land of Ever Winter to the American Southwest: Athapaskan Migrations, Mobility, and Ethnogenesis.* Salt Lake City: University of Utah Press, ca. 2012.

Sharp, Kathleen. "An Exclusive Look at the Greatest Haul of Native American Artifacts, Ever." *Smithsonian*, November 2015, https://www.smithsonianmag.com/history/exclusive-greatest-haul-native-american-artifacts-looted-180956959/.

Sheire, James. *Cattle Raising in the Canyons.* Denver: National Park Service, 1972.

Simpson, Kevin. "More Than a Century Ago, A European Visitor Took More Than 600 Native American Remains . . . ," *Colorado Sun*, October 10, 2019.

Thompson, Gerald. *The Army and the Navajo: The Bosque Redondo Reservation Experiment, 1863–1868.* Tucson: University of Arizona Press, 1976.

Thompson, Jonathan. "A Reluctant Rebellion in the Utah Desert," *High Country News*, May 13, 2014.

Topping, Gary. *Glen Canyon and the San Juan Country.* Moscow: University of Idaho Press, 1997.

———. "Zane Grey in Zion: An Examination of His Supposed Anti-Mormonism," *BYU Studies Quarterly*, vol. 18, no. 4, 1978.

Trafzer, Clifford E. *The Kit Carson Campaign: The Last Great Navajo War.* Norman: University of Oklahoma Press, 1982.

"Treaty between the United States of America and the Navajo Tribe of Indians." Las Vegas, Nevada: KC Publications, 1968.

Trimble, Stephen, ed. *Red Rock Stories: Three Generations of Writers Speak on Behalf of Utah's Public Lands.* Salt Lake City and Torrey, Utah: Torrey House Press, 2017.

"United States of America, Plaintiff-appellee, v. Earl K. Shumway, Defendant-appellant, 112 F.3d 1413," https://law.justia.com/cases/federal/appellate-courts/F3/112/1413/585127/, May 6, 1997.

Utah: A Guide to the State. New York: Hastings House, 1941.

Van Valkenburgh, Richard F. *Diné Biķéyah*. Window Rock, Arizona: Office of Indian Affairs, 1941.

Warner, Matt, as told to Murray E. King. *The Last of the Bandit Raiders*. Caldwell, Idaho: Caxton Printers, 1940.

The WPA Guide to 1930s New Mexico. Tucson: University of Arizona Press, 1989.

Young, Karl. "Wild Cows of the San Juan," *Utah Historical Quarterly*, Summer 1964, vol. 32, no. 3.

Yurth, Cindy. "Manuelito's Legacy." *Navajo Times*, February 14, 2013.

Zwinger, Ann. *Wind in the Rock: The Canyonlands of Southeastern Utah*. Tucson: University of Arizona Press, 1978.

INDEX